MARKETING YOUR SMALL BUSINESS MADE E-Z

William A. Cohen
and
Marshall E. Reddick

MADE E-Z PRODUCTS, Inc.
Deerfield Beach, Florida / www.MadeE-Z.com

Marketing Your Small Business Made E-Z™
© 2000 Made E-Z Products, Inc.
Printed in the United States of America

MADE E-Z
PRODUCTS

384 South Military Trail
Deerfield Beach, FL 33442
Tel. 954-480-8933
Fax 954-480-8906
http://www.MadeE-Z.com

1 2 3 4 5 6 7 8 9 10   CPC   R   10 9 8 7 6 5 4 3 2

This publication is designed to provide accurate and authoritative information in regard to subject matter covered. It is sold with the understanding that neither the publisher nor author is engaged in rendering legal, accounting, or other professional services. If legal advice or other expert assistance is required, the services of a competent professional should be sought. From: *A Declaration of Principles jointly adopted by a Committee of the American Bar Association and a Committee of Publishers.*

Marketing Your Small Business Made E-Z™
William A. Cohen and Marshall E. Reddick

Table of contents

Introduction to Marketing Your Small Business Made E-Z™

We want you to be successful.

Whether your company succeeds or fails depends totally upon your commitment to marketing. Why is this? Because marketing includes all the business activities involved in directing the flow of your products or services from you the producer to the consumer. If you do marketing correctly, your business will grow and you will make money. If you do marketing incorrectly, your business will flounder. Without successful marketing, your sales and cash flow will be reduced to zero.

Most of the information about marketing and the attention given to it are focused on the problems of big business. This is strange, because a big business can survive marketing mistakes much more easily than a small one. Even small marketing mistakes are critical for a small business. Statistically 90 percent of small businesses fail within the first two years. Even into their tenth year, small businesses have a greater propensity for failure than large businesses. Again, the reason is obvious. Large businesses can afford a few mistakes. Small businesses can't.

We are both professors of marketing, but we came to the profession from different beginnings: one through industry and marketing research, the other through industry and government marketing. Both of us have been and are practicing entrepreneurs who have been involved in marketing for a number of small businesses which include consulting, seminars, mail order, import, export, manufacturing, writing, marketing research, publishing, real estate, syndication, literary representation, manufacturing representation, and government marketing.

Through extensive practice and study of marketing and small businesses, we have come to the conclusion that most businesses fail as a result of incorrect marketing, and that most incorrect marketing practices continue even when the basic theories of correct practice are well established.

The interested reader may well ask why. If the basic marketing theories for a small business are established, and if such a high failure rate or at least risk of failure exists, and if this failure rate is attributable mainly to wrong marketing practices, why in the world doesn't the practitioner of marketing for a small business do the right thing? The answer is simply that there is a large gap between theory, as developed by researchers in academia, and practical marketing, as accomplished by the entrepreneur or businessman in the small firm. This gap exists because few people who run small businesses are also professional scientific marketing researchers, and few scientific researchers are in small businesses.

Our basic objective in writing this book is to take the theories of marketing and translate them into practical ideas—techniques and processes you can follow to make marketing for your small business successful.

History is replete with companies that have combined marketing theory with marketing practice to reach success. The Minute Maid Corporation, which produces frozen orange juice, was having serious problems in the 1950s because of the high price of oranges. This forced the company to take losses at a time when sales were slowing down as a result of expanding competition. But through successful practice of marketing theory, the company allocated resources toward new product innovation. With those funds, the company developed the unique machinery that made it possible to process freeze-damaged fruit. During a major frost in the winter of 1957,

Minute Maid sustained major gains over its competition and turned a net loss into a net gain.

After World War II the aluminum industry was left with a tremendous capacity for production but a very small post-war market. Richard Reynolds, of Reynolds Aluminum, using marketing theory, found new post-war civilian markets for his products. New applications for aluminum included everything from lawn furniture to food containers to boat hulls, applications that had been undreamed of prior to the war. Richard Reynolds' ability to transform marketing theory into marketing practice not only saved his company, but made it the multi-billion dollar corporation it is today.

Joe Karbo, the mail-order genius, faced bankruptcy, yet through shrewd application of marketing theory to the practice of mail-order marketing, he succeeded not only in turning his small company around, but in expanding to such an extent that one single product, his book *The Lazy Man's Way to Riches*, which he introduced in 1973, sold more than a million copies in seven years.

T. R. Kennedy, Jr., who is vice president of marketing for Blue Cross and Blue Shield of Texas, says, "If an organization is to be groomed properly for its competitive battle in the marketplace, it must function through a sound, well-planned, and flexible market-oriented program."

In this book we are presenting a marketing program that will help you in many ways. It will:

- Tell you how to organize the marketing function in your company for success.

- Explain how to do marketing research and do it at low cost.

- Show you how to develop a successful product or service strategy.

- Assist you in developing a successful pricing strategy.

- Help you develop a distribution strategy that will maximize your profits.

- Show you the ways of using the promotional variable to skyrocket your sales.

- Explain consumer behavior and show you how to make it work for you.

- Show you how to enter and compete in the industrial market.

- Show you how to do business in the international market.

- Show you how to reach the government market.

Finally, this book will show you how to develop a marketing plan that will ensure your success. So get ready. Our promise to you is that we will show you how to turn marketing theory not just into marketing practice, but into successful marketing practice.

The marketing concept

1

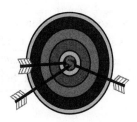

Chapter 1

The marketing concept

> **What you'll find in this chapter:**
> ➠ Understanding marketing
> ➠ Appreciating small business advantages
> ➠ Pleasing the consumer
> ➠ Coordinating corporate efforts
> ➠ Orienting toward profit

Many firms fail because of their tendencies to ignore the customer while selecting the product and developing the business. In order to succeed in today's competitive environment, it is necessary to start with the consumer. This marketing philosophy is called *The Marketing Concept.*

What is the marketing concept?

DEFINITION

The *marketing concept* is a philosophy of how to market a product or a service. It means developing the product or service around the needs and desires of the consumer. Unfortunately, many products and services are not marketed in this manner. Quite commonly a product is developed and then forced onto the market through a strong sales or advertising effort. Such attempts often meet consumer resistance and result in product failure.

The marketing concept begins with total support of the entire staff for the concept of customer satisfaction. This philosophy must pervade the organization from the stock clerk to the president. Salespeople must go out of their way to please the customer. Usually that little extra effort will make a tremendous difference. The rule that the customer is always right is not a bad one. Once the firm is totally committed to customer orientation, the needs and desires of the customer must be determined—not through guesswork, but through appropriate research techniques.

The differential advantage of the small firm

Often we hear that small companies or services cannot compete against large ones. This is true, but a small firm does not have to meet a large one head-on. Actually, the small firm has a differential advantage in its close proximity to its customers. This proximity gives the small firm the potential for satisfying customer needs much more easily and quickly and with fewer dollars. Moreover, the small firm can go after a market segment that is far too small for the larger firm.

> *note* The small firm can implement the marketing concept better than a large one.

How important is the marketing concept for your small business? The president of Burroughs Corporation says this: "Any company is nothing but a marketing organization." But Burroughs isn't the only large company that has adopted the marketing concept with great success. General Electric introduced the concept in 1952, and Ralph J. Cordiver, who was then president, said:

> *This concept, it is believed, will tighten control over business operations and will fix responsibility while making possible greater flexibility and closer teamwork in the marketing of the company's products.*

General Electric has been more successful in the last 30 years of its operations than in the entire history of the company.

> **HOT spot** The greatest success of the marketing concept can be seen in the growth of the small business that adopts it.

Back in 1955, Ray Kroc contacted Richard and Maurice McDonald, who owned a small hamburger restaurant. In those days, if you wanted to buy a hamburger, you went to a so-called "hamburger joint," usually a dirty, greasy place that attracted primarily the teenage crowd. It was definitely not a family-type establishment. Kroc, along with the McDonalds, started the fabulous McDonald chain and franchise of fast food restaurants. Their food outlets were clean, service was fast and efficient, and a conscious effort was made to attract the entire family.

McDonald's practiced the marketing concept by seeking not to sell hamburgers, but to satisfy the consumer's want for buying a hamburger in a clean and efficient setting and getting it fast. McDonald's also satisfied a consumer need by carefully choosing locations and carefully selecting franchise operators. Then, going one step further, the company gave these franchisees thorough management training at a central facility and, finally, supported them with high-powered, high-quality promotion programs.

Has the marketing concept brought success to McDonald's? After 25 years, McDonald's is a multi-billion dollar operation. It has no less than 20 percent of the fast food market, which is far ahead of its nearest competitor.

> *note* The marketing concept enabled McDonald's to grow into a gigantic business from a very small one.

Three principles for implementing the marketing concept

Here are three principles for adopting the marketing concept:

1) consumer orientation

2) coordination and integration of corporate efforts

3) profit orientation

Let's look at each one in turn.

A **consumer orientation** means that you look to your consumer in developing your product and service, not inwardly toward yourself. Like the McDonald brothers, you should seek not simply to sell hamburgers, but to find out what the customer wants and then develop your hamburgers or your hamburger outlets around this want. It means that before developing a new product, you should examine your market and find out what your market wants. It means you should offer a product or service, not because you want to, but because it is something your potential customer or client wants to buy.

Corporate efforts need to be coordinated and integrated on behalf of support of the marketing concept. No matter how small or large your company is, all divisions—manufacturing, sales, research and development, whatever must be coordinated in support of the marketing concept. When Henry Ford started manufacturing his famous automobile, he provided the old Model T in one color, black, which allowed him to provide an automobile at a price that was acceptable to his potential customers. This was correct application of the marketing concept. However, that strategy is not always acceptable; routine introduction of a one-color-only product is not application of the marketing concept. Today the marketing concept would require a number of different colors, even though that would cause a higher price. Today's customer is willing to pay a premium price in order to have a choice of color. This is what the customer wants. He would not be willing to buy the product with no color choice unless the price were significantly lower. The third principle you must adopt as part of the marketing concept is **profit orientation**. Even though your emphasis is on satisfying customer

HOT spot It is the coordination between market research (to find out what the customer wants) and research and development (to develop this item) and finally production (to produce what is wanted by the customer at a reasonable price) that demonstrates the marketing concept.

needs or wants, you must still make a profit. You should not produce any product or offer any service unless it makes an immediate profit by itself or will lead directly to a profit in some follow-up production or service. Adopting the marketing concept does not negate the fact that you should and must make a profit in order to be successful.

Overcoming the problems of implementation

There are five basic problems with implementing the marketing concept:

1) Understanding the difference between marketing and selling.

2) Any new product or service includes features that satisfy some customer needs but hurt others.

3) You must determine—often at considerable expense—what your customers' needs are.

4) Helping and satisfying the needs of one segment of your market may hurt other segments of the market.

5) If your company is already established, morale could suffer during the restructuring a company needs to undertake to adopt the marketing concept. Let's look at each problem in turn.

Small business operators often confuse the distinction between marketing and selling. In some ways, the meanings are almost opposite: in selling, the emphasis is on the product or service that you already have, on

> **E-Z TIP**
> Selling emphasizes what the company needs—sales and profits—whereas marketing emphasizes what the buyer needs.

convincing a potential customer to purchase; in marketing, the emphasis is on what the customer wants. It is up to you to develop the product or service that will satisfy that want. Selling frequently emphasizes internal company organization, such as production or some other functional area, whereas marketing must emphasize an organization working outside the company in order to learn what the customer wants before the production is even conceived.

Clearly, any buyer's or potential buyer's needs are continually changing, whether in response to psychological or other factors. At one time, a need for security may predominate. At other times it may be some physiological need, or perhaps an emotional need. Your product is sure to satisfy some needs, but at the same time may seem to ignore others, so take caution: when you introduce a new product that was based on research into certain customer needs, you should continue your research sufficiently to ensure that the product doesn't cause more dissatisfaction than satisfaction.

It is often difficult to determine your potential customer's exact needs at any given time, but if you cannot do this, you cannot implement the marketing concept. Sometimes needs are totally different in two different segments of one market. Take the clothing market: in the very small sizes for children and infants, the need is for utility; in the teenage market, equal emphasis must be on style and appearance. Therefore it is unlikely that you can satisfy both segments of this market with an identical product that simply differs in size. Therefore, implementation of the marketing concept must consider market segmentation.

If your company is fairly sizable and already established, the initial stages of implementing the marketing concept may be somewhat damaging to morale. Let us say your company has been in existence for some time and has no marketing executive reporting to you, the chief executive officer. If you suddenly elevate marketing to a top-level position, you may have some friction among your older executives. This friction will exist until your marketing executive has demonstrated his value.

Two easy steps will enable you to implement the marketing concept. First develop an information system, and second, reorganize so that marketing reports to the senior executive of your company. The information system is necessary in order to get the customers' input and orientation about potential products and services you can offer. The chapter in this book on marketing research offers many techniques on how to do this.

You may need to reorganize, depending upon the stage of your company at the time, in order to ensure that the marketing concept is adopted. A later chapter will help you to reorganize efficiently and effectively to get the most out of the marketing concept, to satisfy the customer most thoroughly, and to result in your own success.

HOT spot Keep in mind that the marketing concept is an orientation toward customer needs and wants, backed by an integrated marketing effort, and aimed at generating customer satisfaction. This is the key to success and meeting your own profit goals.

How to organize the marketing function

2

Chapter 2

How to organize the marketing function

Without marketing objectives, your firm has no target, no real objective. You cannot decide how to get where you are going until you know where you want to go. Only when you have established marketing objectives for your firm can you begin to build an organization that can achieve these objectives expeditiously.

Defining marketing objectives

Let's talk about what kind of objectives you might establish for your company. Company objectives may be to penetrate a market, to introduce a new product and achieve a certain level of market share by a certain period of time, to achieve a certain level of sales, to introduce a new product line into an industry, or to introduce an old product into a new market or a new product into an old market. Objectives should be quantified. An objective of achieving great profits is not acceptable. You should quantify this to indicate that your marketing objective is to achieve profits of $50,000 by the second

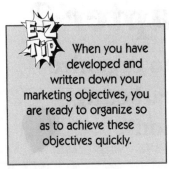

When you have developed and written down your marketing objectives, you are ready to organize so as to achieve these objectives quickly.

month or to double sales by the fourth month, and so forth.

Usually, the marketing organization of a new business is nonexistent. In fact, let's say you, as president, are going to be the entire marketing organization for your company as well as its production head and its chief salesman. It is not going to be very long before your ability to do everything yourself will be severely handicapped. You will need additional people to help you and you will need a marketing organization. Such an organization implies some sort of structure. Some people, especially those who are in a new small business, say that a structured marketing organization is not really desirable. Their theory is that everyone will work to the best of his or her ability and simply get the job done.

The problem is that without structure, even the best people with the best goodwill and the highest energy level in the world cannot accomplish an objective. Without a clear organizational structure, these good people are continually bumping into each other and taking action and expending resources which, although good for their area of operation, may severely undermine, if not destroy, the efforts of someone else who is working toward the same goal.

Even mighty Sears almost went bankrupt during its early years because Richard Sears did not effectively structure the new marketing arm of the company in running its mail-order operation.

Fritos became a household name and went from a small business to a very large one, but only after its founder, Charlie Doolan, restructured his company. He developed a new marketing organization that sold Fritos throughout the United States instead of just locally in Texas.

Max Factor went from a single store in Los Angeles to a worldwide multi-million dollar business when Max Factor, Sr., reorganized his company into a functional organization which allowed marketing and development to operate separately.

Two researchers at Ohio University, Paul Hershey and Kenneth Blanchard, developed a theory about organizations and leadership which they called the Life Cycle Theory. According to the Life Cycle Theory, organizations are operated in different ways depending on their age. A brand new company, for example, might well operate more effectively with a very

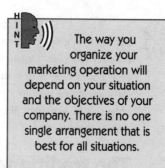

The way you organize your marketing operation will depend on your situation and the objectives of your company. There is no one single arrangement that is best for all situations.

tight structure and with little consideration for the members of the organization than an older company. The reason for this is that in a new organization that has little or no structure but shows high consideration for the members, the members of the organization may construe such consideration as permissiveness and the lack of structure as a sort of I-don't-care attitude on the part of management. As parents with small children know, structure is often very necessary.

As an organization grows older, more trust can be placed in its individual members. In fact, a higher degree of consideration for the individual members of the organization may be just the way to achieve greater effectiveness. In family life, this might correspond to youngsters in high school.

As an organization grows still older, and the members of the organization take increasingly more responsibility for their actions and learn more about how to achieve the objectives of the organization, the structure may be loosened and consideration for members increased even more.

note This is but one example of the Life Cycle Theory in operation. As a young company you will be functionally organized. In a functional organization each suborganization performs a separate function, For example, as president you may have marketing, engineering, and production organizations reporting to you. However, as time goes on and your sales increase, you, as the one final arbiter, will be making more and more decisions that will have increasing impact on more activities in your company. Eventually the load becomes too much, and at this point, many organizations make a transition into some other type of organization where some of the decision making can be delegated to lower-level managers.

While we should keep the Life Cycle Theory in mind when we structure any marketing organization, we should at the same time consider what Peter Drucker has said: "Organizational change of structure is major surgery." The clear implication here is that you should not undertake restructuring unless there are strong reasons for doing so, just as surgery should not be performed unless it is essential. Why? Like medical surgery, organizational surgery connotes risk.

The traditional organization

Traditional organization is based on the concept of line and staff. If you can understand this concept, you will be able to structure any type of organization. Line personnel are people who take action and make decisions that have to do with reaching the primary objectives of the organization. In a traditional organization, there is a chain of command containing line personnel for accomplishing tasks and decision making from the top to the bottom. Their responsibilities and authority are explicit and clear-cut. Everyone knows exactly what he is expected to do, what authority and responsibility he has, and to whom he reports at each level.

In a traditional organization, a decision is made at the lowest working level, as indicated in Figure 2-1. If the matter in question for some reason cannot be made by or is considered beyond the authority of the person at the lowest level, it is passed on to the next higher level. Through this concept, decisions that cannot be resolved are passed up the line to the very apex of the organization, the president.

Staff personnel are not in this chain of command. According to traditional organizational theory, staff includes everyone who is not line. Staff personnel at every level support line functions by providing advice, counseling, and recommendations.

> **HOT** spot According to the basic principles of traditional organizational theory, responsibility is given only with a commensurate amount of authority.

Below: Each position reports to only one other position, so that each individual in the organization has only one boss. Tier lines of authority and responsibility exist from the bottom

DEFINITION

to the very top, and each head of a department has a limited number of persons reporting to him. This is a number that he can control effectively; traditionally it is no more than nine. This number is known as *the span of control*. The design of the job is used to determine the selection of personnel rather than the other way around.

Figure 2-1. A traditional organization

```
                    ┌───────────────┐
                    │   President    │
                    └───────┬───────┘
                            │         ┌───────┐  Planner
                            ├─────────│ Staff │  Financial
                            │         └───────┘  Officer
                            │                    New Business
                            ▲
        ┌───────────────────┼───────────────────┐
   ┌─────────┐        ┌──────────┐        ┌──────────┐
   │   VP     │        │   VP      │        │   VP      │
   │Marketing │        │Engineering│        │Production │
   └─────────┘        └──────────┘        └──────────┘
        │              ┌───────┐  Public Relations
        ├──────────────│ Staff │  Administrator
        │              └───────┘  Customer Relations
        ▲
   ┌────────────┼───────────────────┐
┌──────────┐ ┌───────────┐   ┌──────────┐
│Marketing │ │Advertising│   │  Sales    │
│Research  │ │ Director  │   │ Director  │
│Director  │ └───────────┘   └──────────┘
└──────────┘                      │
                         ┌────────┴──────┐
                    ┌──────────┐   ┌──────────┐
                    │  West     │   │  East     │
                    │ Manager   │   │ Manager   │
                    └──────────┘   └──────────┘
                         ▲
        ┌──────────┬─────┼──────┬──────────┐
  ┌──────────┐┌──────────┐┌──────────┐┌──────────┐┌──────────┐
  │Salesperson││Salesperson││Salesperson││Salesperson││Salesperson│
  └──────────┘└──────────┘└──────────┘└──────────┘└──────────┘
```

(Unresolved decisions
passed up from here)

A manager is given commensurate authority in order to fulfill each responsibility that has been delegated to him. Finally, the manager in a traditional organization can delegate authority to accomplish a task to a subordinate, but he does not surrender the accountability of the task.

This theory has served reasonably well as a model over the last 2,000 years, but within the last 50 years or so behavioral scientists have attacked it.

Their argument is not that a traditionally structured organization won't work, but that human beings can be organized to perform even better.

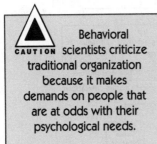

note In a traditional organization, there is no division of responsibility or authority.

The limiting of the individual in a traditional organization to a certain area of responsibility may conflict with his job classification. For example, a marketing manager with broad talents and abilities may be limited in a traditional organization to performing the sales function.

⚠ CAUTION Behavioral scientists criticize traditional organization because it makes demands on people that are at odds with their psychological needs.

Behavioral scientists also say that the basic principles of traditional organizational theory are derived from the incorrect assumption that people do not like work and responsibility and therefore you must closely supervise them to get them to perform. They maintain that this is not true and that people do in fact seek responsibility; they do not necessarily dislike work. They assert that a theory based on an erroneous assumption is not designed to take advantage of the maximum potential for work inherent in any member of an organization.

In addition, these behavioral scientists claim that traditional organization provides for no communication between the manager at the top of the organization and his working people at the bottom, only between him and his intermediate subordinates. Therefore, all information is screened coming up and screened going down, and neither the person at the top nor the people at the bottom receive a true picture.

Nontraditional solutions

The behavioral scientists did not stop at criticizing traditional organization, but also made various recommendations in order to improve what they regarded as the basic shortcoming of traditional organizations.

Their recommendations are known as the human relations approach. It has been characterized by a number of important concepts:

1) Enrichment or enlargement of a job rather than narrow specialization.

2) An emphasis on teamwork and the development of voluntary cooperation.

3) Accountability to peers rather than to superiors.

4) Enlargement of the span of control to encourage delegation of authority.

5) Emphasis on group rather than individual decision making.

6) Use of informal norms rather than total reliance on rules and regulations.

Many of the recommendations made by the behavioral scientists have been incorporated and have had a considerable impact on traditional organizations. They have been adopted by small businesses throughout the United States and throughout the world as well as by many of the largest Fortune 500 companies and some of the largest bureaucratic organizations in the world. As business people interested in structuring marketing departments that will be profitable to our companies, we should use both traditional and nontraditional concepts as tools to help us reach our goal and objectives.

This sensible balancing of concepts has in itself developed into a theory, which organizational experts call "contingency" theory. Its main emphasis is that there is in fact no best approach for all organizations, and that specific situational factors should govern the choice.

HOT spot At any given time, you must select those facets of traditional and nontraditional organizational theory that make sense for the survival and profitability of your marketing organization.

Centralization and decentralization

Before we can begin to design a proper structure for our marketing organization, there is yet another concept which will have an impact on our final design and which we must understand before proceeding. This is the concept of centralization and decentralization. It has applicability to traditional organizations as well as those that are aligned with human relations theories and recommendations.

DEFINITION

Centralized decision making means making decisions at the highest level possible within the organization, at corporate headquarters. One advantage of central organization is that decisions are generally made by the most competent, best qualified people in the organization. Why? The theory is that rising to the top acts as a natural screening process. Better people reach the top, and in the process they acquire the most high-level management experience.

Another advantage of centralization is that the people who are making these top-level decisions are generally all located in the same geographical area or even in the very same building. Because they can communicate with one another readily and deliberate together before the decision making, coordination is much easier and the likelihood is greater that a decision will be supported by overall organizational interests rather than those of any one special interest group or division.

Still another advantage to centralization is that since the divisions of the organization do not operate independently, less staff is required. Most general staff support is needed at headquarters where the decision making is accomplished. Duplicating functions, such as having a new-business development specialist, at headquarters and at each of the suborganizations, is not necessary.

As a final major dividend, the centralization concept allows for standardization. Since the central organization is making purchasing decisions, a buy in quantity is made by the headquarters organization rather than several separate buys of smaller quantity for each of the suborganizations. In this way money is saved. Money may also be saved in maintenance of a standardized item. Also, mobility of managers from one

division to another is much easier and requires less time for familiarization, since standardized operating procedures hold throughout the overall organization and do not differ substantially among the subdivisions.

Are there any advantages to a decentralized organization? Yes, quite a few. In a decentralized organization, responsibility is delegated as far down the organization as possible. This means the individual marketing manager—the one directly concerned with the work to be accomplished—is making the decisions related to it. Clearly, he can react much more rapidly on the spot than he could in a centralized organization, where he would have to spend time collecting information and sending it to higher headquarters, which might then sometimes request additional information. If so, this information would then have to be collected and sent. Finally, after the decision is made at headquarters, it must be sent back to the division. Only then can the subordinate unit implement it. Of course, during this long process the situation may change. This means several reiterations of the process will be required. Sometimes the wrong decision will be implemented because of these changes.

Another advantage of decentralization is that people on the scene have greater knowledge of local conditions and problems, which makes for better quality decisions. For this reason, many multinational corporations are decentralized. If local conditions vary among the different countries in which a multinational corporation is involved, central purchasing or standardized policies may not be possible. Decentralization also permits the development of corporate managers and allows more opportunity for management training than does a centralized organization, which needs fewer managers. Finally, decentralization provides greater job satisfaction to people at the lower levels who have a desire for; freedom of action, more authority, and greater responsibility.

Designing your marketing organization

It is now up to you to translate these concepts into the boxes and lines of an organizational structure. Basically if you are designing the marketing function in a small business, you will choose one of three types: the functional

organization, the goal-oriented organization, or the matrix organization. In rather general terms, the functional organization tends to be more traditional than the others, while the goal-oriented organization tends to be more related to human relations theory, but there are elements of all these concepts in each. The matrix organization attempts to secure the best of both worlds; it too can have underpinnings of all organizational theories in its construction.

The functional organization

Basically the functional organization uses a traditional organizational structure, with a division of labor among the various functions. Figure 2-2 shows a marketing organization that includes sales, marketing research, and advertising.

But a functional marketing organization has other characteristics which, depending upon your situation, may help or hinder you in reaching your organization's goals and objectives. For example, the division of labor is much easier to accomplish in a functional marketing organization than in a goal-oriented organization. If you have a marketing research department that services different geographic areas, you can accomplish the same task with fewer professionals than if you had the kind of

> **E-Z TIP**
>
> Functional organizations tend to work better with centralized types of structures in which the head of the marketing organization makes most of the important day-to-day decisions. Such an organization has both the advantages and the disadvantages of the centralized organization.

organization in which each geographic location had its own separate marketing research department.

note

Your functional marketing department will have a greater likelihood of getting the most out of total personnel resources than it would in a goal-oriented organization. This is because the members of your functional organization can be directed to work throughout your company without making changes in supervision or organizational setup. However, in a goal-oriented organization the work area is more limited in size because of the focus on a certain goal. When there is no work for the goal-oriented

organization to do, its members cannot easily be redirected elsewhere without a change of supervision or a change in organizational structure.

Figure 2-2. A functionally organized marketing organization.

You will also find, if you had a functional marketing organization, that there will be greater professional synergism since members will interact. For example, the marketing research department has professionals concerned only with marketing research and they will interact. Your sales department contains only employees concerned with sales, and they will interact. Thus, in such an environment a new man can be more easily trained in his particular specialty, and all the members will tend to learn more about their individual specialty and improve their technical marketing skills.

On the other hand, each member of the functional marketing organization will understand less of other specialties in the overall marketing organization. A person in marketing research won't know as much about sales as he could, while a person in sales might know less about marketing research. Each marketing specialist may tend to focus more on his particular specialty than on the overall goal of the marketing organization.

You must also consider the fact that your functional marketing organization will have more difficulty coordinating, scheduling, and integrating activities with other functional organizations within the company. This is because of conflict and competition between different organizations and the fact that each functional organization has its own manager. Therefore, you must go to the head of all of the functional organizations for any decision involving a problem within the lower-level organization. This can mean more work for the overall manager.

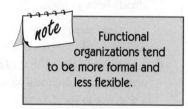

note

Functional organizations tend to be more formal and less flexible.

Since goal organizations are self-contained, they permit informal contact between different specialties, which reduces the need to turn to higher authority to resolve conflicts. But because of the separation of individuals in authority in two or more functional organizations, there is a reduced ability to resolve conflicts between departments.

The goal-oriented organization

In designing a goal-oriented organization you may incorporate elements of the traditional organization as well as those of human relations or other concepts. As the name implies, a goal-oriented marketing organization is designed around the marketing organization's goal by product, geographic area, different category or customer, or different project. Figure 2-3 shows an organization designed to sell a single medical product to three different areas. Each of the subordinate marketing organizations includes retail sales, wholesale sales, and institutional sales. Each division of such a goal-oriented marketing organization is self-contained and can operate relatively independently. Therefore, a geographic goal oriented marketing organization may have its own marketing research,department and its own sales department and perhaps its own advertising department in each geographic area. It is this factor of self-containment and independence that accounts for the goal-oriented organization's greatest weaknesses: duplication of personnel, duplication of skills, and duplication of equipment. Such duplication is obviously unnecessary within one overall functional organization.

Other disadvantages of the goal-oriented marketing organization are less likelihood of maximum utilization of resources, less synergism between the various professionals who make up this organization, and others that have already been mentioned.

One major advantage of every goal-oriented organization may outweigh all else: The goal-oriented organization is dedicated to achieving a goal, not to the day-to-day professional work of a functional organization.

HOT spot When the emphasis is on accomplishment of a specific goal or task, implying schedules to be met, a unique service offered, or special problems to be solved, the goal-oriented design usually works better than the functional design.

Figure 2-3. A goal-oriented marketing organization.

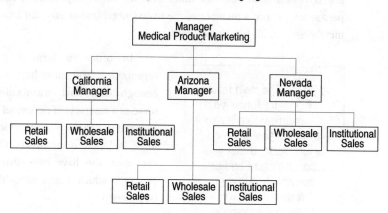

Schedules, coordination, and integration of all the various tasks leading to a specific goal are far more effectively handled when an organization is goal-directed.

The matrix organization

The matrix organization is a relatively recent development. It is an attempt to incorporate the best features of both the functional and the goal-oriented designs. It does not matter whether the matrix organization you form is permanent or temporary; its membership is made up of individuals who are assigned to one or more suborganizations in the overall organizational structure. Because of this, supervision comes from more than one source and the individual often has more than one boss.

In Figure 2-4, which shows a matrix organization of Project A and Project B within an overall functional organization, each member has at least two supervisors. In fact, two members of the organization have more than two supervisors. Each individual reports to his functional manager and supervisor as well as to the heads of Project A and B. The project managers may also have functional jobs: The chief of Project A is also the normal head of the marketing research department.

The primary advantages of the matrix marketing organization are flexibility and goal orientation. But unlike a goal-oriented organization, a

matrix organization does not suffer from the sin of duplication, because a person who is not a member of the matrix organization may still retain his membership in his functional organization.

> **E-Z TIP** The main reason for forming a matrix, which is also true of a goal-oriented organization, is that goal accomplishment and time constraints outweigh requirements for economic efficiency.

In order to form a matrix organization, you must have a large enough functional organization to serve as a reservoir of personnel to be assigned to various projects which are to be included in the matrix. Clearly you must also have more than one project to which these individuals can be assigned.

Finally, you must ensure that whoever heads the matrixed organization or project derives power from some source. The head of a matrix organization has no formal authority over the personnel assigned to him or her from other organizations who are actually doing the work of his project. His authority is over the project only. One means of providing authority to him is through project funding. His project is given authority over a certain amount of money and he is permitted to "buy" various services from other functional departments, including the services of the people who are assigned to him from functional departments.

HINT Let's look again at the life cycle of the organization. If your company is very new and you are in the start-up stage, you will have direct influence on your organization, and you yourself may be doing marketing work in addition to your managerial functions. Such a start-up stage lends itself to a goal-oriented structure, because there are not enough members in the organization for a functional structure. You, as the one in charge of marketing, can have the maximum impact on all the personnel in it. Many small companies never progress beyond this start-up stage, which is not necessarily bad. This may be the best stage for your company to be in at this point, and perhaps this is where your marketing organization should be as well.

However, for many companies, the next step is to move to a functional orientation stage—stage two of the life cycle. In this stage the responsibility

Figure 2-4. A matrix-organized marketing organization.

Marketing Project A

1. Manager (Marketing research manager
2. Analyst A
3. Copywriter B
4. Copywriter C
5. Researcher A
6. Salespersons A, B, E

Director of Marketing

Marketing Project B

1. Manager
2. Analysts A, C
3. Copywriters A,C
4. Salespersons C, D

Marketing Research

1. Manager
2. Analyst A
3. Analyst B
4. Analyst C
5. Researcher A
6. Researcher B

Advertising

1. Manager
2. Copywriter A
3. Copywriter B
4. Copywriter C
5. Artist A
6. Artist B

Sales

1. Manager
2. Salesperson A
3. Salesperson B
4. Salesperson C
5. Salesperson D
6. Salesperson E

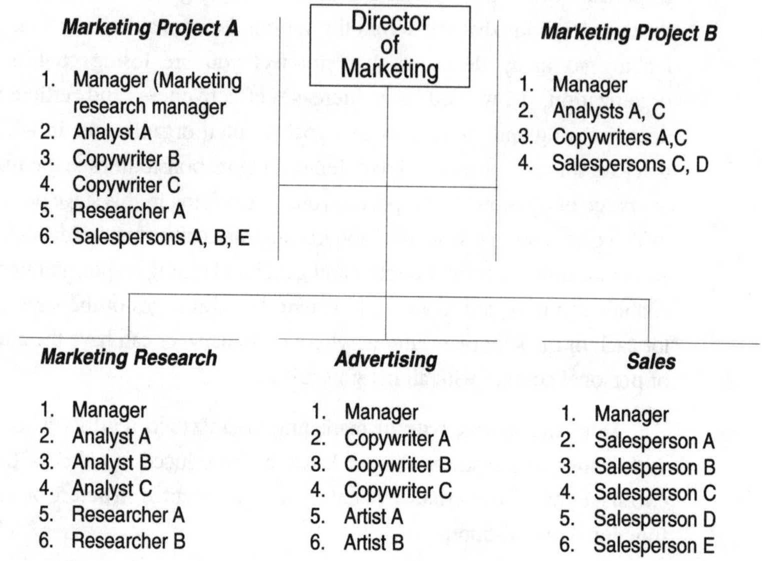

HOT spot The increasing responsibilities cannot be handled by one man any longer, and you now have the specialized personnel available that permit you to build a functional organization.

of your marketing organization will have increased. You hire additional people, and it is now more difficult for you to exert your personality and to have contact with all the people reporting to you. In fact, their number alone makes control more difficult. On the other hand, you don't have to wear as many hats as you did before. Perhaps you had one marketing function that was particularly troublesome, and you have now found someone who is a specialist and can really run with it. Now it is more efficient to organize your business by division of labor by specialty. You may still want to head one or more of the subdivisions in addition to being in charge of the overall marketing organization, but you should think about changing to a functional type of organization. Because of the size of your organization, it is no longer an advantage for you to have direct contact with all your personnel. Many companies stay in stage two for many years, and some never move out.

The final stage of the life cycle is the diversification stage. Here the responsibilities of the organization have increased greatly. You. are continually making decisions that cut across the various functional lines. In fact, you are making so many decisions that you feel you are losing control of the organization. Now you can increase effectiveness and efficiency by decentralizing and going back to a goal-oriented organization, in which you delegate some of the general decision-making responsibilities to the managers in charge of divisions that report to you. Diversifying in this stage permits you to delegate some of your decision-making authority to subordinates, giving you more time for greater control and general planning responsibilities. It also enables you to regain to a certain extent the advantages of the start-up stage for each of the suborganizations, where each manager can have the advantage of personal contact with all his subordinates.

Does the matrix type of marketing organization lend itself to the life cycle concept? The answer is yes. It can be introduced in either of the latter two stages or as an alternative to either the goal-oriented structure or a straight functional organization.

Your aim is to construct a marketing organization that will maximize effectiveness and efficiency and will reach your organizational goals. You develop this organization by first establishing your goals, documenting them, and quantifying them precisely. Then, considering the concepts of traditional and nontraditional organizations, centralization and decentralization, and contingency theory, you structure your organization to maximize the advantages for your particular situation in each stage of the life cycle.

Beat your competition

Chapter 3

Beat your competition

Almost 2,000 years ago Hannibal, general of the relatively minor state of Carthage, almost brought mighty Rome to its knees. He did this not with superior weaponry, not with superiority in numbers, and certainly not with a mighty industrial base. Hannibal's victories were based on strategy.

Typical of the wonders that Hannibal worked with strategy was the Battle of Cannae, fought in 216 B.C. against a superior force of Romans under the Roman general, Varro. Hannibal positioned his troops defensively with strong flanks anchored on the River Aurtidus. His weak center drove forward, inviting the Romans to attack. On his right flank he positioned the weaker of the two forces of Carthaginian cavalry. These engaged and held a superior force of Roman cavalry until the major portion of Carthaginian cavalry, which started on Hannibal's left flank, drove all the way around the two fighting armies to strike the heavy Roman cavalry from the rear and destroy them. At the same time the Roman legions, encountering Hannibal's weak center, rushed their forces forward. Hannibal's center withdrew slowly, sucking the Romans into the center of the Carthaginian mass while the Carthaginian flanks stood fast

and held firmly on the river. When the Romans were totally surrounded, Hannibal gave the order and the trap sprang shut. More than 60,000 of the original 85,000 Roman troops were killed.

> **HINT** Decisive strategy is not limited to warfare. A proper application of strategic principles can win battles in business as well.

Back in the late 1950s both Ford and Chevrolet introduced small subcompact automobiles to compete with the then still growing foreign imports such as Volkswagen, Fiat, and Japanese makes that were beginning to penetrate the market. Despite strenuous efforts, the Detroit-made subcompacts were not totally successful. Ford conducted extensive marketing research to discover who was buying the Ford Falcon, which was Ford's subcompact car, and what features they liked best about it. Over months of research, Ford discovered that although Falcon sales were declining as a percentage of the total sales of the subcompact market and of the total automobile market, sporty features such as bucket seats, higher-powered engines, four-speed gearshifts, and the like were actually increasing in popularity.

With this intelligence, Ford formed a new marketing strategy that came to fruition in 1965 and inflicted a Cannae on its competitors. This product strategy was the introduction of the Mustang, a so-called sports touring car built to satisfy the younger market that Ford had identified as the purchasers who had admired the sporty features of the now defunct Falcon.

Ford's successful strategy left the competition far behind. It was several years before other manufacturers introduced models of the Mustang type.

I think I know what you are thinking: Ford is a giant company, and giant companies have the time to sit back, conduct extensive market research, analyze the results, and develop a successful strategy to beat their competition. But a small company, in which the president/owner wears more than one hat, allows no such luxury. Look at it this way: It is not that you do not have time to work out a successful strategy—you do not have the time *not* to. A small company can be successful in its strategy even when taking on giants. Why? Because a small company can move much faster than a large company in its decision making. Because it can totally change its concept in a day, whereas it

can take a large company a year or longer. Because it can offer more personalized service than a large company can. And finally, a small company can choose one part of the market, go after it, and make it profitable and successful, whereas a large company, because of huge overhead, frequently must ignore small market clusters of profitability. Less than ten years ago, a small company was formed, named International Control Systems. This company took on no less a giant than IBM in the computer field and won by executing a successful strategy of market segmentation. This strategic concept as well as others we will talk about later.

DEFINITION

Under the overall concept of strategy, certain variables can be controlled and certain variables cannot. Those that can are called *strategic variables*. We control these variables—as Hannibal did his cavalry and his infantry—to evolve an overall strategy that will lead to success. There are four strategic variables. In marketing these are sometimes called the four P's. They are:

- product

- price

- place (distribution)

- promotion

The promotional variable includes promotions, personal selling, and advertising.

The product as a strategic variable

There are three things we can do about product: We can introduce a new product, we can change or modify a product, and we can withdraw a product.

Introducing a new product

There are two basic things to keep in mind about the introduction of a new product. The first is that you must introduce new products in order for your business to survive. If you don't your competition will eventually overtake you. Barely seven years ago, a company made millions by introducing a calculator the size of a transistor radio. In 1973 this calculator sold for what was then an unheard of low price, only $80. How many such calculators could

be sold today, when you can buy a calculator the size of a business card for less than $20? Or another example: Could Ford have continued to sell its 1965 Mustang today in this era of fuel economy and subcompacts? No, today's Mustang is much different from the one introduced in 1965.

 Unfortunately, the second point is bad news. It warns us that 80 percent of new products will fail. This failure of new product introduction is due to a thousand and one reasons, and each one costs money. Therefore, as good businessmen and small business managers we must take care to minimize the number of failures among our new products, and to minimize the risks to our financial and other resources in introducing new products. We not only must increase our success rate, but we must make every nickel and dime count.

Before we talk about how to do this, let's talk about how not to do it. While every businessman must use judgment in running his business, he should not allow his emotions or his personal prejudices to cloud his judgmental faculties. In one case, the president of a small engineering and manufacturing firm, which was concerned primarily with developing new products for the government, frequently committed large resources to new product development on the basis of his own or a close friend's observations. This man would make trips to meet with the customer, would talk to one or two friends, then start a new product development program with no more information than that. As

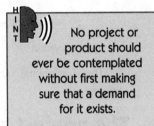

No project or product should ever be contemplated without first making sure that a demand for it exists.

a result, most of the research and development funds necessary for the survival of this company were wasted, since the programs were never fully researched to determine whether the product was actually needed and desired by those in the government who would have to buy it.

You will always have more ideas for new product development than there are resources to pursue them. This means that you will always be faced with making a choice between what you would like to do and what you can actually do. Deciding which new product to pursue and which to hold in abeyance or drop can be done in a number of ways. Sometimes a combination of ways works best. Which method or methods you use will depend on your

situation. Here are some typical ways to make decisions about new product introduction:

- payback

- present value

- internal rate of return

- return on investment (ROI)

- profitability for sales goals, or some other method of comparison that is relevant to your particular new product development decision making

Payback is relevant when you must see a return on your investment within a certain time period. It is calculated by putting the investment in the numerator and your yearly return in the denominator. For example, if your investment was $5,000 and your yearly return in profits was $1,000, the payback period would be five years. It may be that you have a go/no-go situation in which you must see the return on investment within three years. In that case, a five-year project would be unacceptable. On the other hand, your criterion may be the need to see the return on your investment as soon as possible. In that case a two-year payback period would be better than one of three years; or a five-year payback period would be better than one of six or seven years.

DEFINITION

Present value, or PV, is a capital budgeting technique. An analysis based on capital budgeting relates to the time value of money. That is, if you did not invest money in your new product, you might use the money in other ways. For example, you could put the money in the bank and receive an interest of 7 percent per year. You could put the money into home mortgages and receive perhaps 10 percent per year. In other words, there are always choices to make. In using a capital budgeting analysis, you take your initial investment as a negative cash flow at zero years. Every other outflow or inflow of money is figured on a year-by-year basis according to a certain interest or a cost of capital rate. This rate must be determined by your own judgment. Special present value tables are available for capital budgeting calculations. These tables appear in the Appendix of this book.

As an example, let's assume that we use an interest rate of .08. We have a choice between two projects. Project A will require an initial investment of $5,000. The life of the product is five years and so is development time. Therefore, from years six through ten we can expect profits of $5,000 per year. Project B requires an initial investment of $4,000. Its development time is one year. It will bring us yearly profits of $4,000 a year during its product life cycle, which is also five years, but its development time is only one year so that it will be profitable from years two through six. Here are the calculations for this comparison:

	Project A			*Project B*	
Year	Initial Investment =	$5,000	Year	Initial Investment =	$4,000
6	+($5,000)x(.6302) =	+3,151	2	+($4,000)x(.8573) =	+3,429
7	+($5,000)x(.5835) =	+2,917	3	+($4,000)x(.7938) =	+3,175
8	+($5,000)x(.5403) =	+2,701	4	+($4,000)x(.7350) =	+2,940
9	+($5,000)x(.5002) =	+2,501	5	+($4,000)x(.6806) =	+2,722
10	+($5,000)x(.4632) =	+2,316	6	+($4,000)x(.6302) =	+2,521
		+ $8,586			+ $10,787

The multiplying factor is found in Table 1 in the Appendix. The percent value at 8 percent at year 6 yields a multiplying factor of .6302, for year 7 of .5835, and so forth.

This shows why Project B will be more profitable than Project A: profit of $10,787 versus profit of $8,586.

DEFINITION

Internal rate of return, or IRR, is an alternative capital budgeting technique that enables us to compare two or more different projects for profitability considering the time value of money and the fact that we may spend financial resources in other ways. Let us look at the same two projects, using an interest rate of .08, and compute an internal rate of return. In this case we do not know the interest rate, but either we are seeking the highest possible interest rate or, alternatively, our company may have a policy of accepting no project whose internal rate of return does not fall below a certain percentage. We calculate this information as follows.

To find the internal rate of return, we must again consult Table 1 in the Appendix. For project A, look for multipliers that, when multiplied by our return of $5,000 a year for years 6 through 10, will equal our investment of

$5,000. In other words, the sum of the five multipliers in the years 6 through 10 should equal about 1.0. This appears to be a rate of return between 23 percent and 26 percent.

	23 percent		*26 percent*	
year 6	.2751 x 5,000 =	$ 1,375	.0333 x 5,000 =	$ 1,516
year 7	.2218 x 5,000 =	1,109	.2486 x 5,000 =	1,243
year 8	.1789 x 5,000 =	894	.2038 x 5,000 =	1,019
year 9	.1443 x 5,000 =	721	.1670 x 5,000 =	835
year 10	.1164 x 5,000 =	582	.1369 x 5,000 =	685
		$4,681		$5,298

Therefore, for Project A we know that the internal rate of return is about 25 percent.

Now let's look at Project B.

We use the same method, except that we see that for years 2 through 6, the multipliers times our return of $4,000 per year will equal our initial investment of $4,000 and an internal rate of return of between 50 percent and 45 percent.

	50 percent		*45 percent*	
year 2	.4444 x 4,000 =	$1,778	.4752 x 4,000 =	$1,901
year 3	.2963 x 4,000 =	1,185	.3280 x 4,000 =	1,312
year 4	.1975 x 4,000 =	790	.2262 x 4,000 =	905
year 5	.1317 x 4,000 =	527	.1560 x 4,000 =	624
year 6	.0878 x 4,000 =	351	.1076 x 4,000 =	430
		$4,631		$5,173

As a rough estimate, internal rate of return for Project B is 47 percent. Since 47 percent is greater than 23 percent, Project B offers a better internal rate of return.

There are many different ratios and methods of calculating return on investment. A very simple one is by dividing the return by the investment. Thus, if the return were $5,000 and the investment $20,000, the ROI would be

 Definition:

ROI stands for *return on investment*. It is a measurement of our investment against the total return in profit we might expect.

.25. If the return were $5,000 and the investment $50,000 the ROI would be .10. Clearly with this type of analysis, we want to have the largest percentage possible. That will be the best ROI.

Breakeven analysis is another method of comparing alternative projects to decide which is more advantageous. With breakeven analysis, you compare how many units or dollars are necessary in sales in order to break even or make no profit but incur no loss. A breakeven chart is constructed as shown in Figure 3-1. On the vertical axis we have dollars. On the horizontal axis we have units of the new product. The horizontal line drawn at the $1,700 point represents the research and development investment. The $2,000 line represents the total fixed costs including tooling. The line drawn upward and to the right from zero origin represents sales. For example, if each unit sells for $20, then the sale of 275 units represents $5,500, and this point falls on the horizontal line plotted. The line starting at the $2,000 'point on the vertical axis and continuing upward and to the right is the total cost line. The breakeven point lies at the intersection of the total cost line and the sales line.

Figure 3-1. Breakeven analysis.

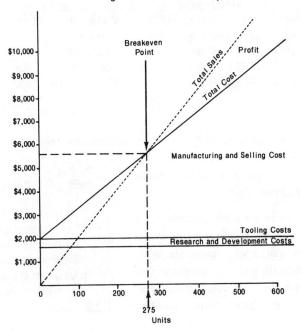

In the example shown in the figure, the breakeven occurs at $5,500 and 275 units sold. At this point we neither make a profit nor incur any loss. Higher up on the sales line, above the breakeven point, we make a profit. Lower down on the sales line, below the breakeven point, we suffer a loss. Although the breakeven analysis shows us how many units we must sell to break even and how much we will make depending on sales volume, it does not tell us how long it will take us to reach breakeven, nor does it show the maximum potential profitability of the product.

Profitability or sales goals may be used to compare competing projects for developing new products for the marketplace. We may use a very simple criterion: the maximum sales possible or the maximum profits possible. You can also substitute any criterion you feel is important for your situation. You could, for example, compare products for development based on the publicity they might bring to your company, ignoring profitability, sales, breakeven, ROI, IRR, or any other basis of quantitative comparison.

Modifying a product or changing its use

note

We modify a product or change its use in order to extend the product's life cycle.

Every product has a life cycle that begins at introduction and goes through various phases until market saturation. You will note by looking at Figure 3-2 that although sales may still be high when the market is saturated, profits may have actually declined. This is usually what happens when competitors produce the same item, or when the cost per sale has risen. The saturation portion of the life cycle is the time to take action to continue high profitability. One such action is, of course, to introduce a new product and begin the cycle anew.

Another method that frequently works well—and is less expensive and takes less time—is simply to change or modify the old product or find a new use for it. Either of these actions extends the life cycle, as shown by the dashed lines in the figure. The hand calculator of 1973 mentioned before had its life cycle extended by a modification that reduced its size by approximately 80 percent and reduced the cost at the same time. Naturally this product has been modified several times—many times, in fact—since that period. Or

Figure 3-2. Declining profits with market saturation.

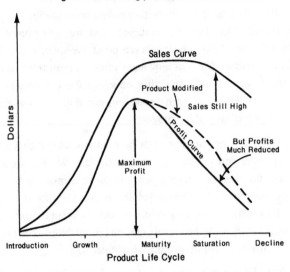

consider the potato chip. This product was revolutionized in its saturation phase simply by repackaging from a bag into a can and changing the chip so that all chips were of identical size and shape, permitting them to stack neatly. This made the potato chip less crushable. The product took a significant number of sales from the product as still sold today in the standard paper bag.

Another example of a change of this type is the decision made several years ago to offer a very old product to fulfill an entirely new need. Here is where Armour took baking soda, a product that had been around for 100 years or more, and offered it as a freshener for refrigerators. This product change extended the life cycle effectively into the dashed line as shown in the figure. When making the decision to modify a product or change its use, we should always compare the altered product and its cost against a proposed new product and its costs in the same way that we compared alternatives among new products. This is the only way we will really know whether it is better to introduce one of our new products into the marketplace or simply to change one that is already there.

Withdrawing a product

The third choice we can make is to discontinue a product. You may wonder why a negative decision to drop a product is important to you as a head of a small business. It is important because dropping a product frees resources that will allow you to develop or promote other possibly more profitable products. Furthermore, retaining a product while introducing a replacement at the same time means that you will lose some sales from your old product to the new product. You will also lose some potential sales for the new product because of continuing sales of the old one.

 You must always run a continuing review of the products in your current product line to see whether they should be dropped or continued.

The review of the wisdom of dropping products should be continued throughout a new product's development, since changes in the marketplace as well as progress in technology or lack of progress in program development can always affect the product decision.

Pricing as a strategic variable

Controlling the price of a product is another way to win in the marketplace. In general, there are three basic strategies available to you: You can have a high price, a low price, or a meet-the-competition price.

There are many cases where a high price is the correct pricing strategy. In fact, one of the most common errors in small business marketing is to use a low price when a high price is the one that will actually maximize profitability. A high price may be useful for image. If, for example, you are a consultant, the fact that your price is low may lead to the inference that you are not as expert as a similar consultant who has a high price.

Going in with a high price for a new product has the additional advantage that the higher price recaptures the initial investment sooner. Then, when the competition rushes in with an identical or similar product, more financial resources are available to the small firm to counter this and initiate

action to maintain profitability. Finally, high price may be used to maintain or initiate distribution channels. Joe Cossman, the distributor and promoter of the flexible tube sprinkling hose, had the entire market to himself with his new product during the first year of sales. The second summer, however,

 HOT spot Remember that the consumer, or your customer or client, is looking at price as only one component in the overall value he receives.

many competitors rushed in with similar products. Since this item was not patented, and since it was very easy to construct tooling to manufacture the product at relatively low cost, all these competitors used penetration, or low, pricing tactics, to attempt to break into this market. But Joe Cossman actually raised his price, and at the same time he raised the discount to retail distributors. This meant considerably more profit for these distributors, many of whom chose to carry the Cossman sprinkler rather than the lower-priced brands that would have given them a much lower profit margin.

A low price is really a penetration price. It is the most frequently used strategy to break into a new market. You need to see that the low price does not negatively affect your image. You do not want your customers or clients to get the feeling that your product or service is inferior in value or quality.

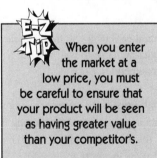 **E-Z TIP** When you enter the market at a low price, you must be careful to ensure that your product will be seen as having greater value than your competitor's.

The me-too price, or meet-the-competition price, assumes that your product or service possesses special features that greatly increase its value. You cannot expect to use a me-too price to break into any market with a new product and take market shares away from your competitors if you do not offer something different or extra to increase the value, at least as perceived by your customer.

Distribution as a strategic variable

The distribution variable refers to the choices you can make about the best way to get your product to market. You must consider the fact that

distribution channels compete with one another and that, depending on your situation and your new product, certain channels will be more successful than others. Certain channels will be more efficient than others in terms of cost. Certain distribution channels are traditionally used for some products and in some industries, and although other

Do not make the mistake of assuming that any single distribution channel can be used under all circumstances or with all products. This is just not true.

distribution channels exist, it would be unwise to use them because breaking the tradition may negatively affect sales.

On the other hand, sometimes a well-thought-out plan will enable you to succeed in using a distribution channel that has never been used successfully before for your particular product or service. For example, one does not normally think of automobiles being sold by direct mail, but several years ago someone won the Direct Mail Marketing Association's Golden Mailbox award by successfully selling diesel-powered Mercedes Benz automobiles just that way. The initial idea behind this campaign—long before the energy crisis—was simply to sell an overproduction of automobiles that Mercedes Benz had supplied with diesel engines. Diesel engines were considered a decided disadvantage in many respects. They were noisier than conventional cars, and diesel fuel wasn't always easy to find.

They were harder to repair, too. The director of the mail campaign concentrated on the advantages. He noted the differential in selling price between gasoline and diesel fuel, and he called the engine noise an advantage in that unlike gasoline-powered cars you really could hear the engine roar and know when it had been started. So successful was this campaign that Mercedes Benz not only sold the automobiles it wanted to dispose of, they had to open up the production line for additional diesel-engine automobiles to meet the demand. As a spin-off, various organizations have been formed to permit consumers to buy automobiles through the mail directly from Detroit at reduced prices simply by calling a toll-free number, giving information about the car they want, and sending a down payment. Again, a new distribution channel was successful.

Promotion as a strategic variable

Promotion is made up of three components: special promotion campaigns, personal selling, and advertising. Promotions must occur throughout a product's life cycle in order to maximize the profitability of the product. And, of course, promotion should occur throughout the existence of a business. When business is good, promotions should be done to increase market share; when business is bad, they promote the sales that are necessary to retrench and survive. The timing of promotions is critical. When timed correctly and used with other strategic variables, the sum of the parts of the marketing mix and strategy is greater than the summation of each of the strategy's different parts.

> **HOT spot** The biggest mistake that people make about special promotions is the idea that they should be done only when a new business starts or a new product is introduced.

The personal selling strategic variable is self-explanatory: salesmanship done on an individual basis by company or representative salesmen. A sales training course, for example, might be a strategy in personal selling. Or increased numbers of salesmen might be a part of the personal selling component of this strategic variable.

 The advertising component of the promotional strategic variable can be subdivided into three separate areas. First, what kind of medium to advertise in (radio, television, direct mail, handbills, and so forth). Second, which specific outlets to use of the kind selected (which magazines, which radio stations, or which television stations). Finally, when to advertise. Timing is very important. Should you advertise every day, every week, once a week, once a month, three times a year? All these questions are important in manipulating this strategic variable.

The marketing mix and how to use it

Every strategic variable can be manipulated in two ways. First, a decision can be made to use it or not to use it. Second, a decision can be made

regarding the amount of resources to be placed on the particular strategic variable. This gives us a very sizable number of combinations to construct our overall strategy. We might choose to manipulate only the product variable, or we could combine it with different quantities of the other three strategic variables. The combination of what resources to use of the four strategic variables makes up the overall strategy and is called the *marketing mix*. Given a certain fixed amount of dollars, different mixes of strategies can be purchased for this dollar figure.

DEFINITION

The *strategic variables* are variables that can be controlled by you. In addition, there are certain variables that are very difficult to manipulate or control. These variables, known as *environmental variables*, are demand, competition, distribution structure, and legal constraints.

DEFINITION

The environmental variables

Demand

Demand is an environmental and not a strategic variable because it is extremely difficult to change it. It is far better to accept demand as a given than to try to create it. In other words, in your business if demand is not there, do not attempt a strategy that requires building a demand.

Frequently a demand exists and is only waiting to be uncovered. This is quite different from having to build the demand from nothing. Frequently you will hear an inventor or promoter praising his product very enthusiastically even though it is untested in the market and the demand for it is unknown. When questioned about the existing demand, this promoter will sometimes say the existing demand is

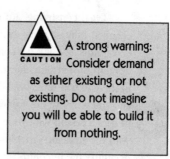
A strong warning:
CAUTION Consider demand as either existing or not existing. Do not imagine you will be able to build it from nothing.

unimportant because he will build a demand for this product. The fact is that before the demand can be built, he has gone broke.

Competition

As an environmental variable, competition can be controlled only with great difficulty. If you had unlimited resources, I suppose it would be possible to drive a competitor out of business. However, this can only be done at great expense, and in the attempt you might yourself be driven out of business. The way to handle this environmental variable as you develop your marketing strategy is to imagine what steps your competition will take to counter your strategy. Think several steps ahead of the countermoves that

In developing your strategy, always look first for existing distribution structures for this particular business or product area.

he will make for every move you make. Be assured that competition will always react in some fashion to any new strategy you introduce.

Distribution structure

Distribution structure is considered an environmental variable because, like the other two environmental variables, it must be built at a price if it does not already exist.

Legal constraints

Legal constraints are environmental variables because the law can be changed only at some price in resources, time, and effort. Therefore, legal constraints should be considered fixed and any marketing strategy you develop should allow for this fact. A marketing strategy that requires a change in the law will probably be unsuccessful because your firm will lose money and you will lose the money before you can get the law changed. If you want to be successful with your marketing strategy, you must emphasize and work with the strategic variables while at the same time you use to the best effect or nullify the uncontrollable environmental variables.

Low-cost marketing research and test marketing

4

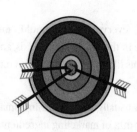

Chapter 4

Low-cost marketing research and test marketing

What you'll find in this chapter:

- ➡ Determining a method of data collection
- ➡ Selecting a sample audience
- ➡ Choosing a type of sample
- ➡ Surveying and understanding results
- ➡ Test marketing pros and cons

What is the demand for my idea? Will my idea be accepted? What is its proper price and how should I promote it? These are all questions that marketing research and test marketing can answer. Marketing research is a fairly new phenomenon in business. Its use has been prompted by the many new product and new service failures that most firms, large and small alike, have experienced.

Large companies were the first to adopt sophisticated research techniques and they have reduced their failure rate dramatically. Entrepreneurs may feel that it is impossible for owners of small businesses to conduct research, but that is not true; market research can be conducted easily and inexpensively by the entrepreneur himself.

The entrepreneur and research

Many managers of small businesses and many new entrepreneurs fail to understand why they should spend the time and money to do research. They

reason that since they like their own idea, everyone else should, too. Unfortunately, customers are individuals, unique in their wants and needs, and it is difficult to predict their behavior. What seems like a useful product to one person might appear useless to another.

Research is a form of insurance that can usually tell the businessman whether he is offering the consumer the proper mix of marketing ingredients, including the characteristics of the product itself, the price, the size and color of the package, the promotion, and the kind of distribution. If research is not undertaken, the entrepreneur may be missing one of the key ingredients that can make the difference between success and failure of a new product or service.

The entrepreneur seldom has prior experience and would be likely to base decisions exclusively upon intuition. Normally, when most persons think of research, they think of interviewers who ask questions, but there are many other invaluable sources of information, most of which are free and available for the asking.

> **HOT** spot A new business cannot afford to take the chance of introducing a new product or service without proper preparatory investigation.

Primary research, performed by professional researchers, is relatively inexpensive in comparison with the cost of failure. A complete study, including analysis of results, will normally cost from $2,000 to $6,000, depending on the method of interviewing and the complexity of the study. Although he would find it time-consuming, the entrepreneur could do the same study within the company for $100 to $1,000.

Research can tell you nearly anything you want to know, provided it has been gathered properly. Some of the more common questions research can answer are:

- What is the nature of the demand for my product?

- Who will buy my product?

- Where are my potential customers located?

- What product features do most customers really want?

- What prices are my customers willing to pay?

- What media should I use to advertise and promote my product to my customers?

- What kind of outlet should I sell my products through?

Conducting marketing research

Finding the solution to any problem follows the same process, whether it is a problem in pricing, advertising, or consumer behavior. A problem-solving process has been developed that assures valid results. It includes the following steps:

Determining the problems and objectives of the study

When research is conducted without careful evaluation, it may be wasted.

When you consider promotion, for example, it is essential to determine who the customer is so that advertising is not wasted on noncustomers. Research can determine whether or not promotion should be used at all, and it assures that the appropriate advertising and promotion message is used. The medium to use is important; radio, television, newspapers, magazines, and billboards are only a few that are available to the entrepreneur. Finally, plan the timing of the promotion. With newspapers, certain days and certain spots in the paper are much more effective than others.

A good rule of thumb is to determine the who, what, why, where, and when of the four elements of the marketing mix: product, place (channels of distribution), price, and promotion.

It is also vital to identify problem areas so that research can be directed specifically toward them. If the firm has a serious cash problem, and a great deal is spent on advertising, research should be conducted to determine the effectiveness of the advertising. Determining which specific things to look at in the research is extremely important. A new technique for accomplishing this is the Focus group involving a group of about 15 consumers similar to the ones you wish to study. This group is asked about the product or service. Their responses help to develop the questionnaire.

 Before beginning the process of gathering data, determine what studies have already been undertaken. This can save hours of expensive primary research effort. Certain aspects of the research may have already been done. A careful review of competitive practices should be undertaken. Such a review may turn up questions that need answering in the research, or it may answer questions previously thought to require research. Many times, the research results of competitors may be found in annual reports or magazine articles. Disclosures for selling stock required by the Securities and Exchange Commission are very informative.

Secondary research (data that has already been gathered) is usually available free, or at a fraction of the normal cost for gathering such information. The Small Business Administration of the federal government, chambers of commerce, trade associations, and periodicals, as well as your competitors, are good sources of secondary data. University students who are studying marketing can be hired inexpensively.

Developing ideas and hunches

Throughout your research process, develop hunches or hypotheses. If these hunches are important ingredients of the business plan, test them. For example, one might have a strong feeling that the product should be priced much higher than any competitor's products. If you are an entrepreneur, your own feelings will generate the best hunches. It is usually difficult to identify a particular source—it is just a feeling. Many successful managers and owners in the early 1900s based all their decisions on hunches. Often they were extremely effective.

If you can become sensitive to others you will gain insight into consumer actions. This is one reason why the small business has a distinct advantage over national corporations. The owner of a small business is in close association with customers and can become more aware of their needs.

The new entrepreneur may wish to discuss his ideas with someone who has experience in the area. Many consultants have experience and

> **CAUTION** It is dangerous to base decisions exclusively on hunches today, because the environmental and consumer factors are much more complex than they were in the early history of American business, though they still have validity.

expertise in an entrepreneur's area of concern. These consultants can provide insight throughout the development of the firm at a relatively low price. Colleges and universities are an excellent source for obtaining help. Ask for references to assure the quality of the people you hire.

An individual frequently has personal biases that will color the way he views something. Brainstorming with others is a way of obtaining divergent points of view. It is preferable that participants in brainstorming sessions be from different backgrounds, especially from management, finance, and marketing. Some common types of customers should also be included to contribute their ideas. In brainstorming sessions, ask structured questions, such as, "What price do you think should be charged?" Once answers are offered, ask participants why they feel the way they do.

DEFINITION

Anticipate the results you expect and then make sure you have asked the questions that will get the information needed. This will ensure that information you want will be gained, even if the results are entirely different from what was expected. Technically, this is called *hypothesis testing*. When you do this, make sure you do not bias the way the questions are phrased; they must be worded so that they elicit the actual attitudes of the respondent.

Determining the method of data collection

The common ways of collecting data, each of which has advantages and disadvantages, are the mail interview, the telephone interview, and the face-to-face personal interview.

The mail interview is usually the least expensive. If time is not a problem and a good mailing list is available, this procedure is most advisable. The only cost is questionnaire development, printing, and mailing.

A 10 to 15 percent return is considered excellent, so a large mailing must be used to assure the proper number of responses. Include a return envelope with the questionnaire to encourage people to complete and mail back their responses.

Telephone interviewing is appropriate only when phone numbers are available or when the questionnaire must be administered quickly and only a few questions asked. Telephone interviews are more likely to make people irritable, so if the sample is made up of customers, this technique should not be used.

The personal interview is the most expensive—from $4 to $5 per interview when done professionally. Supervisors all over the country have trained men and women to conduct interviews. They can be found in the *Yellow Pages* under Marketing Research and Analysis.

Personal interviews should be used when probing questions must be asked. People are less likely to give incorrect responses in a personal interview. These three approaches are compared in Figure 4-1.

Designing a questionnaire is complicated. It must be written carefully in order to get reliable information. Figure 4-2 summarizes the procedure.

A common weakness in questionnaires is crowding, so be sure to leave plenty of space for answers. Placing a period at the end of a blank line encourages the respondent to fill up the allotted space. Have the questionnaire printed clearly.

Figure 4-1. Comparison of data collection through mail, telephone, and personal interviews.

Survey Aspect	Mail Interview	Telephone Interview	Personal Interview
Questionnaire			
Length of interview	20 minutes or less	Less than 10 minutes	Longer (one hour or more is possible; plus possible mail-back). Usually, though, not longer than 30 minutes is a good rule
Complexity of questions	May be moderately complex	Fair	Can be more complex; can use cards or probes.
Flexibility (skipping)	Poor (skipping dangerous)	Fair	Excellent
Probing	Poor	Fair	Best
Getting at reasons(determining why)	Poor	Fair	Best
Handling touchy subject	Relatively good	Risky: Respondent may hang up	Risky: May bias replies
Control of question order	Problem—Respondent may read ahead	Excellent	Excellent
Sample			
List availability	Good mailing lists are available	Free, renewed annually	Area sampling a problem. Must get maps, population estimates by sub-areas.
Interviewing			
Response rate	Low—0 to 15% for single mailing to general public, higher for special groups, especially professionals, and for several mailings.	Good—roughly 70%	Excellent—about 80%
Interviewing bias and cheating	None	Can occur. Supervisor can counteract to considerable extent.	May occur. Should telephone a sample of respondents to check cheating.
Identity of respondent	Not certain	Known	Known
Administration and Cost			
Cost	Low, especially if response rate is high and telephone sample not necessary.	Moderately expensive	High—three or more times costs of mail or telephone.
Administrative load	Light	Heavier—must hire, train and supervise telephoners.	Heaviest—must hire, train supervise, check, and pay at a distance.

It is always advisable to pretest the questionnaire on about 10 to 20 persons who are similar to the consumers to be surveyed, to be sure that you are getting the kind of information you hope for and need. Make sure your instructions are clear, simple, and easy to read and that your questions are simple to understand. They should be phrased so that the answers are easy to interpret and tabulate. The questions should be preceded for easy key punching. Avoid ambiguous and leading questions. The order in which questions are listed should be logical, with only one idea in each question.

Selecting a sample

Before a sample can be selected the universe of customers must be determined. The universe comprises all the individuals who have the characteristics the businessman is interested in. In some cases, it might be possible to interview the entire universe, but this is usually very costly and unnecessary. When a sample is taken of the universe, it must be representative of the members. Some random process should be used to assure that no subjective selection might bias the sample. The most common approach to selecting a random sample is to use a random number table. Random number tables list the digits 0 through 9 in a purely random way— that is, each digit has an equal chance of selection at any draw. Table 1 is an example of a random number table.

Suppose you want to interview a random sample of all males who surf in Fort Lauderdale. First prepare the largest possible list of names of individuals in that universe. Let's assume that your list contains 500 names, and that you want to randomly select 50. Assign a number to each name so that your list is numbered consecutively from 001 to 500. The random number table will help you select 50 three-digit numbers from 001 to 500. Choose any column and use any three consecutive digits. You may start anywhere in the table. Read to the left or right, up or down, until you have accumulated 50 three-digit numbers. Discard any numbers greater than 500. The 50 names whose assigned numbers are chosen become your random sample of Fort Lauderdale surfers.

However, you must take into account that you will have difficulty tracking down and interviewing every person in your sample. To be safe (and realistic), your sample should contain 50 percent more names than you actually want to contact. In the above example, 75 names should be randomly selected in order to ensure that 50 people will be interviewed.

> **HINT**
>
> Lists for the universe may come from a telephone book or other directory.

Mailing list companies can provide a list of customers with virtually any set of characteristics you desire. They can even provide a list selected at random from the universe you are interested in. Lists from mailing companies are inexpensive, and companies can be located in the *Yellow Pages*.

If in-store personal interviews or house-to-house canvassing are being used, you can achieve randomness through one of several sample selection methods.

> **E-Z TIP** The advantage of stratifying is that it limits the size of the universe and the required size of the sample.

Stratified random sampling is a method of selecting a homogeneous segment. For example, we may take a random sample of blondes (for hair coloring) or dog owners (for pet food). It also saves time and money. Area sampling, sometimes called cluster sampling, occurs when certain geographic segments of a universe are selected.

The following pages (Figure 4-2) summarize the design of a questionnaire:

Figure 4-2. Designing a questionnaire.

Very basic classification data can usually be filled in by the interviewer before the interview. Complicated or very personal classification data should go at the end of the questionnaire.

The introductory statement establishes rapport with the interviewee. It should not be read, but rather put in the interviewer's own words. This introduction will make the difference between success and failure for the interview.

Product description tells the interviewee about the product or service. It should be a complete description of the product. Do not try to oversell the product; that may bias the results.

Initial impression questions should appear first. They should be uncomplicated, nonpersonal, closed-end questions. Attitude scales are used to determine the intensity of the respondents' feelings.

Open-end questions are useful for determining why the person feels the way he or she does.

Buying intentions are important to determine. People may like the idea, but not want to buy it. If one can determine why they would not, perhaps the product can be revised to meet more of their demands.

Name of Respondent _____ Name of Interviewer _____

Address _____ Date _____

Phone _____ Time _____

Other (nonpersonal) relevant data _____

Good morning, my name is , and I am conducting a marketing study for a new product (service) called The answers you give to the following questions will help determine whether or not to introduce this new product (service) idea, and what features to incorporate into the product. May I have a few minutes of your time?

The name of this product is _____ It is a

_____, and its functions/purposes are _____

_____.

The benefits of this product are _____

_____

1. What is your immediate reaction to this idea?

Positive		Negative	
Great	_____	So-so	_____
Like it very much	_____	I do not particularly like it	_____
Like It somewhat	_____	I do not like it at all	_____

Why do you say that? Explain. _____

_____

_____

2. Which of the following best expresses your feeling about buying this product if it were available to you?

Positive		Negative	
I'm absolutely sure I would buy it	_____	I probably would not buy it	_____
I'm almost sure I would buy it	_____	I'm almost sure I would not buy it	_____
I probably would buy it	_____	I'm absolutely sure I would not buy it	__

Why do you say that?

_____	_____
_____	_____
_____	_____

Figure 4-2, *continued*

Product appeals must be determined, so as to be able to promote the product effectively. Such information will indicate what to emphasize and what to de-emphasize.

Pricing is an important aspect. Here, one can determine a relative demand curve for the product. It is difficult for the consumer to answer this question precisely, but it should at least give the entrepreneur an idea of the price range.

The retail outlet, where the product would be most likely to be found, is important.

The advertising medium to use must also be determined.

Sometimes consumers do not like a product for minor reasons, and when these reasons are eliminated, they will buy it. The more difficult, tiring questions should be placed at the end of the interview.

Classification data of a personal nature should be asked at the end of the interview. Never ask for a person's specific age or income, because they will become suspicious of you and may become angry.

Always ***close*** with a friendly thank you. You may wish to interview this person again.

3. All things considered, what is there about this product idea that appeals to you most. What do you consider its most important advantages?

	Appeal		Advantages
1>	_____	1.	_____
2.	_____	2.	_____
3.	_____	3.	_____

4. How much do you think such a product would cost? _____

5. Where would you expect to buy such a product? _____

_____

6. Where would you expect such a product to be advertised? _____

_____

7. Are there any suggestions you would care to make that you think might improve this product? _____

Classification data:

1. In what category does your age fall:

    under 15   _____

    16-21   _____

    22-29   _____

    30-49   _____

    50-60   _____

    over 60   _____

2. Please tell me where your total family income falls:

    below $5,000   _____

    $5,000-$9,999   _____

    10,000-14,999   _____

    15,000-19.999   _____

    above 20,000   _____

3. Check one

    Female; single ____ married ____

    Male; single ____ married ____

Thank you for your cooperation!

Table 1. A table of random numbers.

57278	28133	04340	19889	27266	77468	02509	27534	00342	30727
97953	43227	41110	86887	19559	64945	54520	90528	18850	43610
07431	45121	73187	80431	57245	77311	44596	23531	63637	47042
20930	54735	95568	86799	49721	89049	01791	81084	03284	24096
78003	86322	23893	19483	18624	78634	31967	06395	34924	67283
48541	02641	89681	97881	69919	24170	85386	25834	75945	90965
52684	87995	43702	10623	95580	75795	59360	87848	83250	41168
44032	67360	54462	31774	01629	03406	81878	92801	27984	89892
40757	07266	13231	93527	51509	19550	24785	11136	35905	44879
42290	21749	34505	46547	03354	83574	17762	07646	66469	61568
37592	08604	53542	99986	26017	84967	96696	19155	88259	03612
32583	59967	64315	84822	74950	80322	10037	19425	96714	97330
75625	48032	05891	58701	91532	81253	87706	42235	44799	58271
91808	34409	59390	38399	09462	07373	19799	04132	31531	16485
19926	91034	26756	37752	47276	70856	94741	55372	50250	48775
78782	17338	68884	04609	03479	59241	39569	13351	64340	34108
54319	43047	73502	30408	94554	18640	91396	16242	96184	64191
34359	78839	55454	08551	19021	56584	84609	26286	31079	89061
52871	79550	40787	87299	70144	45090	45199	80127	21304	88681
69226	39419	66757	59927	04968	56061	66103	59708	36607	79140
07575	58710	92577	67823	52832	36514	56137	11321	62025	09049
91682	48619	15333	05876	20802	39128	75562	10170	72858	07010
62040	64062	70625	57559	46143	46638	37861	12551	58076	87218
80099	81346	54688	70326	22662	08106	82354	94331	29618	38043
77758	41609	69027	03208	28505	06689	61270	67122	45496	30345
20009	11788	77442	46535	09576	24905	46353	63277	36064	58249
52091	84347	27681	24853	68826	04138	83340	96698	89529	46622
19569	02594	04226	93412	36370	16393	05509	43349	01135	92264
48286	19309	39931	61597	95916	59340	30322	56291	45847	85836
44400	82261	21889	89837	64397	05508	31365	36334	08765	89749
19322	99470	86311	96458	84173	06386	39946	49558	80223	69513
21704	81386	35499	57991	05992	47982	01949	50203	45471	18610
59506	33660	80198	19429	26262	42605	64807	29526	50672	49761
69876	11749	18876	54501	71446	40239	42174	14601	51255	24318
47268	55681	53952	54010	24425	21284	90929	05499	37739	88835
80651	73964	85491	79648	30293	31305	96030	25760	85013	03763
91894	81410	81245	09998	80494	86183	01343	82296	80842	58427
40239	16519	23159	32970	91162	40386	81829	16582	45640	07032
88212	51975	93468	83446	94238	48944	63226	05278	32797	27430
55103	14461	92774	26397	46587	51470	41598	29070	26690	69567
15360	93359	86173	53747	03141	75425	69947	37188	30936	99987
70678	38035	89688	64524	08530	87826	82214	05660	04461	28460
23620	33295	98309	16475	26722	92523	62702	02103	38482	28012
71594	59029	79559	67497	56559	05538	38354	61813	04816	66451
63723	62966	40545	65085	77086	03427	62353	77932	81281	32626
24852	88450	99212	80393	72573	59370	75741	05229	43644	29794
80184	48999	76580	84648	04210	76599	43704	23101	06957	66554
46973	78646	73852	44752	50849	07905	65120	48320	23223	96491
18043	96840	23148	89768	10865	45987	55568	08478	73137	03867
84956	48341	26773	23897	70640	75961	04522	09761	81718	63357

San Diego is often selected as a test market for the western states. This type of sampling simplifies the interviewing process and lessens the required sample size.

Quota sampling is the best method to use when a specific type of individual must be selected from a homogeneous group. Persons are selected at random until a certain number of the type of persons needed are interviewed. For example, we may seek customers who purchase items in our store at least four times a year.

Systematic sampling is a process by which a formula for selection is used—every other house, or every tenth person may be interviewed. Some statisticians argue that this is not truly a random process, but it is often used because of its simplicity.

DEFINITION

Judgment sampling refers to the conscious subjective process of selecting individuals to be interviewed. This requires the interviewer to exercise human judgment, thus introducing possible biases. This process is often used in cases where an in-depth, motivation research questioning procedure is required and only a few interviews (20 perhaps) are to be conducted. Judgment sampling has no statistical validity, but it is very popular among some large companies. It takes a highly trained interviewer and analyst to use such techniques.

Figure 4-3. Sample with identical means but different dispersions.

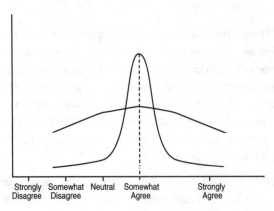

How many responses do you need in order to reflect the nature of the universe? There are no easy ways of determining sample size. It depends upon the standard deviation or dispersion (standard error of the mean) of the responses the consumer may give. Figure 4-3 shows two curves with identical means but different dispersions. In both cases, 100 persons were sampled; the means are identical. In the case of A, there was strong agreement when persons were asked whether they thought the product was a good idea. Most of the persons (90 percent) said they "somewhat agreed" that it was. Roughly 2% percent strongly agreed, and the rest (2% percent) were neutral or negative toward the product idea. Thus, we are relatively certain that the answers received from the sample were representative of the universe.

In the case of B, however, the results are not as clear-cut. Only 50 percent "somewhat agreed," 25 percent "strongly agreed," and 25 percent were neutral or negatively predisposed.

It is not clear whether this is the true distribution. More individuals probably need to be sampled. If this were done, and the distribution were to stay relatively the same, then the distribution would indeed be representative. Thus, an effective and easy way to determine proper sample size is simply to sample until you are sure that additional interviews will not change the average responses you have received. If nine out of ten randomly selected customers answer "Because of price" when asked why they patronize the store, then the sample is representative. If seven different answers are given, then additional people must be interviewed to determine the important reasons.

Those who want a more scientific approach may use another procedure. First, estimate how many individuals will be in agreement with most of the questions. This can be determined by trying the questionnaire out on, say, ten people. Then use the figures given in Table 2. If one or 99 percent were in agreement, this great similarity in opinion calls for a small sample size of only 20 persons. If, however, the percent of affirmative answers was not in agreement (say 50 percent for and 50 percent against), then the largest sample size (410) would be required.

This chart is also useful in determining how representative each question is. In most of the questions, a sample size of 20 is enough. If a 50-50 response is given, however, the sample size of 20 is too small for that particular question, and the responses from that question should be considered suspect.

Table 2. Determining the proper sample size.

Percent of Affirmative Answers to a Question	Sample Size to Use
1% or 99%	20
3 or 97	50
5 or 95	75
10 or 90	150
15 or 85	200
20 or 80	250
25 or 75	300
30 or 70	350
35 or 65	375
40 or 60	380
45 or 55	400
50 or 50	410

Conducting the survey

If the universe consists of the entrepreneur's present customers, questionnaires can be administered randomly in the store or through a mailing. An entrepreneur should keep an updated list of his customers. Names and addresses may be obtained from checks, credit accounts, drawings, contests, and various other kinds of record-keeping.

> *note* The actual process of collecting the data is mechanical and not difficult. One must simply decide what procedure to use.

If the businessman feels that mail is appropriate and wants to sample in a particular geographic area—perhaps around his business—mailing list companies can provide a random selection of mailing labels by zip code or street. Addresses for personal interviewing may also be obtained this way at roughly $20 to $50 per thousand names.

Interviewers can be hired by calling local high schools or college placement offices. If a larger sample (of several states, for example) is required, the entrepreneur may require the services of a marketing research firm. All the aspects of research can usually be performed by professionals for $10 to $25 per interview.

Assessing the results

The first part of editing is to determine that the correct person completed the questionnaire. Random calls to some of the interviewees should be made. Sometimes a secretary, spouse, or child, rather than the targeted individual, may complete a questionnaire.

> **HOT spot** Editing is a very important element in marketing research, but it is often neglected. Edit questionnaires to make sure that useful, relevant information has been gained.

Make sure that useful information is present on the questionnaire. Sometimes irate respondents will complete the questionnaire with malicious intent. They may not be consistent, and some of their answers may be extreme. This kind of questionnaire should be thrown out. One must be careful not to exclude relevant questionnaires, however.

 Definition:

Tabulation is the process of transferring the data from the questionnaires to a useful format that can be easily understood and analyzed.

The normal process for closed-end (yes or no, for example) responses is simply to add up the total number of specific responses and find the percentage, as in Figure 4-4. Percentages are usually more relevant than the absolute number, unless the sample size is extremely small. The base (the total number of persons answering the question) should always be shown.

Figure 4-4. Tabulation of closed-end responses.

1. Question: Do you buy your own sport shirts?		
	Yes _____ NO _____	
	Total Number	
YES ~~HHL~~ ~~HHL~~ ~~HHL~~ IIII	19	70.3
NO ~~HHL~~ III	8	29.7
Total	27	100
Base = 27		

Figure 4-5. Tabulation of open-end responses.

1. Question: Why do you buy your own sport shirts?

I want a certain type of shirt.   III

My wife doesn't know what I want.   卌

I have better taste   III

My wife pays too much for my shirts   卌   卌   I

I know what I want   III

I don't trust my wife to buy what I want.   III

My wife buys cheap stuff.   III

My wife is color blind. III

My wife buys terrible stuff   IIII

I like bright colors.   IIII

Actually, I don't usually buy my own shirts.   IIII

Other.   I

No particular reason. III

No answer.   IIII

Answers Consolidated	#	%
I don't care for what my wife buys me.	28	51.9
I know what I want.	15	27.8
I don't buy my own shirts.	4	7.4
No particular reasons/no answer.	7	12.9
	54	100%

Tabulation of open-end questions is tricky. One must take many diverse responses and combine items into relevant categories that represent the diverse responses. Figure 4-5 is an example. The tabulator has the power of completely changing the true results by the way he combines responses. He must be as objective as possible. Too much combining will result in information lost. Try to combine the total responses into a minimum of 13 categories, or one fourth the total responses, whichever number is smaller.

Analyzing the results

In analyzing the results, try to point out relevant data and important relationships that will help you make decisions. Take each question and ask, "Who said this? What is actually being said? Why did he respond this way? Where and when would this be most likely to happen?"

For example, the following conclusions might be made about the results of the responses in Figure 4-4:

Who: Men prefer to buy their own sport shirts.

What was said: For a variety of reasons, there seems to be resistance by men against having their wives buy their sport shirts. The assumption that wives pay too much for the shirts seemed to be one of the most important reasons given.

Where and when: Since men prefer to buy their own sport shirts, they will do so when they have the time. They will probably make their purchases during lunch hour, after work, or on weekends. Very likely they would go shopping without their wives because of the differences in taste. Therefore, noon shopping trips would make the most sense, since weekends are often devoted to family shopping.

On the basis of the results, recommendations for action should be made.

Report writing

The entrepreneur may question the need for writing a report if he has already conducted the research. The research report can be a very handy tool for obtaining funds or convincing others about the merit of the idea. It should be professionally presented. The format of a marketing research report is reasonably standardized, and follows the one illustrated in Figure 4-6.

Figure 4-6. Format of the marketing research report.

Title Page	Name of the study, who the study is for (the individual or organization who conducted the study), and the date
Table of Contents	(detailed)
Part I	Purpose of the Study—Background for understanding the problem, and objectives of the study.
Part II	Summary Results—On a different color paper.

Figure 4-6, continued

Part III	Procedure Followed—Details of methodology including the research design, who was interviewed, how the interview was administered, and when the study was conducted.
Part IV	Results and Analysis—All tables and detailed analysis.
Part V	Recommendations—What steps the results indicate should be taken.
Conclusions	Implications, relative success of the study, suggestions for further research
Appendixes	Statistical analysis, lengthy tables

Test marketing

DEFINITION

The research practice of actually trying out the marketing plan to determine if it works as expected is known as *test marketing*. Even after marketing research has been conducted, test marketing is a valid idea, since only practical experience can truly indicate the success or failure of a business. If it is not difficult or expensive, test marketing may be used instead of marketing research.

When trying out your marketing plans under real-life circumstances, your first task is to select a representative market area. It may be a local market or a city, state, or region. Make sure your market is not one that has been overtested, and that it is representative of the actual market you want to reach later. It should not be dominated by any industry or government facility (such as an Air Force base), or any customer type (such as senior citizens). Your market should not be too small or too large (150,000 to 500,000 is a good size), and it should be free from unique conditions such as nonrepresentative climate or income distribution.

Advertising and merchandising programs, product packaging, effect of pricing, and store displays all require test marketing. Test marketing has many advantages: It provides decision making guidelines and evidence of actual performance; it can predict the influence of advertising, or what the volume of sales will be; and it points out weaknesses in the plan that need to be overcome. Your test market may be in a single store, several stores, or all stores of a particular chain in a town, state, or region. The important consideration is that the test market is representative. Testing may be done by observation or

sales measurement, or customers may be asked to fill out a coupon. Shelf counts might be taken at the end of the day, or after an advertising program has run.

It is a good idea to have a control group identical to the test market group but not exposed to the factor being tested. For example, if you want to measure the impact of an advertisement on your business, you would advertise, then question consumers, and then measure the difference in sales between those who had seen the advertising and those who had not. The use of a control group is advisable, because

Test marketing should not be used if timing is important in introducing the product ahead of competitors, since test marketing forewarns the competition, giving it a chance to enter the market or to counter with competitive measures.

sometimes other factors can influence results. Let us say that we advertised raincoats, and on the same day it happened to rain. Without a control group, we would never know to what extent the increase in sales was the outcome of advertising or simply the result of the rain.

In recent years, with product failures becoming so expensive, mini-marketing has found favor with the larger firms. Mini-marketing is a term used when a small market is singled out as a sub-market. All the market strategy is tried in the mini-market. Necessary alterations are made in the marketing plan, and the company, as soon as it is sure it has the optimum marketing mix in the area, jumps to the next market. Profits from the first market can be used to set up the new one, and so it goes until the firm has expanded to the desired extent.

Marketing research is an important area that is too often neglected by the new entrepreneur. Often, he thinks he lacks the time or money to conduct research, or he is so absorbed in the mechanics of getting the business started that he forgets to think about research. Without it, the entrepreneur is frequently guessing who his customers are and what they want in the way of a product. He is not sure what promotion, price, channel, and service mix will be appropriate. Without having a clear understanding of these vital areas, it is no wonder that so many new businesses fail so rapidly. When research is conducted, however, the entrepreneur can save a great deal of time, effort, and expense. Perhaps it will even help him save his business.

Making buyer behavior concepts work for you

5

Chapter 5

Making buyer behavior concepts work for you

The concept of a behavioral environment is an exciting new approach to understanding consumer behavior. The firm is a behavioral entity. In order to survive, it must adapt to and, when possible, influence the behavioral environment that surrounds it. The objective of this chapter is to acquaint the small business marketer with the dimensions of the behavioral environment in which he will be required to make his decisions.

The study of consumer behavior in colleges and universities is quite new. Those who understand consumer behavior will possess unique expertise in behavioral marketing that even most businessmen do not possess. Knowledge of consumer behavior will enable you to advance rapidly and become more successful. Learn the concepts well and make them part of your thinking. They will be highly relevant and helpful in your problem-solving.

The marketing manager's role

In the behavioral environment, the marketing manager must be concerned with many psychological factors. Some of these aspects of behavior

are beyond his control and influence. In order to be successful in today's competitive environment, the marketing manager must be in tune with the uncontrollable variables of culture, society, and reference group influences, which exert a strong influence on the consumer's willingness to buy products. Let's define our terms.

DEFINITION

Culture is the distinctive lifestyle (mode of living) of an aggregate of people resulting from their adaptation to their environment. Cultural influences are usually very basic, but are not always obvious. They are enduring and do not change rapidly. They shape our basic attitudes, ideas, beliefs, values, language, religion, and so on. Ethnic restaurants are examples of businesses catering to culture-based needs.

DEFINITION

Social influences are concerned with the individual's interaction with groups. Humans are social animals in the sense that they form groups and strive to be compatible with the society around them. Social influences are also enduring, but are subject to more rapid change than are cultural ones.

DEFINITION

Reference groups are groups with which an individual identifies. People seek reference groups that they either feel compatible with or aspire to, and are influenced by the actions of the members of such a group. A person's reference group will probably have a substantial influence on the choice of products he purchases, the stores he patronizes, and the area in which he chooses to live. The family unit exerts a tremendous amount of influence on all its members, and can be considered a small reference group. Children usually form many of their behavior patterns by the age of 16. Parents influence the types and brands of products that the child will use in his adult life, since habits formed at an early age tend to be very enduring. McDonald's has successfully advertised to children by using Ronald McDonald, while Wendy's has chosen to cater more to adults.

Marketing in the behavioral environment

For each marketing function (product development, pricing, channels of distribution, and promotion) there is a parallel behavioral aspect. For example, the marketer is concerned with the development of an appropriate price for a product. A traditional approach to the selection of a price would involve a

> **HOT spot** When one begins to consider the behavioral implications of marketing, the door opens on a new and unique way of formulating a marketing plan.

consideration of demand curves, costs, and basic company financial requirements. The behavioral aspects of price must also be considered. An understanding of the psychology of pricing is essential if the marketer is to attach an appropriate price to the product.

Briefly, a marketing strategy is a plan for reaching a predetermined objective. It differs from a traditional marketing strategy in that it begins with the consumer and is complete only when customer satisfaction is achieved: The whole marketing process evolves from an emphasis on the consumer. Developing this marketing strategy in the behavioral environment involves the following systematic process:

1) understanding the behavioral environment

2) selecting the target customer

3) selecting the product idea

4) developing the product image

5) determining consumer perceptions

6) selecting the retail institution

7) developing the distribution system

8) organizing the firm

These eight steps will now be considered in detail.

1) Understanding the behavioral environment

The entrepreneur must recognize that his potential customer is not the traditional Economic Man who was thought to be completely rational and therefore to exhibit predictable buying patterns. Rather, the consumer is "Psychological Man," or "Woman," exhibiting psychological needs as well as rational economic ones. Thus a consumer's emotional buying behavior is a far

cry from the strictly rational and problem-solving model of the consumer as Economic Man.

2) Selecting the target customer

DEFINITION Usually, the marketer is not interested in all consumers, nor is it possible to reach all consumers with a single strategy. The marketer attempts to aim his product at a specific group of customers. The *target market* is the group of consumers which the market singles out to attempt to satisfy. This group is selected on the basis of common psychological and physiological needs and desires for the product idea, which may be vague at this stage in the process. The target market must be large enough and have sufficient buying power to make it profitable to sell the product.

3) Selecting the product idea

Depending upon the circumstances, this step may occur before or after selecting the target customer, and the concept or idea may come from any of several sources.

Many fine products, such as nylon, would never have been developed if such discoveries were postponed until consumers requested them. If a laboratory process is used to generate product ideas, and the product is then adjusted to the consumer's wants, needs, and desires, then the firm can be considered customer-oriented.

> *note* Many large firms have technicians and creative personnel working full time to research and develop new product ideas. This approach to product development is not directly customer-oriented, but is sometimes necessary because customers do not always know what they want.

Some firms attempt to develop new product ideas by surveying the consumer to determine what people want. Laboratory personnel are then asked to develop a product to meet that need. This process may take the form of going to the consumer with product ideas and concepts and asking for a reaction to the product. Sometimes product concepts are overwhelmingly accepted and desired by the consumer, but the product cannot be developed in the laboratory. An example is the

desire for a completely non-polluting automobile. It is needed and desired, but so far it has not been produced.

 A firm may find that one of its products is not selling satisfactorily or the company may desire to expand the market for its product. In such cases, the company may seek out new target markets to satisfy. For example, a company may be selling its soaps to industrial users only, and they may wish to adapt the soaps to the consumer market. The product Janitor in a Drum is a good example. Such a change in strategy requires an entirely different marketing mix. Usually the pricing practice, channels of distribution, promotion, and packaging all have to be changed in order to reach the new consumer market segment.

Private sources of new ideas should not be overlooked. It has been said that necessity is the mother of invention. Every person in his lifetime probably dreams up at least one valuable idea but, because he lacks marketing know-how, cannot convert that idea into a product and get it to the marketplace. Yet thousands of ideas do reach the marketplace from amateur inventors. Many hundreds of companies are started every year for the purpose of marketing these ideas, and sometimes they are very successful.

4) Developing the product image

Once the product idea is developed, the marketer must create an image for his product that will appeal to the target customer.

Few consumers buy products because of basic utility alone. Most consumers evaluate the worth of the product on the basis of how it contributes to their self-concept. Cigarette manufacturers, for example, have taken fundamentally similar brands and differentiated them psychologically by image. The Marlboro man is a different image from the "springtime freshness" of the Salem campaign. All the factors comprising the marketing mix—the brand name, the package, the price, the promotion, the channels of distribution, and the product itself—combine to make up the product image. Each of these product features should be compatible with, and complementary to, the desired image, so that the image is clear. This image should also be developed with the behavioral factors of motivation, cognition, and learning in mind.

The product image is essentially the blend of product stimuli which are projected to the consumer. This image includes both the psychological and physiological aspects of the product and all the various stimuli used to market it. If the product image is not compatible with and appropriate to the target customer's own selfconcept, he will reject it.

5) Determining consumer perceptions

The traditional, nonbehavioral approach to selecting a channel of distribution usually involves selection on the basis of availability and the expense involved. Such a process, however, does not consider the desires and habits of the target customer. The channel of distribution a product follows is one of the important ingredients of marketing strategy and product image, and should therefore be selected on the basis of the target customer's self-concept and his perception of the product. Consumers perceive products in five different ways.

First are **convenience goods**, those products the customer wants but is not willing to spend much time shopping for. They include such items as cigarettes, soap, newspapers, chewing gum, candy, and most grocery products. Staple convenience goods, such as foods, are purchased frequently and with little thought, though brands and prices are sometimes important. If a particular brand is not readily available, most consumers will not make an effort to find it at another store. Convenience goods bought on impulse, such as ice-cream cones, popcorn, and *TV Guide* purchased at the checkout counter, are goods whose purchase is not planned. Emergency convenience goods, such as tow service in the desert, are sought only when a need is urgent. Price and quality are of little concern in such instances.

Second, there are **shopping goods**, which are those products that a consumer feels are worth the time and effort to examine carefully and compare with competing products. Homogeneous shopping goods are perceived to be very similar in quality by the customer, so he or she shops around to find the best price. Heterogeneous shopping goods are products which the consumer sees as different in quality and suitability. Carpets and clothing are examples where quality is most important to the customer and price is secondary.

The third classification, **specialty goods**, includes products that a significant group of buyers want and will make a special effort to buy. Singer sewing machines are sought out by customers who are loyal to Singer machines. Usually this willingness to search on the consumer's part is due to strong brand preference, but it may also suggest strong store preference. Saks Fifth Avenue, for example, commands a strong store preference for some consumers, while others prefer Bloomingdale's.

Unsought goods are products that potential customers do not presently need or want, and therefore do not search for. The benefits of these products are not immediately obvious and therefore require personal explanation or demonstration. Life insurance, encyclopedias, and high-quality soaps, knives, and cosmetics are examples of this fourth category of goods. The purchase of such products can be put off indefinitely.

Finally, **new products** are those brand-new items that have not been widely advertised; consumers do not know about them. The new product also is unsought, but as the consumer learns about it his demand for the product may develop.

These five classifications are the direct result of the nature of the consumer's preference for the goods. Let us take one product—the bandage—as an example to clarify how these classifications are developed.

First, consider the consumer preference. One consumer may have no preference for brands at all. She is in the store and passes a display of bandages. She places a box in her basket and pays for it at the counter. To this customer, bandages are a convenience good, since the product was purchased on impulse; she probably would not shop around for it.

HINT
Convenience goods are also purchased because of circumstances that arise. If the consumer's small child cuts a finger and there are no bandages in the house, the consumer will probably go to the nearest store and purchase the first box of bandages she sees, without consideration for brand or price. This form of purchase would make the bandages an emergency convenience good. Consider next the shopper who is getting low on bandages. She puts them on her shopping list, goes to the grocery store, but finds they are more expensive than she is accustomed to paying (homogeneous shopping goods).

She then goes to the discount store and finds they are lower in price, but she is concerned that the quality may be low (heterogeneous shopping goods). She ends up buying them in a drugstore at her own perceived appropriate price and quality. To this consumer, bandages are considered a shopping good.

Specialty goods imply a strong preference for one particular brand. A small child asks her mother to get the bandage that all the kids on the block have—the one with the blue stars. The mother looks all over town before she finds the right brand. To this mother, the good is a specialty good since there is strong brand preference for that product.

In the case of unsought goods, a bandage manufacturer might come up with the ultimate in bandages, but his product is very costly. Consumers may not be susceptible because of the high price, and they may not believe or understand the features of the bandage. The manufacturer finds that the only way to sell the product is door to door. This product would be unsought because of its nature.

A new product could involve a bandage company that produces a bandage with a special nonstick pad and a color that blends so perfectly with the skin that it can hardly be seen. Marketing research has indicated that there is a great demand for the product, but because it is so new, no consumers are seeking it out. The product may have to be introduced to doctors who will be asked to give the new bandages to their patients until publicity and promotion take effect.

6) Selecting the retail institution

The retail institution system is composed of the many outlets involved with selling to the ultimate target customer. The system is made up of many intermediaries and is extremely complex. The choice of retail institutions will depend on the buying habits of the target markets. Naturally, the product should be distributed through those retail institutions that cater to our target markets.

If the customer perceives the product as a convenience good, it should be sold through as many outlets as possible. This intensive distribution might include variety and grocery stores, vending machines, and so forth.

If the customer shops around for the product, it can be sold through a more selective outlet where comparative shopping is done for either quality or price. For example, department stores and shopping centers might be used.

> **HOT** **spot** The consumer perceives the product in different ways, and only by understanding these perceptions will the marketer be able to select the correct retail institutions.

If the product is perceived as a specialty item, and if strong brand preferences exist, the product can be sold on an exclusive basis. Specialty stores and shops might be used, factory-owned or -controlled stores might be developed, and even mail order might be desirable.

Products unsought by the customer usually require door-to-door selling. Usually no other channel system exists for these products. In many instances, salesmen for these products work on straight commission.

New and unknown products usually require personal selling to the channel systems to inform them about the features of the product and to get them to carry it in their stores. All products begin their life cycle in this new product category, but through proper promotional efforts the product can become a specialty good and may ultimately move into the shopping or convenience goods classification.

7) Developing the distribution system

The distribution system includes the retailer, wholesaler, broker, transportation, and storage institutions. This system traditionally evolves without much consideration for the consumer. Usually the choice of retailers will determine the specific channels to be used, since these channels service the specific retailers.

> **note** Under the behavioral approach, the distribution system is purposely organized to service the target customer.

There are of course other reasons for selecting a channel of distribution, but the target customer

must be of prime consideration. Other considerations might include the cost of the various channels, what channel competitors use, the efficiency of the channels, and the power of the manufacturer.

8) Organizing the firm

> **HOT spot** A firm which is marketing concept-oriented must be able to direct its entire operation toward satisfying the consumer at a profit. Departments must work together closely for the achievement of this end.

From a traditional point of view, the firm is composed of a number of business functions—production, marketing and sales, finance and accounting, management and personnel, and legal. Each of these departments has a particular role and these roles are mutually exclusive. There is competition among the departments for salaries, manpower, and prestige. Jealousy between departments usually exists. Under the traditional philosophy of business it is difficult to coordinate each function and particularly so to direct the entire firm's efforts to achieve a specific objective.

Is the consumer rational or emotional?

For centuries, there has been argument concerning the rationality of the consumer. Some marketing behaviorists have argued that the consumer is basically rational. Others are convinced that consumers purchase products on a fundamentally emotional basis. There are no clear-cut answers to the question, "Is the consumer either truly rational or truly emotional in patterns of buying behavior?" For purposes of clarity, *rational behavior* is defined as behavior that is explainable and

> **note** Depending upon the individual and the situation, consumers exhibit both rational and emotional behavior, sometimes simultaneously, toward product selection.

DEFINITION predictable. *Emotional behavior* is confined to behavior that is not predictable. From these definitions it should be noted that emotional behavior,

once it is understood and predictable, becomes rational behavior. As marketers learn about consumer behavior, more behavior will seem rational. This is the goal toward which the marketing discipline is working, because greater understanding of consumer behavior means greater potential for consumer satisfaction.

The list below shows the type of behavior that each category of product tends to elicit.

Product Type	Behavior Elicited
Convenience Goods	
Staples	Rational
Emergency	Emotional
Impulse	Emotional
Shopping Goods	
Heterogeneous	Emotional
Homogeneous	Rational
Specialty Goods	Rational
Unsought Goods	Emotional

In general, staple convenience goods are purchased with price in mind, and rational behavior is usually exhibited. However, if an item is not very expensive, the consumer may not bother making a rational decision, and emotional behavior may take over. Impulse goods are an example of products that are selected on a very emotional basis, for example, because of pretty packaging, great visibility, and intrigue.

HOT spot Because of their high price, shopping goods tend to be purchased on a more rational basis.

Homogeneous shopping goods are perceived as very similar from brand to brand. Therefore, price is the major consideration. For example, color televisions are probably purchased on the basis of price comparisons, since picture quality is quite similar. This does not apply to heterogeneous shopping goods, however. Products such as clothing are perceived as being very different both in quality and style. Most consumers have a difficult time determining and comparing quality, and therefore exhibit more emotional behavior.

Specialty goods are usually purchased rationally, since the consumer has developed a strong brand preference. The fact that a consumer chooses a particular brand over other alternatives indicates that rational reasoning helped develop the consumer's strong brand preference in the first place.

If goods are not sought by consumers because of the nature of the products, they usually have to be sold based on emotional appeal; rational appeal does not withstand the scrutiny of the consumer. This is one reason that such products usually require personal selling. As every door-to-door salesman knows, if a potential customer has a chance to think about purchasing the product or service, the purchase may not be made. That's one reason that legislation was sought and passed giving the consumer a 4% hour cooling-off period. The salesman must use logic to win a customer, must test for closing points, and must get a signature on the dotted line before the consumer's own logic is brought into play. This is not to imply that the product lacks merit. Products sold door to door are frequently of good quality and are sometimes important to the well-being of the consumer. Insurance, for example, is extremely important, but consumers will delay purchasing it because of the cost. They use the rationale that, "it will never happen to me." Products sold door to door are relatively expensive, and features that overcome objections to price must be emphasized by the salesman.

> *note* New products are usually bought on a relatively emotional basis because consumers have not had enough experience on which to base rational decisions.

New products may be purchased just because it is exciting to try new things. For people who enjoy spending money (and who have the money to spend), buying new products is like a continuous Christmas or birthday celebration.

Theories of consumer behavior

Consumer behavior is a complex process, a mixture of both rational and emotional reasoning. In order to understand such behavior, a brief summary of the various types of behavior will be helpful. Most of the theories and their applications in marketing will be covered in greater depth later. The theories differ because each theorist identifies different determinants of consumer

behavior. Each theory presents the behavior process that the consumer will use and follow.

The theory of Economic Man

Economists made the first organized efforts at describing and explaining consumer behavior. Alfred Marshall was mainly responsible for developing the economic view of consumer behavior. He looked at the consumer largely from a very theoretical basis. At the center of his model was Economic Man, and the assumptions placed upon Economic Man were very restrictive:

- The consumer has complete information needed to make the buying decision.

- The consumer exhibits completely rational buying behavior.

- The consumer will attempt to maximize his utility with each product he purchases.

The method of the economist is to start with these simplified, general, and often unrealistic assumptions and then to note the effect of changing such factors as price or quality, while holding the other factors constant. The theory of Economic Man has since been refined to the modern utility theory of today. The economist studies the ways in which consumers earning a certain income maximize their utility (satisfaction).

Economists have contributed a great deal toward the understanding of business and marketing through their theoretical models. However, many practitioners object to the restrictive assumptions of the theory of Economic Man. Let's consider some of their objections to the theory:

- It deals only with the act of purchase and not with what leads up to the purchase.

- It does not indicate the reasons that consumers act the way they do.

- The influences of culture, society, reference groups, and family are disregarded.

- The basic assumptions of the model are overly restrictive.

- The model does not handle the problems of post-purchase behavior.

The economists' failure to deal directly with these objections forced practitioners to develop their own theories, which have since strongly influenced marketing thought.

Alderson's problem-solving model

An extension of the theory of Economic Man evolved that considers the problem-solving aspects of consumer behavior. Wroe Alderson (the Father of Marketing) was largely responsible for applying a problem-solving model to consumer behavior.* This school of thought assumes that the consumer enters the marketplace as a problem solver. The homemaker becomes a kind of purchasing agent engaged in building an assortment of products for use by herself and her family. She develops and replenishes an inventory of goods for future use. She must make her buying decisions under uncertainty because she cannot know for sure what relative probabilities or chances are for future use of the products.

She must also decide on how many of the various marketing functions to perform herself and how many she will allow to be performed for her by the marketing process. It is a rule in marketing that all of the marketing functions have to be performed by someone. The consumer may decide to perform the functions of distribution, grading, seeking out information, and placing a value on the good, or she may decide to have all the functions performed for her. As the chart below indicates, the more functions she performs herself, the less her financial outlay. Conversely, the more functions she leaves for the marketer to perform, the more expensive the product.

Function	Cost	Time	Effort
Pick wild vegetables	Lowest	Greatest	Greatest
Go to farm to select vegetables	Low	Great	Great
Purchase frozen prepared vegetables at grocery store	High	Least	Least

Starting at one extreme, the consumer could go out into the wilds and find wild vegetables, pick them, take them home, and can them. The cash outlay would be very little. However, the time and effort involved would be great. She could purchase the vegetables partially prepared in frozen

---

* Delbert Duncan, ed., *Proceedings: Conference of Marketing Teachers from Far Western States* (Berkeley: University of California, 1958), pp. 15-28.

containers ready to eat. This, of course, cuts down measurably the time required, but increases the cost. Consumers, then, are involved in evaluating their perceived utility in doing things themselves as opposed to conceding the effort to the marketing process. The typical problem-solving process that the consumer might use is:

- *Define the problem.* In other words, determine how to satisfy the wants, needs, or desires of the members of the family through the purchase of products or services.

- *Gather information* about available products that will probably satisfy the household.

- *Evaluate each alternative.* Consider its advantages and disadvantages, including such things as price, quality, and how well the product will satisfy the family.

- *Select* from the alternatives the best product available.

- *Evaluate the product* to determine if it lived up to expectations.

- If the product is satisfactory, *adopt the product,* and maintain an inventory for probable future use.

This problem-solving process may seem unrealistically complex, so let's consider a real-life situation: the purchase of toothpaste. First, the consumer would gather a great deal of information about all the toothpastes available on the market. Then each toothpaste would be tried and rated, and the best toothpaste selected. At first glance this process may seem cumbersome. However, consider the tremendous speed with which the individual can actually analyze information. The human mind is far more rapid than modern-day computers are. It is possible that each time the consumer is confronted by a new toothpaste, he subconsciously compares it to his past experience with other toothpastes. This past experience is probably broad, varied, and complete. Through the consumer's exposure to advertising,

> *note* The problem-solving process may take place subconsciously, but it is a very real part of the decision-making process of consumer behavior.

Consumer Reports, free samples, word of mouth, and actual experience, the individual has a tremendous storehouse of information. For the more important products, those which are relatively expensive or are an important part of the consumer's self-enhancement, the problem-solving process will probably be more obvious.

A consumer's experience using problem-solving skills will influence the extent to which the problem-solving process is used. Usually, college-educated consumers have more experiences requiring problem solving and will be more inclined to use this process when purchasing products. These consumers require more detailed information before they will purchase a product.

The theory of cognitive dissonance

The theory of cognitive dissonance is concerned with the way in which consumers deal with anxiety or conflicting stimuli in product selection. When the individual is stimulated by a new product, new advertisements, or dissatisfaction with a product, and such stimuli cause conflict, that individual will be motivated to make the stimuli consonant (consistent) with one another or reduce the conflicts. Festinger is responsible for applying the dissonance theory to marketing.[*]

Every purchase decision involves dissonance of some kind because dissonance occurs when a person has to decide between two or more alternatives. There is always the alternative of making no decision at all, but choosing between purchasing a product or not purchasing a product may also cause dissonance. Dissonance also occurs when a consumer has to choose between alternatives that are perceived to have equally bad outcomes. Dissonance also occurs when the choice is between two positive alternatives. In this case, the consumer may desire two products very much but can afford only one of the products. The easiest dissonant situation to handle is the one in which a decision must be made between a positive and a negative alternative. The only reason dissonance might be present at all is that the individual is not completely certain that he has all the information. For example, suppose a close friend offers you a free sample of a product. If you do not accept the sample, the friend might be offended. However, you may be

[*] Leon Festinger, "Cognitive Dissonance," *Scientific American*. March 1962, pp. 93-102.

uncertain of the intentions of your friend or you may not be confident in the product itself. The theory of cognitive dissonance has a great deal to offer the marketer in the quest for understanding consumer behavior.

Since dissonance will probably be involved in every attempt to sell a product, the marketer must learn to help the customer decrease the amount of dissonance.

Whenever a customer selects a product, dissonance is likely to occur. Not only is the consumer spending money for a particular product, he is also giving up the ability to buy other products. If the customer is confident that the value and use he will receive from the product is greater than the sacrifice, then dissonance will be minimized. Marketers can use the four principles discussed below to help potential customers reduce dissonance.*

- *An individual is able to reduce dissonance by eliminating one of the cognitive elements, his responsibility for a decision, or his control over an act.* Advertising may employ a bandwagon approach in order to enable the individual consumer to submerge his actions in mass behavior. Alternatively, an advertisement might show why potentially dissonant elements are unimportant or not true.

- *Information can be denied, distorted, or forgotten to reduce dissonance. Selective forgetting is the process by which unpleasant or unreconcilable elements are dismissed from awareness.* Advertising audiences will often seek out information that is consistent with their own views. Advertisers ought to make follow-up advertising readily accessible for consumers who need help rationalizing their purchase behavior. Product (as well as political) advertising can be couched in vague terms that allow the listener to interpret the comments in the way most compatible with his own beliefs.

- *A person will actively avoid situations and information that are likely to increase dissonance.* If products can be shown to have a

* *Ibid.,* pp. 96-102.

benefit that alleviates dissonance, the product will probably be purchased.

For example, if the customer is convinced that a brand of mouthwash will improve his breath and reduce the chances of offending others, then the product has appeal. The Dial phrase, "Don't you wish everybody did?" employs this concept.

- *Dissonance can be effectively reduced by minimizing the importance of the issue, decision, or act that led to the dissonant state.* The marketer can show how a potentially dissonant situation can be handled easily and simply, thus reducing dissonance. For example, General Motors Acceptance Corporation shows how purchasing an automobile can be financed simply and easily.

> **E-Z TIP**
> Rather than trying to reduce all consumer dissonance, the marketer needs to alleviate enough of the dissonant factors so that the consumer will try the product and become a repeat customer.

Most products contain some dissonance-producing elements, and these elements detract from the product's total image. The price of the product can cause dissonance because it involves a part of one's income. The price can, however, be surrounded with so many positive stimuli regarding features of the product that it does not seem to be too objectionable. When several dissonant factors are present, one may be far more influential than the others.

Risk-reduction theory

Risk-reduction theory is based on the premise that consumers will select those goods that decrease their chances of being "hurt" or of being "wrong." This theory has strong social implications; the term "hurt" refers to social suffering. The risk-reduction element may be found, for example, in consumers who are insecure about their social position or are new to a particular social class. A new college graduate may find himself in a middle-management position, in a new town, with a new circle of friends. He may not

be sure which automobile to purchase. His wife may be insecure about the proper furniture to buy, the foods and drinks to serve at parties, and the china to place on the table when guests arrive. People seeking to reduce such risks may act in the following ways:

- They purchase name brand products.

- They purchase from stores with favorable reputations or from stores where members of their reference group purchase their products.

- They equate price with quality (the higher the price the better the quality).

- They observe and copy the actions of the members of their reference group.

The marketer can appeal to such a consumer by showing him how others like himself use the product.

Emotional behavior theories

Emotional behavior theories deal with consumer behavior that is not completely understood and is therefore not predictable. In man's attempt to understand emotional behavior, the following theories have been developed:

- Psychoanalytic Theory
- The self-image purchase
- Psycho-social models
- Impulse buying
- Ecological/environmental theory
- Organizational factors models

It will be of use to consider briefly the main concepts of some of these theories.

Psychoanalytic Theory

DEFINITION

Sigmund Freud's theory that man has a psyche of which he is largely unaware set the world back on its heels. This psyche, said Freud, has tremendous influence over the individual's behavior. This theory is called *Psychoanalytic Theory.* Prior to Freud, it was thought that behavior could be

explained on purely a biological level. Freud identified several psychological mechanisms that comprised man's psyche.

Freud described the personality of an individual as a total process, but proposed that the psyche had three mechanisms: the id, super ego, and ego.

DEFINITION

The *id* represents instinctual needs that are innate to everyone. The small babe as he is brought into this world is basically pleasure seeking; the pleasure principle states that the child desires warmth, oral and sexual gratification, and the avoidance of pain. If the id is constantly gratified and the child is pampered to excess, this mechanism will overdevelop and the individual will grow up to be impulsive. He will not be able to tolerate tension and will always seek immediate gratification. The id drives may also be satisfied by defense mechanisms of imagination, fantasy, and dreams. If the id were allowed to become extremely overdeveloped, the individual would become animalistic in nature.

DEFINITION

The *super ego* results from a socialization process that is learned basically from the child's parents. In order to help the child get along in society, the parents present a moral code or conscience to the child. The super ego is an emotional manifestation of the parents.

DEFINITION

The child immediately begins to recognize that he must control his drives, must repress the id process in order to conform to the socialization process of his parents and the surrounding environment. This is the so-called reality principle. In a well-adjusted personality the *ego* acts like a thermostat and automatically adjusts to the surroundings. It enables an individual to maintain an equilibrium between the impulsive id and the external social environment of the super ego.

Uses of Freudian psychology

Freud's theory was initially significant because it identified the mental process of personality, but of perhaps greater importance is its effect on subsequent theories. It led to the discovery that a person's behavior is influenced by mechanisms of which the individual is not aware. In an attempt to cope with the environment, a person may unconsciously use many defense mechanisms such as rationalization, repression, and projection. Marketers may need to apply the research on psychological motivation in order to understand and ultimately predict consumer behavior.

In one case, research showed that successful greeting cards contained sexual symbolism of ovals and circles.* Other campaigns have revolved around the theme of "reward thyself." This theme may be successful because of the strong id influence.

> **note** Motivation researchers, using Freudian psychology, have made many contributions toward understanding consumer behavior.

Freud's theory dealt heavily with man's desire for sex (the libido) and his attempt to resolve this drive. In line with this, many products have been sold as "love objects." For example, motivation research findings suggest that men buy convertibles as a substitute mistress. It is interesting that a disinterest in convertibles coincided with the occurrence of the so-called sexual revolution.

Freud identified the importance of touch and feeling (tactile relationships) to the child's sense of security. Soaps, bottles, and boxes may be developed so that the design is sensually appealing.

> **HOT spot** Advertisements that allude to sex usually attract attention to the advertisements themselves, a requisite for effective advertising.

The theory of the self-image purchase

Probably one of the most unique and startling approaches toward explaining and predicting consumer behavior is the concept of the self-image purchase. This theory states that a consumer will purchase those products that enhance his self-concept. Ernest Dichter, the father of motivation research, was probably one of the first individuals to use this concept in explaining and predicting consumer behavior. Schooled in Freudian psychology, Dichter has taken these principles and made a career of the study of consumer behavior. The theory shows how a consumer uses products to express his self-concept and how every purchase can be related back to this self-concept.

* Vance Packard, *The Hidden Persuaders* (New York: McKay, 1956).

Impulse buying

DEFINITION

The *impulse purchase* may be defined as one that is not planned. The impulse purchase is becoming more and more important: Recent studies have indicated that between 50 and 85 percent of all goods purchased at the grocery store are bought on impulse.

There are several forms of impulse buying: impulse purchase, impulse shopping, impulse situation, and new product impulse purchase. Let's examine each of these four impulse purchases. The "normal" impulse purchase, the one most authors define, takes place when the consumer disrupts his normal buying pattern to purchase a product with which he is confronted. For example, an individual who usually purchases Campbell's soup sees a special display of another brand, and decides to try the new brand. Special displays or other in-store promotional efforts may be necessary to encourage people to adopt, or at least try, a new product. Introductory offers with special price appeals and preferred display positions are most effective.

Many consumers today let the grocery store finalize their shopping list. They go to the store with the intent of purchasing food, but with no particular products in mind. As they roam up and down the aisles, they select the products that most appeal to them. This form of shopping is encouraged by self-service merchandising and the wide selection of products and brands available to the consumer today.

Gaining preferred shelf space is important for the marketer who relies on impulse shopping. The package, too, is important, for it is the silent agent that causes the impulse purchase. The impulse situation occurs when the consumer is in a situation that encourages the purchase of the product. In such an instance, the consumer may pass a popcorn stand that is exuding such a tantalizing aroma of fresh popcorn that the individual buys a 50-cent bag. The same thing could occur in the bleachers at a football game when the concession boy comes around with a hot dog.

> *note* When a new product is introduced it may be purchased on impulse simply because it is promoted as being new. The marketing implications are that new products should appeal to a person's tendency to buy an item on impulse.

Another consumer may find himself standing in a checkout line surrounded by racks of impulse goods. Having nothing better to do, he may squeeze, pinch, smell, or read about the product and ultimately place the product in the basket. *TV Guide* and *Playboy* have used this form of impulse selling very effectively. Most of us have generally accepted the concept that trying new products is an enjoyable experience.

Special offers, displays, and preferential dealer efforts are required with such new offerings. Many companies with maturing products find that bringing the product out with a new box or new features can be effective in attracting new customers. Some caution should be taken, however, for if a product idea is too new and unique, or perceived as being expensive, then it may be resisted. Consumer education may be necessary before consumer acceptance occurs. For example, consumers were initially skeptical that microwave ovens could cook foods as rapidly as manufacturers claimed and that they were safe for home use.

Ecological-environmental theory

Ecology is a biological science dealing with the interaction of an organism with its environment. In order to reduce any possible threat to survival (either psychological or physiological), people join organized behavior systems. These groups may be large social groups or small, specialized reference groups.

> **HINT**
> As applied to marketing, ecology considers how man adapts physically, socially, and physiologically to the stresses produced by his environment.

People attempt to interact successfully with their environment. This includes seeking stability in interactions while at the same time improving upon one's situation. Man suggests his social position and relative success at adaptation through the products he displays. A person who does not adapt successfully indicates this through inconsistent purchasing behavior. For example, a husband and wife who are not compatible will not purchase products in the same manner as a compatible couple will. Each member of an incompatible family will purchase products that are self-oriented rather than family-oriented. Instead of buying a home—something they can enjoy together—the husband may buy a sports car for himself and the wife expensive clothing for herself. In any case, the adaptation of the individual to his environment may influence his behavior as a consumer.

Figure 5-1.   Consumer

	1. Innovators (2-3%)	2. Early adopters (12-15%)
Personal characteristics		
1. Social class	Lower-upper	Upper-middle
2. Income	High income (inherited)	High income (earned from salary and investment)
3. Occupation	Highest professionals Merchants Financiers	Middle management and owners of medium-size businesses
4. Education	Private schooling	College
5. Housing	Inherited property Fine mansions	Large homes-good suburbs or best apartments
6. Family influence	Not family oriented Children in private school or grown	Children's social advancement important Education important
7. Time orientation	Present oriented, but worried about impact of time	Future oriented
Psychological characteristics		
1. Nature of needs	Self-actualization needs (realization of potential)	Esteem needs (for status and recognition by others)
2. Perceptions	Cosmopolitan in outlook	Prestige Status conscious Aspire to upper class
3. Self-concept	Elite	Social strivers, peer group leaders, venturesome
4. Aspiration groups	British upper class	Innovator class
5. Reference groups	Sports, social, and travel groups	Dominate industry and community organizations Golf, college, and Fraternity

Characteristics

3. Early majority (33%)	4. Late Majority (34%)	5. Laggards (12-15%)
Lower-middle	Upper-lower	Lower-lower
Above-average income (earned)	Average income	Below average income
Owners of small businesses Nonmanagerial office and union managers	Skilled labor	Unskilled labor
High school Trade school	Grammar school, some high school	Very little-some grammar school
Small houses Multiple-family dwellings	Low-income housing in urban-renewal projects	Slum apartments
Child centered and home centered	Children taken for granted	Children expected to raise themselves
Present oriented	Present (security) oriented	Tradition oriented, live in the past
Belonging needs (with others and groups)	Safety needs (freedom from fear)	Survival needs (basic needs)
Local aspirations and local social acceptance	Home and product centered	Live from day to day
Respectability from own reference groups and home	Security, home, centered, aggression apathy, no hope.	Fatalistic, live from day to day
In own social strata Dissociated from upper-lower	Others in this classification and in early majority Dissociated from lower-lower	Don't aspire
Social groups of this strata: chambers of commerce, labor unions, family, church, P.T.A., Auxiliaries	Family Labor unions	Ethnic group oriented

Figure 5-1. Consumer

	1. Innovators (2-3%)	2. Early adopters (12-15%)
Marketing functions		
1. Adoption process	The first to try new products influence the early adopters	The opinion leaders, taste-makers (most important)
2. Reasons for buying	Like to try new, innovative ideas	Because product is sign of social status To emulate upper class
3. Shopping patterns	Very little shopping or purchasing	Specialty stores with status
4. Spending emphasis	Hedonic products Large homes, trips to Europe Expensive cars, yachts, fashion	Prestige products Social-status products Education, investments

Categories of consumers

This chapter has shown ways that the business person can evaluate the market and the behavioral environment of the consumer, and then select a target customer for a specific product or service. One of the most effective ways to select a consumer is by identifying the categories of consumers and by understanding the characteristics of each category. (See Figure 5-1).

Innovators

Innovators have the psychological characteristics that predispose them to try new products and the financial means to afford such products. These people are often members of the upper class whose wealth is inherited. They are generally cosmopolitan people who travel widely. They comprise 2 to 3 percent of the population. Most new products are adopted by this group. first, and other groups will not buy them until the innovators have.

Characteristics, *continued*

3. Early majority (33%)	4. Late Majority (34%)	5. Laggards (12-15%)
First individuals in middle class to adopt	Major market, identify with early majority	Adopt because of direct contact with product
Desire for group acceptance	Out of necessity	Impulse or tradition
Shopping centers, Sears, Ward's Discount stores for branded products	Local stores Discount houses	Door to door Convenience stores
Status and anxiety products Home centered, children's products Savings important	Safety products Heavy appliances	Spend on impulse as soon as money is available

Early adopters

This group consists of upper middle-class individuals—the people who hold middle-management positions or own medium-size companies. They have attained success and wealth through their own endeavors. They have aspirations of becoming innovators, and therefore emulate the behavior of that group by buying the goods and services that innovators purchase. Early adopters make up 12 to 15 percent of the population, and are the country's opinion leaders.

Early majority

This group is composed of lower middle-class people who fall into two distinct groups: (1) owners of small businesses and (2) nonmanagement white collar workers or union managers. They identify strongly with members of their own group, but will purchase the goods and services bought by the early adopters because the early adopters are the leaders of the organizations. Thirty-three percent of the population belong to the early majority.

Late majority

The late majority is composed of people in the upper-lower class; they are primarily skilled workers. They look to the early majority to find out how to purchase because they want to put distance between themselves and the laggards. The late majority is most concerned about security—that is, they concentrate on holding their own and in general do not aspire to higher social status. They account for 34 percent of the population.

Laggards

The laggards are lower-class people who work at unskilled labor and live from day to day. Their living conditions are very poor, and they buy products primarily on impulse. They do not use problem-solving processes in purchasing; they adopt products because the items are necessities.

note Rather than being concerned with demand curves, demographics, and numbers, the professional marketer focuses his emphasis upon the qualitative psychological considerations of consumer behavior.

The professional small business marketer of today is confronted with a new means of viewing the marketplace and his customer. The business person must become committed to understanding the various aspects of the behavioral environment because excessive product failures and competition are forcing it on him. An awareness of the behavioral environment broadens his understanding of the marketing process and increases his ability to achieve success.

Developing a successful product strategy

6

Chapter 6

Developing a successful product strategy

One of the most significant problems plaguing the business person today is obtaining an answer to the question, "How do my customers regard my product?" From a technical standpoint, a product consists of a group of raw materials fashioned together to create a certain effect or perform a specific function. A car, for instance, represents such engineering features as power brakes, power steering, and manual or automatic transmission, and such tangible values as comfort, appearance, ease of upkeep, and trade-in value. An engineer would perceive an automobile in this way, and many top managers also consider the product from this rather technical viewpoint, because of their concern about costs and profits. The fact that many of these top managers come from the ranks of production rather than marketing may be a reason for their emphasis on product features.

Service organizations often (mistakenly) think of their "product" in a mechanical way. Banks think of their various services—checking accounts, certificates of deposit, loans, and check guarantee options, for example—as *things*. Beauty salons sell various kinds of hair styles and insurance brokers

offer insurance plans as if they were items. This traditional means of describing a product or service must include the intangible but very real psychological factors which combine to make up the product/service image.

Examining the product image

DEFINITION

The *product image* is the way in which the consumer perceives a product. The marketer must approach the product from an image-conscious viewpoint, since the consumer is not nearly as concerned with the functional or technical aspects of the product as with the psychological satisfaction to be gained from buying and using it. The consumer wants to express and enhance his or her self-image, and one way of doing this is through products. Virtually all the products we use express our self-image—the clothes we wear, the house we own, the car we drive, the colognes and perfumes we use.

Product personality, then, consists of two parts, the physical and the psychological. Physically a bar of soap may be round, square, or octagonal; it contains lye and coloring. In personality, soap is boldly masculine or softly feminine, modern or old-fashioned, of high status or low, light and delicate or heavy and coarse.

Although most consumers buy most products out of a desire to enhance their self-concept, they do not realize or are not willing to admit that this is what motivated their purchase. When asked why they bought a particular product, consumers give very rational reasons: "It's a good value, of high quality," or "I needed it." Let's look at an example of a buyer's reasoning.

> *note* The consumer does not make a distinction between the physical and psychological characteristics of products. To the consumer, the product has a unique image.

John Smith, who considers himself rational, is very careful with his money. He is making only an average income and prides himself and his family on being economical, sensible shoppers.

John's boss is invited over for dinner. The boss tells John not to make the dinner fancy, but the preparations will probably go like this:

John's wife will purchase a better cut of meat than she usually does. She will also buy name brand vegetables and desserts instead of local store brands. She'll buy a new tablecloth, borrow china from a neighbor, and purchase a new dress for the occasion. She will visit the hairdresser. John will wash the windows of the house and the car and will pull a few weeds in the garden. The overstuffed comfortable chair with a few holes will be moved to the basement.

> **E-Z TIP**
> While product features are easily duplicated in today's rapidly changing technological environment, a favorable product image is difficult to compete against.

It seems funny when it happens to someone else, but haven't we all acted this way at times?

An even more important reason for focusing on developing a favorable product image is that it will give your small firm a definite competitive advantage. It is easier and less expensive for smaller companies to develop effective company and product images because they are more a part of the local community. Large corporations must develop general images that will appeal to a large mass market.

A competing company's attempt to copy a successfully established product image usually results in promoting the originator's product image as well. The reason for this phenomenon should be obvious: When two ideas (images) are of equal strength but of unequal age, repetition increases the strength of the earlier idea more than that of the newer idea. If there are two ideas of the same strength but of unequal age, the older idea will not be forgotten as rapidly as the new one.

The implications are that the competitive firm is forced to develop an alternate but equally effective product image which will also attract the customers. This task is difficult, slow, and expensive. Usually new competitors are forced to seek out a different target market with a unique product image.

Elements of the product image mix

The product image is a complex combination of many ingredients. One must consider them all so that the final product—the product image—is clear, vivid, and acceptable to the target customer whom the marketer wishes to reach. Let's consider some of the major elements of the product image mix in detail.

The institutional image

The institutional image is the image of the generic product and not of any particular brand or company name. One could think, for example, of the institutional image for milk, oranges, canned soups, bananas, or butter. Such images are of major concern to trade associations composed of firms who sell the same generic type of product. Firms may combine into trade associations for the purpose of increasing primary demand for the product in the industry, rather than the secondary demand for a particular brand or company. Each firm will benefit from this increase in primary demand. Small companies should investigate the possibilities of organizing to stimulate primary demand for their products. If the industry is suffering from a poor image, all the firms in the industry may suffer.

Several years ago, the prune industry was suffering from a poor image. Many small growers had gone out of business. Motivational research studies were conducted for the industry, and it was discovered that the typical image of prunes was associated with old ladies and constipation. The suggestion was made to associate the prune with youth and a healthy diet. Prune consumers were portrayed as being smart, young, modern, and conscious of their figures. The prune industry began to revive.

The corporate image

The image of a corporation consists of a combination of all the images of the products of the various divisions of a firm. General Foods, for example, handles hundreds of different products, from coffee to dog food. This image, which is usually fuzzy or vague, is a complex one to develop.

> **note** If a favorable corporate image is achieved, it will benefit all the various product lines of the firm and add to the prestige and image of these products.

The corporate image is important since it does contribute to the product image. A strong corporate image can also make it easier to introduce new products, since favorable images of the corporation already exist. It is an easy task for Campbell's to introduce a new soup, whereas some unknown company would have a problem because no one is familiar with the name. Smaller companies must anticipate the corporate image by planning for it early in the growth of the company. The name of the firm should not limit the scope of the company's operations; it should be appealing and say what the company does. Developing a favorable image initially will make it easier to add new products.

Services, guarantees, and warranties

These give the impression of quality. Products that suffer from a poor image or products whose quality or safety may be in question need services, guarantees, and warranties in order to survive. The psychological implications are that a firm offering warranties or guarantees probably has a quality product. This is particularly important for small companies.

 Available servicing is particularly important for products which the consumer perceives as being mechanically complicated. The knowledge that servicing is available relieves pre-purchase tensions, reduces customer anxiety about possible failure of the product, and may help him to rationalize the purchase of an expensive, complicated product. For the smaller company, it is essential to provide good service. That is often the greatest competitive advantage it will possess against larger companies.

Price relationships

The price of a product is a strong image factor. Many complex mechanisms are at work in the psychology of pricing. The price of a product means different things to different people. To some consumers it adds value, as in the case of a status product, and to others it has a negative aspect, as in the case of the rational shopper who shops for the best buys.

Many consumers feel that there is a price-quality relationship: the higher the price, the better the quality, and vice versa. If the unknowing marketer were to price a status product too low his price might detract from the product. One would not expect to find a $4.99 dress at Saks Fifth Avenue.

Users of the product

Since many consumers use products to express their self-concepts and social class, the persons who use these items may influence the consumer image. Consumers also belong to and identify with reference groups. Members of the group are influenced by other members' buying behavior. Research has indicated that some people are extremely important in establishing an image for products. Fashion leaders set the trends for certain categories of clothing. Early adopters of these trends seem to have a tremendous impact on 'product acceptance. If this group does not accept a particular product, chances are great that the product will not become acceptable to the remainder of the consumers.

The promotion mix

Advertising has been the most effective form of promotion for creating the product image. However, the other ingredients in the promotional mix are important and are used to supplement or reinforce the advertising program.

> **E-Z TIP**
> Price is an important ingredient of the product image. If the price is not compatible with the other ingredients (packaging, advertising), the consumer may become confused and frustrated. This anxiety may cause him to consider some other product.

> **note**
> Promotion is one of the major tools for developing the product image. The mix includes advertising, personal selling, sales promotion, publicity, and branding and packaging.

Personal selling includes all sales efforts of an interpersonal kind and is very useful for introducing new product concepts and products which require some explanation of their characteristic features. Door-to-door salespeople have created a negative image for themselves by misrepresenting their products to the extent that personal door-to-door sales efforts suffer from a rather poor image, although

companies like Avon have done a great deal to change this image. Personal selling in specialty and exclusive shops, on the other hand, commands a highly favorable image. Clients feel that personal selling in such shops is a necessary part of the store's services.

Sales promotion includes all the contests and giveaways that are used to supplement other forms of promotion. Display also plays an important part in impulse merchandising. Publicity is any free form of promotion. This form of promotion includes press releases and editorial comments about "a startling new product.* Publicity has proved to be very useful for introducing new product concepts.

Brand and package image

DEFINITION

The brand and package image is an important visual form of identification. A *brand* is "a name, term, symbol, or design, or a combination of them, which is intended to identify the goods or services of one seller or group of sellers, and to differentiate them from those of competitors."[1] The brand name is usually associated with a company, firm, or organization. General Foods and Del Monte are examples. Strong brand identification is important because of its pre-selling capability. Once a strong, favorable brand image is established, it is relatively easy to introduce new products under the established brand name. The brand image is the mental picture the consumer has of the company and the behavioral way of looking at the brand name. The brand image influences the consumer's perception and acceptance of the product itself.

> **HINT** The marketer should consider the nature of each of the products in the firm, and should select a brand name that represents all the products in the line as well as the image of the firm itself.

Motivation research indicates that consumers cannot tell the difference between brands of cigarettes when blindfolded, but they have very clear-cut images of the various brands. The consumer seems to associate a definite type of person with each of the brands of cigarettes. Consider the contrast between the traditionally feminine image evoked by Eve cigarettes, and the gutsy, no-nonsense Virginia Slims woman.

---

* Committee on Definitions, Ralph S. Alexander, Chairman, *Marketing Definitions: A Glossary of Marketing Terms* (Chicago: American Marketing Association, 1960). p. 8.

A brand name must be psychologically meaningful. Some examples of effective brand names may make this clear:*

Armorkoat	promise of results in use
Easy-Off	ease of use
Taster's Choice	quality
Leathercraft	ingredients of product
JOY	pleasant association
How to Win Friends and Influence People	a reward for using

Here are some dos to keep in mind:

- Understand the nature of your firm's product image, and develop a brand name that is consistent with that image.‡

- Use a name that suggests prestige and self-enhancement (*Vogue* magazine).

- Use a name that is sexually suggestive (My Sin perfume).

- Make sure the brand matches the desired feminine or masculine image. Suffixes of -la, -na, -ine, and -ette usually have feminine implications.

- Try to make the name as personal as possible to achieve wide popular appeal (Mrs. Paul's Fish Sticks).

- Keep the name short (Tab).

- The name should become an easily visualized symbol (EXXON).

Here are some don'ts:

- Avoid names that are in poor taste. Avoid slang and blasphemy.

- Avoid names with strong seasonal connotations, if the product may ultimately be used in other seasons.

- Avoid overemphasis of one feature or insignificant features.

- Do not use names that are difficult to remember or to pronounce.

- Avoid geographical names that will hurt future nationwide sales.

* Steward Henderson Britt, *Consumer Behavior* (New York: John Wiley, 1967), pp. 378-379.*

‡ Adapted from James M. Vacary, *How to Think about a Brand Name for a New Product*, SALES MANAGEMENT, Vol. 77, April 3, 1956, pp. 34-38.

Only complementary products should be sold under a single brand name. For example, it would be unwise for Gerber baby foods to come out with Gerber dog foods, since the mental pictures of baby food and dog food are not compatible. Separate brand names should be used in such cases.

Psychology of the package

DEFINITION

As the consumer walks down the aisle of the typical self-service store, certain products will attract his attention; others will not even be noticed. The combination of stimuli which cause a product to be noticed is called the *package image*. Since self-service shopping is an extremely important form of selling today, the package, in many cases, must sell the product.

Through emotional needs, the consumer sets up very demanding standards of product packaging. Packages may make the difference between success and failure for some products, and although they do not create the product image, they can measurably detract or reinforce and enhance it. For some products, the package may be the consumer's only contact with the product. A cheap looking package should not be placed around a product which the manufacturer feels is of high quality. An importer of Swiss watches found that when he packaged his watches on a card with clear plastic, sales were limited, but as soon as he placed the watch in a handsome box with red and black velvet, his sales increased measurably.

In developing packages, the following behavioral aspects are of enormous importance.

- *Serving size.* Careful consideration should be given to the size of the box and the amount of the product supplied. If the box holds more than a person can use, the consumer may feel he is wasteful when he purchases the product; if the container does not hold enough, he may feel dissatisfied or cheated, Normally, it is better to give the consumer a little more, rather than less, than he would normally use, since people usually think that "the more the quantity, the better the deal." With many products, the item itself costs less than the package. Problems of size can usually be remedied by offering different sizes, but this is costly for the manufacturer.

- **_Informative._** Some packages must carry information about how to use the contents correctly. Unclear directions may confuse and discourage the consumer from buying the product, or he may misuse it and become frustrated and dissatisfied. It takes real talent to write good directions. Diagrams may be employed to show the proper use of a product and to help the consumer identify with it. Important factors such as guarantees and warranties should be kept as simple as possible and displayed prominently on the package.

- **_Communicative._** The package is an important form of visual communication. It must attract attention, arouse interest, and move the consumer to action. The combination of all the graphics—brand name, letters, colors—must communicate the image you want to project. It must say "try me." It must attract, and yet not be pretentious. It must sell, but not oversell.

- **_Confidence._** The package must express the quality which the consumer can expect from the product. Its message must be believable, but at the same time it must create an emotional response in the individual so that he will try it. The feel, shape, graphics, and brand name must say to the consumer "If you'll buy me, you won't be sorry."

- **_Status._** Status, or prestige, involves the social acceptability of a product. Some products are proudly displayed in the home because their presence proclaims that the owner is an excellent shopper. A customer may be more inclined to leave Crest toothpaste outside the medicine cabinet since Crest has been accepted by the American Dental Association as "an effective preventative against tooth decay." Some products, on the other hand, may be hidden from view because they have no particular social image but were purchased because they are convenient or inexpensive. The products which are proudly displayed have a greater chance of being accepted by reference groups and reinforced by word of mouth. This has backfired in a few instances where the product is displayed but not really used: A person, for example, may fill his Cutty Sark bottle with a cheap brand of liquor.

  The social display appeal of a product can be encouraged by making the package attractive. Facial tissue companies have done this by

making their packages pleasing to the eye and by having them fit in with the color decor of most bathrooms.

• *Dependability.* The package should allude to confidence in the product and the manufacturer. Bold colors, like red and black, have been found to be better for packaging automobile accessories. These colors apparently express strength and durability to the customer. Softer colors, such as the pastel combinations, are useful for cosmetics since soft colors express femininity and high quality. Warranties and guarantees may also be used to give the image of dependability.

• *Esthetic satisfaction.* The design, color, and feel of the product can be very important. Lettering and colors communicate different meanings. Certain shapes exude greater psychological satisfaction than others. The Coke bottle has been refined to the point that it now feels natural in the hand. Ernest Dichter, the outstanding motivation researcher, found that the feel of the doorknobs is one of the few tangible ways a person has of relating to his home. Other products have been so poorly designed that they have been discontinued. Several companies have attempted to change the shape of the catsup bottle, with little success: it is just right the way it is.

• *Identification.* Often the purpose of the package is to make the product easily recognizable by the consumer. Trademarks, brand names, distinguishing shapes, or profound color combinations are all means of facilitating identification. With the large number of manufacturers competing for the attention of the consumer in the self-service store, successful product recognition is important.

Product classification

In order to understand the concept of product and product images, marketers have found it useful to classify products into relationships that can be used to explain and predict the consumer's reactions to various product images.

Several ways of classifying products have evolved. The marketer must decide whether one or several of the following classifications are useful for understanding the customer and developing an appropriate product image.

Consumer product perception

Products can be classified as specialty goods, shopping goods, convenience goods, or new or unsought goods. Specialty goods, because of their strong brand preference, command the strongest search appeal. Shopping goods are perceived to be either different in quality (heterogeneous) or similar (homogeneous); shopping therefore occurs because of the consumer's desire to compare quality or price. There is a strong inclination on the consumer's part to shop around for these goods, but the desire is not as strong as it is for specialty goods. The consumer who perceives the product as a convenience good (including impulse goods, emergency goods, and staples)

> **note**
>
> One means of analyzing products is by classifying them according to the consumer's willingness to seek the product out.

has a low predisposition for shopping for these types of products. Unsought goods such as life insurance, encyclopedias, and expensive kitchen equipment must be marketed to the consumer by means of personal selling or direct mail because the consumer considers these as purchases that can be put off.

A new and unknown product is usually resisted. There is little or no willingness on the part of most consumers to shop for new goods. Once the product can be classified, the appropriate marketing strategy (plan) for selling the product can be determined. The way in which the consumer perceives the product will also determine the amount of control the marketer has over the product and product image. A firm introducing a new product possesses great control. Because the consumer is unfamiliar with the product, the marketer can shape the image in almost any direction he desires. Since personal selling and direct mail are the main means of initial promotion, and since these forms of promotion are directly controlled by the marketer, excellent control is gained. The dilemma lies in the fact that the product's unsought status must be changed to a sought-after one; in the process, loss of control may result.

The unsought good. Since personal (door-to-door) selling and direct mail are again the main means of sales, the marketer can establish any image he desires. Unfortunately, however, door-to-door sales have developed a poor image because of past use by swindlers or companies with devious sales

methods. Door-to-door salesmen were often individuals who were basically uneducated and "hard up." Their sales methods reflected their situations in the

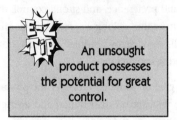

An unsought product possesses the potential for great control.

hard sell approach, or through the devious gimmicks used to make the sale. Companies now using door-to-door sales are keenly aware of this stigma and are attempting to change the unfavorable image through the use of professional, educated individuals. Also, sales calls are typically made on a referral basis only. Direct mail also suffers from a poor image. The term "junk mail" reflects the feeling of many consumers toward this form of sales effort.

Specialty goods, shopping goods, and convenience goods. If strong consumer brand preference can be achieved, strong control over the product and image can be maintained. Specialty goods can be sold on a very selective basis through factory-owned stores, franchising, or exclusive dealings, with the product still under the control of the manufacturer.

For both forms of shopping goods (heterogeneous and homogeneous) distribution can be on a selective basis, and control can be maintained over the methods of marketing. But when a product becomes perceived as a convenience good and requires intensive distribution, much of the control over the product and its image is lost. Convenience goods are sold through many types of outlets including discount stores, grocery stores, and vending machines. The methods of promotion, selling, and pricing vary greatly among these outlets. The convenience good may be used as a loss leader in a discount store or as a high-ticket item in some fashion store; the manufacturer has very little

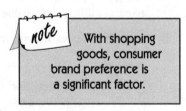

note With shopping goods, consumer brand preference is a significant factor.

say in this decision. Mass media advertising is required to stimulate demand. Any form of image-building at this level is expensive and difficult to achieve and maintain.

While the customer's classification of a product is dependent upon how he perceives it, most products will progress through each classification,

beginning in the new or unsought stage and ultimately becoming a convenience good. If the business person prefers limited, exclusive distribution, high price, strong brand preference, and strong control, then he should attempt to keep the specialty status as long as possible. This situation is particularly attractive for small, new manufacturers who do not have extensive manufacturing or marketing capabilities.

If the proprietor is willing to give up some control over the product and product image in return for more widespread distribution and greater sales volume, he may allow the product to slide into the shopping goods classification. Finally, if he desires a mass distribution situation with low profit margin per product but high sales volume with little control, he may allow the product to become a convenience good.

A few companies have been able to maintain a specialty good status and also obtain excellent market coverage at the same time. Corning Ware is an excellent example. This phenomenon usually requires some artificial mechanism such as superior patents or the use of resale price maintenance which establishes a uniform price. These methods of control are very difficult to achieve and expensive to maintain.

Product life cycle

The product life cycle shows the total sales volume of the generic form of a product (food blenders, cameras, or automobiles) over a period of time. The typical product life cycle can be divided into five stages, each of which requires a different marketing strategy and a unique marketing mix.

These stages include Introduction, Growth, Maturity, Saturation, and Decline. The type of consumers and their perceptions of the product vary from stage to stage. This form of analysis is an exciting one, since it considers a product as dynamic rather than static and allows for a variety of strategies over its entire life. Figure 61 shows a typical product life cycle indicating the sales curve for both the innovating company and the total industry sales.

note — Products, like people, pass through many stages: birth, life, and eventually, death.

Figure 6-1. Product life cycle.

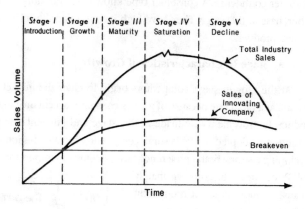

- **Stage I: Characteristics of introduction**

In the introductory stage, usually only one firm exists. The volume of sales of the product rises slowly and production costs are high because experimental production methods are used and frequent product modifications are made. Distribution is limited because of the newness of the product, and because the development of primary demand (demand for the generic product itself) is necessary before it becomes important to develop brand preference. Prices are relatively high in order to cover the high marketing and production costs. Typically, there are no profits experienced at this stage because these high initial development and marketing costs must be recouped. Production and marketing facilities are tested in order to determine whether the products are measuring up to the original standards and expectations.

> ⚠ **CAUTION** The introductory stage is a very critical one for the firm; between 50 and 85 percent of all new products fail in this stage.

Since the average consumer resists new products, the entrepreneur must concentrate on familiarizing the consumer with the new product idea, showing how it may be used, and indicating what results may be expected. Some type of technical explanation

about the nature and use of the product may be necessary to develop consumer confidence. A consumer type known as innovators are most likely to purchase at this stage. They have high incomes and the self-confidence to try new products.

- **Stage II: Characteristics of Growth**

At the growth stage, competitors begin to enter the market. Total sales increase at a rapid rate because of greater consumer acceptance of the generic product. Improvements are made at this stage and efficient line production methods are adopted. There is some competition for distribution outlets, and developing a strong brand preference now becomes an important competitive tool. Prices begin to go down mainly because of more efficient production methods and distribution procedures. Profits are extremely healthy because production and marketing costs are getting lower while sales volume is getting higher.

> *note* The originating firm will usually recover costs and break even at a point between the introduction and growth stage so that the growth stage is one of the most profitable.

While sales are growing rapidly at this stage, the majority of the market may still be skeptical and may wait for the price to decline before trying the product. Early adopters are the most likely to purchase the product at this stage, and for many products this consumer group must be reached before the majority consumer groups will buy. Like the innovator, the early adopter has the income and confidence to try the new product. Early adopters aspire to be innovators and will be influenced by them.

- **Stage III: Characteristics of Maturity**

The first part of the mass market is reached and sales increase, but not as quickly as they did in the growth stage. Parts and service requirements increase. Prices drop dramatically due to pressure from competition and each firm's desire to reach as many consumers as possible. Dealer margins and profits shrink, as do the firms' profits. Early majority consumers purchase the product because others in their reference groups are using it. By this stage, there is little doubt in the mind of the early majority consumer that the

HOT spot During the maturity stage, many competitors enter the market.

product is desirable and safe. The product is offered by many outlets and the consumers have frequent contact with it. Late adopters have not purchased the product yet; early adopters, trying to achieve social distance from their late adopter counterparts, will use the product as a symbol of success. The price seems right, and so they will buy.

- **Stage IV: Characteristics of Saturation**

By the fourth stage there are a number of competitors but only the most efficient firms will prevail. The market is saturated; trade-ins appear, and the replacement market becomes important. The logistics (distribution) is very complex with companies using as many outlets as possible to sell their product. Late majority consumers perceive the product as being a necessity item since so many consumers have adopted it by this stage.

- **Stage V: Characteristics of Decline**

At the decline stage total sales begin to drop. Other types of products may have been developed which are substitutes for the declining one. The number of firms also begins to decrease, and only the manufacturers with favorable cost pictures will survive. Prices are forced down to only a reasonable rate of return for the most efficient manufacturers, and then stabilized. Market exposure is not as important and, as product offerings narrow, survivors tend to specialize and gravitate back to a core market.

A firm which finds itself in a declining market may want to get out as gracefully and as profitably as possible, or it may wish to innovate the product and try for additional sales and profits. Typically, the consumer who adopts at this stage is old, of an ethnic group, or with a low income. Products are purchased only if the individual has the money at the time and are usually purchased on impulse.

The fad life cycle

While most products progress through the five stages and conform to the near normal curve characteristic of the product life cycle, the period from introduction to decline varies considerably from product to product. An item

that passes through the five stages in less than a year is considered a fad product. The life cycle of a fad shows rapid growth and decline with extremely short maturity and saturation stages. Fads occur because the products are visible (the sack dress or hula-hoop) to the general population. Other fad items may be extremely stylish (mini-skirt) or may require skill (skate boards and roller skates) in use. In both cases, the bandwagon effect (where everyone is wearing or using the product) plays an important part. Because of the extreme visibility by the whole market, adoption is rapid. Such products are usually easy to manufacture, with low fixed costs and overhead. Therefore, many competitors exist who force prices down rapidly. Sales for fad items drop off as rapidly as they originally increase, because of loss in stylishness or uniqueness.

Psychological dimensions of the product

As a product moves along in its life cycle, the consumer perceives it differently in each stage. At their inception, products are new to the customer, who perceives them first as luxury items, then as prestige products, and then as status products. They finally are perceived as necessities, and by the time of the decline stage, no interest is left in the product. It can then be called an indifference item.

When the innovation is new and unique, the consumer does not know a great deal, if anything, about the concept. People are drawn to new ideas, but to most the new item is out of reach financially and too new to be trusted. Fear and suspicion are prevalent since the unknown, for most consumers, is psychologically uncomfortable. A good example is the microwave oven. It has been on the market for years, but because of its initial high price and unique features, it was resisted by the mass market.

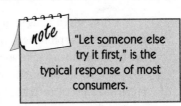

note "Let someone else try it first," is the typical response of most consumers.

In the introductory stage a product is typically priced above the reach of most consumers, and is considered a luxury good. Only the innovator will be interested since he has the money, the curiosity, and the confidence to try new and unique products. Often such products are not purchased for functional reasons, but out of curiosity or to express one's status.

During the growth stage, the consumer will perceive the product as a symbol of prestige and success. For example, a microwave oven will be displayed as proof of social achievement by the early adopter. The consumers who purchase such a product consider themselves leaders in product adoption. Usually the product is still priced relatively high by the manufacturer at this stage. Because of the average consumer's lack of experience with such products, the mass market may perceive that the price is too high.

At this stage, the consumer may develop a strong image for the product. It may be considered a symbol of success, and will probably be coveted by the major market.

HOT spot Consumers accept the fact that they would like to own the product eventually, when the price goes down or their incomes rise.

Because there are several manufacturers at this stage, greater exposure of the product is likely, and familiarity and acceptance will probably occur. Price is the deterrent for most consumers; to purchase the item now might seem extravagant or wasteful. Status products usually imply class membership. Members of this early majority group usually identify strongly with their reference and social groups. Status products representing class membership are important to them, and they use these products to obtain social distance from the late majority class. The microwave oven, by this stage, has become inexpensive enough for the early majority consumers to purchase, and is, therefore, a very visible source of affluence.

By the time the product reaches the next stage of the product life cycle, it probably will be considered a necessity to most consumers. A large number of persons have purchased the item and it enjoys widespread distribution. The late majority consumers who purchase at this late stage are home-centered, and the product will probably be perceived as necessary for comfort in the home. If the household does not have the product, the housewife may fear that others will think of her as a poor homemaker. The price is low enough at this stage for most individuals to be able to afford the product. Recent mass media advertisements and the dramatic lowering of the price of the microwave oven indicate that this product is approaching this stage.

In a declining market situation, most consumers take the product for granted. Other, more exciting goods are on the horizon or are already replacing the use of the declining product. The only person to buy the product at this stage is the laggard who tends to be very traditional and who is older.

Psychological classifications

Certain groups of products appeal to certain needs. Some products are only for grownups, some alleviate anxiety, while others give pleasure or are primarily useful.

Maturity products, because of social custom, are usually withheld from young people. Cigarettes, cosmetics, coffee, and liquor are important for the new users for expressing maturity. Anxiety products are those which are used to alleviate some presumed personal or social threat. Products fitting this classification would be health and dietetic foods, deodorants, and mouthwashes.

Hedonic products are highly dependent on their sensory character for their appeal. Examples are snack foods, certain types of clothing, fad items, and the design of certain automobiles. Functional products are those to which little cultural or social meaning has yet been attached. Examples are staple food items like fruits, vegetables, flour, sugar, and some conventional clothing and home necessities.

The physical nature of the product

From this discussion, the reader may have the idea that the quality of the product is not important—that all businesses have to do to sell a product is develop and promote an attractive product image. This limited sense of product image is misleading. If the product is bad, the best package and

> **note** The consumer does not perceive the package, brand, trademark, and product as separate; to him, it is all one.

marketing program ever developed cannot sell the product over the long run. A few venturesome persons may purchase it once, but if they don't like the product they won't buy it again. By word of mouth, dissatisfaction will spread

quickly to other consumers and government will prosecute attempts at any dishonest presentation of the product.

The proprietor must start with a basically sound product or service if he is to succeed. There have been many situations, however, where fine products have not succeeded because the manufacturer was not sensitive to the product image. A firm that is able to establish a favorable product image in the minds of its consumers gains a competitive advantage which is difficult and expensive to challenge in the marketplace.

In this chapter a great deal of emphasis has been placed on developing the psychological nature of the product. That is not to say, however, that the physical nature of the product is unimportant. It is impossible to sell a poor product in the long run; it must be basically sound before a favorable product image can be developed. It is through the marketing manager's expertise that the successful product image is developed to match the firm's target market.

E-Z TIP

Gaining an understanding of what constitutes the product image is important for the business person since the consumer is striving to express his self-concept through the use of products.

Developing a successful distribution strategy

7

Chapter 7

Developing a successful distribution strategy

DEFINITION

A *marketing channel* for products is the path goods take as they proceed from production to points of intermediate and final use. For services, it is the method of providing the service to the consumer. Finding a channel to carry a product can be difficult and frustrating. Often no channel will accept a new product, and sometimes no channels exist for the new company. In these cases, the entrepreneur has to develop new channels from scratch. A channel of distribution is made up of intermediaries which facilitate the pathway of products from the producer to the consumer or user. The intermediaries, such as wholesalers and the retailers in this pathway or system, are customers of the manufacturer. If a new manufacturer cannot find wholesalers and/or retailers to distribute his products, it will be difficult, if not impossible, to time the selling of the product to the ultimate consumer. The only means of distributing it may be the more expensive routes of franchising, factory-owned stores, or personal sales—alternatives that tend to limit the number of products to be distributed.

Channels are efficient for the same reason manufacturers must be efficient—competition. Wroe Alderson, an expert in the development of marketing channels, gives an example of why channels are efficient: If five households were to exchange their surplus with one another (five articles), ten separate exchanges would be made. However, if this market is replaced by a central market (channel), only five trips are necessary. The greater the number of transactions, the greater will be the difference between the two types of exchanges.

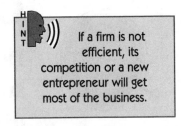

If a firm is not efficient, its competition or a new entrepreneur will get most of the business.

The intermediary can increase the efficiency of exchange, even when producers and consumers are close together (place utility), but the efficiency is greater at greater distances. Retailers may create time utility simply by holding stocks of goods or by selling on credit. Channels are also efficient because routines are possible. When a task is done over and over, the most efficient way of doing it can be developed.

The functions of distribution channels

Businesses in the United States have a far easier time distributing their products than do their counterparts in other parts of the world. Most of the highly industrialized nations of Europe have relatively few retailing specialists, but in the United States, businessmen can obtain effective distribution simply by selecting the types of resellers that best meet their needs. Why has this system of resellers evolved?

Channels exist because they can perform a service at a lower cost than anyone else, including the manufacturer. Specialization has decreased the costs of manufacturing and reduced the costs of distribution. As distribution needs change and new ones develop, specialized channels will be organized to service these new needs. Channels exist to bridge the geographical gap between the producer and the consumer, to provide the storage of goods, and to form a bridge of communication between the producer and the consumer. Because the intermediary is in constant contact with the consumer, it is possible to provide the services needed to get the product to the consumer.

The division of tasks works better when the channel team is closely integrated with the producer. A continuing relationship and healthy profits on both sides preserve the relationship. A realization that the objectives are the same (profits) is important, even when the producer's line constitutes an essential part of the whole. The use of marketing channels implies the delegation of marketing tasks to others. Quality and intensity of performance of desired activities may be sought through persuasion, incentives, and control.

The consumer's use of the channel system

Let's look at the varying degrees of dependency within the marketing process and see how they affect the consumer.

> **HOT spot** The consumer usually has a choice in how many marketing and distribution functions he allocates to the marketing process and how many functions he will perform himself. Usually the more functions he elects to have performed for him, the more it will cost.

- At the first level, the consumer is completely involved in the marketing process. The housewife, in this first example, desires to perform all the functions of food preparation herself. In this rather extreme instance, she would search out a supply of wild vegetables and trap wild animals. She would then prepare the food herself, canning fruits and vegetables and preserving the meat.

- She might decide to buy seeds and livestock and produce the food herself. This would cost a little more, but she would not be as dependent upon the environment to furnish her the food her family requires.

- She may turn the growing (production) function over to someone else. For example, she may drive to a farm and gather the vegetables and select the livestock ready for slaughtering.

- She may require the farmer and rancher to perform the selecting (grading) and place function. She will go to the roadside stand where the fruit has been cleaned and graded, and the shop where the meat is already butchered.

- The housewife might desire even more preparation and easier accessibility of the food. She may go to a nearby grocery store and buy packaged fresh produce.

- This degree of dependence involves further preparation of the food. The consumer may go to the store and buy canned fruits, frozen vegetables, and frozen dinners, ready to heat and serve.

- This degree requires further refinement of place utility. Here, the customer places a call and has the food delivered to the door, all prepared and ready to eat. No effort is required on her part for gathering or preparing it.

- The consumer gives up the entire preparation of the food. She and her husband go to a restaurant where the food is already prepared. All they need to do is select the food items desired.

> *note* Most instant forms of food products have not enjoyed rapid adoption because these products threaten enduring roles.

- In this final stage the housewife gives up all the preparation functions. She has the meal catered in her home where everything is prepared. This is perhaps the ultimate in consumption: All the necessary marketing functions are performed by the marketing intermediary and none by the consumer.

When consumers buy anything, they have the choice of which functions they want to perform for themselves and which they choose to have performed for them. The fewer functions they are willing to perform, the more expensive the process. It is easier to have the marketing intermediary perform the function, and increased discretionary income makes it possible, but few consumers really desire to have all the functions performed for them. The reasons lie in deep-seated psychological needs.

Everyone has been raised with certain perceived roles in mind. There are stereotypes for the roles of the housewife and the husband. These roles usually include the performance of certain marketing functions. For example, it is traditionally the role of the housewife to prepare the meals. When the marketing process performs some of the functions, she may feel that her role is threatened. Household appliances such as dishwashers, clothes dryers, and electric can openers have also lacked immediate acceptance because they challenged traditional roles.

Consumers may find great satisfaction in performing some or all of the functions. A banker may choose to change the oil in his Cadillac himself; a stockbroker may sense a feeling of accomplishment when he grows food in his greenhouse; a housewife may find satisfaction in re-upholstering the furniture.

HOT spot

This offers an interesting challenge to the marketer who is responsible for developing both labor-saving and time-saving products as well as products to provide pleasure for consumers during their leisure time. A dishwasher may be sold on labor-saving appeals, and then hobbies sold to fill the time saved. From the economist's viewpoint, channels of distribution develop and exist because of purely economic reasons, but other factors of a behavioral nature have become evident.

Channels as a behavioral system

CAUTION The advertisement that asks the consumer to request the product at his favorite store is an example of a "pulling" strategy. This strategy is costly and may fail if strong consumer demand is not stimulated quickly.

The particular channel or channels a manufacturer selects usually becomes a behavioral system. Every member of the system (wholesaler and retailer) is a subsystem, but does not operate independently. They are, in fact, highly dependent upon one another for survival and success, and only the interlocking relationships they develop will enable them to survive

the competitive environment in which they operate. This channel system may become closely allied to the manufacturer they serve; and the manufacturer will, in turn, strive to maintain a harmonious distribution system. Most channel systems seek stability; they may resist new manufacturers trying to enter the marketplace. For example, a new soup manufacturer may find that Campbell's has the channel system for soups completely under its control. It may require costly promotional programs to "pull" the product through the channel system. This is accomplished by a strong advertising program designed to stimulate consumer demand. This strong demand may force the channel system to reconsider the new product and start carrying it.

Channel systems develop for economic reasons—to deliver the product to the consumer for a profit—yet the reasons for a successful system go beyond economics. Wholesale and retail intermediaries, like individuals, are motivated and influenced by emotional, sometimes non-rational needs and desires. The customer, by the same token, selects a retailer for many psychological reasons.

The psychology of shopping

Shopping is an important ritual in American culture, as it is in most cultures. One must gain an understanding and appreciation of the shopping ritual before it is possible to predict which store will be selected and by whom.[*]

When shopping, a person feels pampered and catered to. Purchases represent the individual's ability to shop successfully. Self-service shopping has made the process even more of an adventure. Shopping also has strong social overtones. It is a form of social contact, and the stores selected usually exhibit the life style of the shopper. Shopping in small stores, for example, gives the customer a feeling

> **note** Shopping is an expression of freedom for some customers and of affluence for many others.

of belonging to the economic system. By patronizing a small store, customers feel they are enabling the store to stay in business against their large

---

[*] Wroe Alderson, "The Analytical Framework for Marketing," in Delbert Duncan, ed., *Proceedings: Conference of Marketing Teachers from Far Western States* (Berkeley: University of California, 1959), pp. 15-18.

competitors. The retailer who understands these psychological dimensions can adjust the store to serve the customer's psychological and social expectations. Proprietors must also familiarize themselves with the reasons why people shop. Basically there are five types of shoppers.

Personalized shoppers desire personal recognition from salespeople. They like it when sales personnel remember their names, their preferences, and something about their personal life. ("Good morning, Mrs. Thompson. How is that son of yours doing at Yale?") These people will usually develop strong store loyalty. The products carried and the prices charged are secondary in importance. Roughly 28 percent of consumers fall in this category. Small companies can cater to this segment very effectively.

The *ethical shopper* develops a strong identification with the small retailer and feels that by catering to the small firm he is enabling that firm to compete successfully against the large chains. He feels obligated to patronize the local small stores. Approximately 18 to 24 percent of customers fall in this classification.

The *economic shopper* is concerned with the price-quality relationship. For heterogeneous shopping goods, he wants help from salespeople; personalized service is needed to help him decide if the price-quality relationship is a favorable one. For homogeneous shopping goods and convenience goods (with the exception of impulse goods), price is this shopper's most important consideration. Discount houses and some chain department stores appeal to the economic shopper.

> **HOT spot** Between 24 and 33 percent of shoppers are generally motivated to patronize a particular store for economic reasons.

To a large number of consumers, shopping is an adventure, and products are purchased on impulse. For them, a shopping expedition is like Christmas morning when gifts are opened and tried. Many consumers shop for the sake of shopping, with no preconceived intent to purchase a particular product. It has been estimated that nearly 85 percent of all convenience goods are purchased on impulse. The number of *impulsive shoppers*, in the shopping goods classification, is approximately 26 percent.

The *apathetic convenience shopper* is one who does not enjoy the shopping process. Location and convenience are the major consideration for store patronage—the closer the better. Roughly 17 to 26 percent of shoppers fall in this classification.

The results of patronage studies indicate that 24 to 33 percent of those who purchase shopping goods products are price-conscious. This category seems to be growing. Most customers seem to be more interested in the amount of personalized service available, and 17 to 26 percent are mainly interested in location. Approximately 26 percent shop for the sake of shopping and purchase on impulse.

These results indicate that the most favorable combination for a retailer is a relatively small store with personalized service in a convenient location. This is probably the reason why specialty shops in covered shopping malls are popular.

Figure 7-1. Using classification of goods to select channel intermediaries.

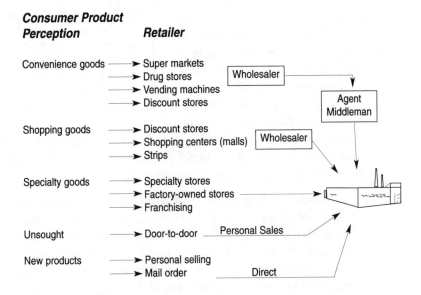

Willingness to shop

The readiness of the consumer to expend effort in buying a product depends upon how the customer perceives the importance of the product in satisfying wants, needs, and desires. As we have seen, products can be grouped under several classifications: convenience goods, shopping goods, specialty goods, unsought goods, and new products. Let us again consider these classifications, this time in the light of consumer willingness to shop.

When a consumer considers a product to be a convenience good, it means that he is willing to purchase a number of known substitutes rather than make the additional effort to shop for a particular brand. If he doesn't find the brand he usually buys, he will purchase another rather than shop for this preferred brand. Most cigarettes and grocery store items are in this classification. It is essential, therefore, that the consumer be able to find his preferred brand easily. This requires intensive distribution (see Figure 7-1) through grocery stores, drugstores, vending machines, and discount outlets. Wholesalers should also be used.

When consumers perceive a product to be a shopping good, they feel that the effort of shopping is worth the potential benefit gained. Consumers shop either because they believe they can buy the product for less money (homogeneous shopping good) or because they can find a better quality product for relatively the same price (heterogeneous shopping good). Such goods should be distributed in a way that facilitates customer shopping. Department stores and shopping malls encourage shopping.

> **note** Dealers handling shopping goods may situate themselves close to one another. This is typical of automobile, mobile home, and furniture and appliance dealers and is known as strip location.

Consumers will usually visit at least three locations before purchasing. The last place a person shops has a slightly higher probability of getting the sale. Promotion campaigns that say "shop around and then come and see us," have been very effective. If your company is the first to be visited, tell the customer about other competitors that you know you can beat.

If a consumer perceives a product to be a specialty good, he will have strong brand preferences. He is willing to exert a great deal of effort to purchase a specific product, even if it means driving across town or waiting for the product to be ordered. Because of this willingness, exclusive and limited distribution is possible. Specialty stores, factory-owned stores, or franchises may be used to distribute such a product.

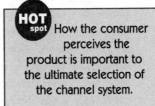

An unsought product is usually one which requires strong persuasive techniques, usually through personal selling, on the part of an intermediary. Unsought goods are of a relatively expensive nature because of this personal selling requirement. Personal and direct selling (mail order) are required because the consumer feels that the product is not absolutely necessary at any particular point in time. Insurance is such a product.

New products are also unsought because consumers do not know about them. The manufacturer must inform the potential customer of the new product and its positive characteristics. Because of its new status, the wholesaler and retailer must also be sold on the attributes of the new product. This involves personal selling at the intermediary level. Wholesalers may be convinced to put up special displays and to conduct special forms of sales promotion to introduce the new product.

Determining consumer perceptions

To select the proper type of retailer, the manufacturer must select the target market and then choose the channel system that will most effectively serve this customer. The proper retailer can be determined by measuring the customer's willingness

HOT spot How the consumer perceives the product is important to the ultimate selection of the channel system.

to exert effort in shopping. Product classification can be influenced by the entrepreneur.

When a firm is selling the product directly, the company manager has a great deal of potential control over the selling practices and the type of consumers the product reaches. As distribution moves from the unsought to the convenience goods classification, however, the manufacturer loses control;

the distribution becomes broader and more diverse. Such products are being sold to so many different forms of wholesalers and retailers that the firm may not even know where its product is being sold and who its target customer is. Price and local promotion are also out of the firm's control. Important ingredients of its marketing strategy and product image are out of its hands.

Table 3. Distribution coverage.

Product Classification	Type of Distribution	Control	Extent of Coverage
Convenience goods	Intensive	Poor	Broad
Shopping goods	Selective	Fair	Fair
Specialty goods	Exclusive	Very good	Limited
Unsought goods	Direct sales	Potentially excellent	Very limited
New products	Personal selling	Excellent	Extremely limited

Looking at the classifications from the aspect of the extent of distribution we can see from Table 3 that the degree of penetration into the market is quite limited at the unsought goods end of the continuum. Direct forms of distribution through mail and personal selling are relatively expensive, and the extent of distribution is limited. For specialty goods the type of distribution is rather exclusive and the degree of coverage is also limited. At the other end of the continuum, convenience goods have an intensive form of distribution.

For higher-priced goods, the specialty or the shopping goods classification works best when the proprietor develops strong brand images and retains control over the image of the product. For inexpensive, highly competitive products, where images would be very expensive and perhaps impossible to maintain, the loss of control may be an appropriate trade-off for widespread distribution and a convenience goods classification.

E-Z TIP

There must be a trade-off between the extent and cost of distribution and the degree of control over the product image.

Developing the store image

Once the general nature of the distribution system is determined the proprietor must consider the image of the specific retail establishments, particularly for the selling of services. One restaurant in a highly competitive market thrives, while the others barely survive. These restaurants' food, prices, services, and advertising are relatively similar. Why does one particular restaurant do so well? It may be because of the image it has projected.

> **note** The image of a store is based upon the consumer's perceptions of the functional and psychological aspects of the store. Much research has been conducted in this area.

When a loyal customer thinks of the store he regularly patronizes, he perceives it in a personal way: "This is my kind of store." In other words, the store is compatible with, and reinforces, his or her self-concept. The individual feels comfortable in the store and enjoys the shopping experience.

Let's look at the factors that make a person feel that this store is the best place to shop.

What the store is like

Sometimes a store has such a strong image that its customers gain a great deal of satisfaction by simply buying its products; in fact, they receive more satisfaction from purchasing an identical brand at this store than at another. Stores like Saks Fifth Avenue, Tiffany, and Macy's have developed such store image appeals. The architecture of the store is important. You cannot tell a book by its cover, but most consumers develop a definite image of a store simply by what it looks like from the outside. Many stores lack imaginative and distinctive design and therefore never entice potential customers into the store.

The location of the store can also influence its image. The physical presence of a store in an area determines whether or not it will appeal to the residents. Location is least important for the store that handles specialty goods

E-Z TIP

Decor is very important for establishing an image. There is a great difference between a stained cement floor and plush padded carpeting, between fluorescent tubes and chandeliers.

with great appeal, but even in this case business can be improved through a wise choice of location. Store layout affects the store's image and patronage. The more consumers who pass a particular product, the greater the probability of purchase. The longer the time a consumer spends in the store, the greater the number of purchases. Traffic patterns should be set up so that customers will be exposed to the whole store. Stores with wide aisles will be perceived as spacious, with high quality products. Stores with long narrow aisles will be perceived as having a lower-status image, like that of a bargain store.

The products it carries and how much they cost

The nature of the products will determine the clientele and the ultimate image of the store. When a customer enters a store, he usually has some expectancy as to the breadth and depth of the assortment of products carried. Breadth refers to the degree to which products of a different nature are sold. For example, a drugstore carries a lot of products besides drug items, but usually has a depth in the drug line, which is to say it probably offers six different brands of vitamins.

note

Price structure will also determine the clientele. Consumers will often pay more for an identical product at one store than another, usually because of the store's image. Displays with special price appeals can be effective for encouraging the customer to survey the entire store. Displays work particularly well for introducing new or novelty items.

Many chain stores and some small retailers offer private brands at a lower price than the national brand, even though the basic product is the same. Though research is sketchy, the following observations are possible:

- The larger the family, the greater the likelihood of using private brands.

- The more of a product the family uses, the greater the probability of using a private brand.

- The greater the feeling of loyalty to the store, the greater the chance the consumer will purchase its private brand.

- The higher the social class of the customer, the less likelihood of his buying private brands.

The people who work there

Every consumer has a preconceived idea of the appropriate roles that salespeople and store personnel should assume. It may be a passive role, a helpful one, or even a very assertive role; it depends upon the nature of the customer and the type of product.

Unfortunately, many managers employ low-salaried salespersons who show little concern for their personal qualities. It takes a truly sensitive, perceptive salesperson to be able to help a consumer with the purchase of most products.

> **HINT** The salesperson may be the only personal contact a customer has with the store. This contact is very important for the establishment of the store image.

The clientele

People tend to surround themselves with others like themselves in order to reinforce their self-concept and to avoid potentially dissonant situations. Consumers will look for stores that are patronized by others like them. The image of the store and its salespeople do a great deal to signal to consumers the type of clientele to which the store caters. A store manager makes a big mistake when he tries to attract many different types of consumers, for this can only result in a confusing image, and consumer loyalty will be difficult to attain.

Consumers are usually very sensitive to the buying habits of members of their own reference group, particularly the buying of clothing, automobiles, and home furnishings. Individuals may seek out retailers who cater to the other members of the group. These reference groups may establish the image for the retail outlet. A bank may be reputed to cater only to businessman; a coffee shop may focus on teenagers.

Most stores have their own social image. The store that does not possess a clear-cut image will probably fail.

While most stores require a social image, some products do not. If a product has an identifiable quality image, even customers of a high social class may be willing to purchase it at a discount store. For example, a General Electric television set might be purchased at a store such as K-Mart. Where brand identity is lacking, as in the case of furniture, clothing, and rugs, the middle and upper-class consumer will prefer the higher-status stores.

Upper middle-class customers are more confident in their shopping ability and are more likely to try new stores, browse through shopping malls, and investigate specialty shops. They travel greater distances and indulge in shopping sprees when traveling and vacationing.

People in a lower social class tend to be limited in their range of stores and refrain from extensive shopping. They usually patronize the stores near home. These stores often have a limited product line, but they provide credit, and the customer feels comfortable there.

Promotion

The nature of the promotion and advertising communicates the image of the store. There is a great difference, for example, between a fashion newspaper advertisement for Saks Fifth Avenue and one for a cut-rate

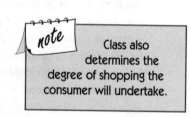
note
Class also determines the degree of shopping the consumer will undertake.

discount house. Newspaper advertisements that are cluttered appear to entice on a low-price basis, but a low quality image accompanies the appeal. Advertisements utilizing a lot of white space and listing higher prices project a quality image. Customers who have never been in a store will immediately develop an image from the advertisement alone.

Shelving and displays

Experience has shown that the location of a product on the shelf in self-service retailing is very important. Studies by market researchers Ronald E.

Frank and William F. Marsy * indicate that, in general, the following order of shelf location is most effective:

- Eye level for lightweight, packaged products.

HINT

Window and in-store displays are a useful means for communicating store image.

- Waist level for baskets of loose, unpackaged items and displays.

- Knee or ankle level for large or heavy products.

- Above eye level for inexpensive, light, bulky items (such as soap or toilet paper).

Stores seeking a high-quality image should not use shelving above waist level. Displays on tables and in glass cases are usually very effective. Stores interested in projecting a low-price image should place products above eye level.

Some stores spend thousands of dollars on their displays, while others have none at all. Window displays are a preview of what to expect inside the store. In-store displays are equally effective. One study indicates that 44 percent of consumers use displays as a guide for purchase decisions; 33 percent of the 5,215 shoppers randomly interviewed purchased one or more items from the available displayed items.[‡] Point-of-purchase displays have been found to be very effective for introducing new products. End-of-aisle display positions are also favorable. The nature of aisle displays definitely contributes to the image of the store.

Studies vary, but the following general conclusions can be made about displays:

- Displays will generally result in increased sales of between 100–500 percent.

- The most effective displays combine several complementary products such as crackers and cheese, lemons and tea.

---

[*] Ronald E. Frank and William Marsy, *Shelf Position and Space, Effects on Sales,* Journal of Marketing Research, February 1970, pp. 59-66.

[‡] *Awareness, Decision, Purchase* (New York: Point-of-Purchase Advertising Institute, 1961). p. 14.

- Newspaper-advertised displays are the most effective, with "cents-off" announcements and product identification next in importance.

- Special-item displays are effective for only about a week, but displays of seasonally related items are effective longer.

- Check-out stand displays and end-aisle locations are most effective, with outer-perimeter areas next, and inner-aisle locations last.

 The point to be made about the importance of shelving and displays is that it is very difficult to come up with an image that will satisfy a diverse group of consumers. Such an attempt may result in having no distinctive image at all. Beware of contradictory images, also, as they may confuse and frustrate the customers.

Selecting channels of distribution

Economic considerations are relevant when choosing a channel of distribution, but behavioral patterns must first be considered when exploring potential channels. The channel with the lowest cost may not be the best choice. It may not achieve the objective of channeling the product, or it may not appeal to the appropriate target customer. Also, it may not meet the behavioral requirements of the customer.

When selecting a channel of distribution, consider the image of the outlet.

Your behavioral screening process should focus on the selection of intermediaries that will project the proper image, satisfy the customer's needs, and form a harmonious, cohesive channel system (See Figure 7-2 on the next page). The loyalty of your intermediaries will also be an important factor. Retail outlets, like products, project different images and attract different types of consumers.

Door-to-door sales

Personal door-to-door selling, while not a retail institution, does sell a lot of products. Companies such as Avon and Tupperware have done a great deal to upgrade the image of the door-to-door salesperson, and many low-priced products are also sold in poor neighborhoods by means of personal selling.

Mark-ups are typically high, and credit is easy. Local and state laws have been enacted to protect the consumer from improper door-to-door sales practices.

Factory-owned and factory-controlled stores

Many manufacturers desire, or require, a great deal of control over the sale of their products. They may, therefore, develop and run their own retail outlets, often referred to as factory-owned or specialty stores. Singer Sewing Centers are an example. The use of franchising by manufacturers is also an attempt at controlling the sale of the product. In this approach the dealer agrees to certain conditions in return for permission to sell the manufacturer's product. Such outlets usually have a high-quality image. The customer who patronizes such a store expects sales information and service.

Figure 7-2. Using a behavioral approach to select a channel of distribution.

Manufacturers	Wholesalers	Retailers	Consumer Satisfaction with Intermediaries
1) Select a retailer with appropriate image	Find wholesalers who service retailers with appropriate image	Retailer's ability to reflect appropriate image Door-to-door Factory-owned specialty store Department store Drugstore Discount house Shopping mall Supermarket	Favorable consumer image of retailer
2) Select intermediaries that are sensitive to consumer's needs	Find wholesalers who satisfy retailers	Find retailers who are able to cater to consumer's needs	Satisfaction of consumer's requirements
3) Manufacturer develops harmonious channel system	Role expectancy of wholesaler achieved	Role expectancy of retailer achieved	Customer satisfaction
4) Gain intermediary loyalty	Gain wholesaler loyalty	Gain retailer loyalty	Gain consumer loyalty

The specialty store

Specialty store customers are usually brand-conscious. They may be heavy risk-reducers; they do not want to risk making a poor decision, so they only patronize the well-known, quality dealer, literally letting the retailer select the product for them. This is particularly true for furniture and many other shopping goods. Sales personnel in specialty stores are usually available and are looked to for advice and guidance in product selection. The salesman should provide assurance to the customer that he is making the correct decision.

Service is also provided to further assure the customer that the right decision is being made. Furniture stores may provide free interior decoration service. Specialty store customers expect to be pampered and do not mind paying higher prices for personalized service; they want to be recognized as individuals. Salesmen should remember their steady customers' names, as customers will expect credit without question. These customers are usually status-conscious; stores should be conveniently located near the type of consumer to whom they are trying to appeal.

Consumers who shop at these stores tend to be of an upper-middle social and economic group. They like to try new products and are known as early adopters. A few early majority shoppers also patronize these stores. They have high incomes, are socially conscious, and typically come from middle-management positions. Such a customer may be the owner of a medium-size business. They tend to be in their late thirties or early forties.

The department store

The department store used to appeal mainly to the lower-middle income groups. The old Sears, Roebuck and Company and Montgomery Ward and Company had a strong price appeal and reached grass roots (the farmers and their wives) through their catalogues. Discount houses, with their even stronger price appeal, have encouraged department stores to trade up; strong attempts are now being made to establish a higher-quality image. Many products are sold under store names. Ward's, for example, has its Power Kraft tools, and Sears its Kenmore appliances. These products take advantage of the department store's image. Factory-owned or -controlled specialty store retailers

appeal to the same type of customer. The image is not prestigious, nor is the customer preference as great for the store. Prices are not quite so high, and there is less emphasis on personal selling.

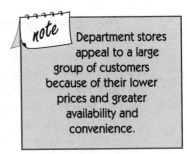

note Department stores appeal to a large group of customers because of their lower prices and greater availability and convenience.

Customers are risk-reducers, but not too status-conscious, and their incomes tend to be lower than those who frequent the specialty stores. Department store chains attract a large proportion of younger customers. Private local department stores may attract higher-income, higher-social class, older (40 to 50) consumers.

The drugstore

Drugstores have expanded their product line to the extent that they have become small department stores. In recent years they have shifted from a high-price image to a lower-price one for many of their product lines in order to maintain store traffic for the high-priced, high-margin, ethical drugs. This practice was forced upon them when discount houses began operating pharmacies. Loss-leader practices are particularly obvious in discount operations such as Thrifty-Drug and Sav-On Drugstores.

The discount house

The discount house has always had a strong price appeal and a relatively low-quality image, although strong attempts have been made by management to improve this image through store guarantees and warranties. Service is typically sparse, check-out lines are long, and variety is lacking. Affluent, upper-class individuals may go there, but only to purchase nationally branded items, such as appliances and television sets. Consumers who are "on the way up" may purchase essentials such as nonprescription drugs, garden hoses, and hairdryers. Consumers with children are likely to use discount stores.

Blue collar workers visit the discount store often. They are not concerned about nationally branded items because they are not particularly status-conscious. Contrary to popular opinion, discount houses are not often frequented by low-income, lower-class consumers; these individuals usually lack transportation to travel to the outlying discount house.

Studies have indicated that distance is an important criterion for shopping.* Very few consumers will travel more than 15 minutes to a shopping area. Discount houses have been able to maintain their low-price image, while at the same time gaining acceptance by most consumers as a good place to shop. They still have a relatively impersonal image, and the low-quality stigma has discouraged them from developing store brands to any great extent.

> **HOT spot** Customers who patronize the discount store do so because of the price appeal only.

The shopping mall

With its temperature-controlled environment, the mall has become a popular and innovative retailing institution. A large number of specialty stores congregate near a central core store, such as a Sears, to create customer traffic. Such an atmosphere encourages impulse shopping. Malls have a fairly high status image, but allow the shopper of average means an opportunity to explore the specialty shops without the social overtones normally associated with specialty stores.

The supermarket

There has been a radical change from the "ma and pa" type of store found on nearly every street corner before the Great Depression. The average supermarket of today carries more than 50,000 items, Many of these are non-food products that have been added because of the ease of carrying

> **note** The 7-Eleven small convenience stores are a good example of how small retailers can thrive alongside giants by providing unique services, such as remaining open 24 hours.

them and the 50 to 100 percent markup that is common for such items. Rack jobbers usually supply the goods, providing and servicing the racks.

* James A. Brunner and John L. Mason, "The Influence of Driving Time Upon Shopping Center Preference," *Journal of Marketing*, October 1970, pp. 12-17.

Sensitivity to consumer's needs

Different consumers require different kinds of treatment by the retailer. In every case, the business person should determine the target customers' unique requirements and make sure the intermediary will cater properly to them. These requirements include basic physiological, social, and esteem-fulfilling needs.

Physiological needs include the basic essentials of getting the product from the manufacturer to the target consumer who expects a minimum degree of accessibility to and availability of the retail establishment. The consumer's desire for the product and its degree of availability must be equated. The greater the desire or preference for the product, the lesser the requirements for availability.

For some consumers, shopping is a social outlet; they look forward to it. For many housewives, shopping is a major social event; they may fix their hair and wear a sporty outfit just to go to the supermarket. Customers will select those retail outlets that cater to customers like themselves. The location, sales personnel, and general image all combine to appeal to people in a particular social class.

The importance of an individual's self-concept cannot be mentioned too often. To the retailer it may mean requiring the sales personnel to remember the customers' names, or provide personalized credit cards and home delivery. In the discount store, it may mean assuring the consumer that he has truly purchased a "good deal." This may be accomplished by offering money-back guarantees, if the customer is not satisfied.

A harmonious and cohesive channel system

Once a channel system has been selected, the manufacturer hopes not only that it will be effective, but that a favorable, cohesive relationship will develop among all the intermediaries. There are various ways of gaining cooperation, such as dealer and trade discounts.

Power problems

At times there is need for power to be exerted in order to change some aspect of the developed channel system. If channel systems are resistant to change, each member will be interdependent, and will attempt to maintain a status quo relationship. If a change is required—getting rid of a channel member or adopting a new or competing product line—power may be needed to implement the change. Power may also be required in the case of disagreement among channel members.

The basis of power is reward, coercion, expertise, legitimacy, and identification. Reward and coercion seem to be used most often. Coercive power is blunt and will probably be resisted; it should be considered as a last resort. If expert and legitimate power is established in the early stages of development of the channel system, coercion may not be necessary. These forms of power must be accepted as legitimate roles of the participants and must be the result of proven experience.

The power of the manufacturer has long been resisted by wholesalers and retailers. This resistance can be explained by a phenomenon called "The Principle of Countervailing Power." This principle, developed by John Kenneth Galbraith, states that a growing concentration of power in one sector will be met with power from another sector. Retail power has developed in the form of centrally owned chains, cooperative chains, consumer cooperatives, department stores, and discount houses.

Pushing and pulling

Two strategies exist for getting a product through a channel system: They are called *pushing* and *pulling*.

A manufacturer may push his product through a channel system when he is fundamentally stronger than the retailer who handles his product. For example, a large manufacturer of soups could force a supermarket to handle one of its products. If the manager refused, he might risk losing the rest of the line or some form of promotion benefit. While "tying" contracts are usually illegal, subtle forms of pushing go on all the time.

Pulling occurs when a manufacturer, usually through consumer advertising, develops a demand for his product at the consumer level. The consumer will request the product from his retailer. "If your grocer does not have it, ask him to order it for you," is the plea of a number of manufacturers. It does not take many of these queries before the retailer will seek a source.

Pushing and pulling are not necessarily optimal strategies, nor are they the only ones that exist. Pushing may create ill will with retailers and wholesalers; loyalty is diminished and will shift as soon as another manufacturer offers a favorable alternative. With the advent of cooperative retail buying groups and large discounters, pushing has become more difficult.

Pulling is achieved when the manufacturer stimulates consumer demand. It is usually attempted by a weak manufacturer who has found it impossible to obtain a channel who will handle his product. Stimulating demand at the consumer level is very expensive, requiring several hundreds of thousands of dollars worth of advertising. Working from an initial position of weakness may hurt future dealings with the intermediaries in the channel.

The influence of roles

DEFINITION

A *role* is a pattern of behavior which is expected of a particular position. When a channel is first formed, stereotyped roles may exist. After a period of time, each of the members of the channel system has the opportunity to experiment with this role. If they are successful, the other channel members will probably follow those members and assume the new role. If a member is not successful he will forfeit that particular aspect of the role, or he may find himself excluded altogether. Other members will then attempt either to assume his function or to turn to an outside source. This outside source may eventually become a member of the channel. The success of a channel depends upon how well each intermediary performs his role. Each should specialize and perform his function better than any other member. Every function must be performed by someone. These functions include ordering, transportation, order-taking, selling, and promotion. They also include determining customer requirements, financing, breaking bulk, grading and sorting, and storage.

For a channel system to operate successfully, all members must feel that they are performing their role well, and that that role is the one they want to perform. Conflict arises when one member feels that another is not performing his role, or that another member is impinging upon some aspect of his own role. A channel system emerges through a process of interaction and experimentation. This channel can be efficient and harmonious; the members work together as a team and help one another out when necessary. Roles develop and are necessary because of the complexity of the channel system. Each member must know what to expect from the others. Lack of information within any system tends to create fear and discontent. Roles tend to lessen the need for a great deal of communication.

> *note*
>
> Customers patronize stores where they feel comfortable, seeking out the ones that most closely satisfy their preconceptions of what a store should be.

The channel system is a complex network of agent middlemen, wholesalers, and retailers. A manufacturer's channel of distribution evolves because of economic and behavioral pressures. Shopping is potentially a dissonant activity. Because of social and psychological factors, however, it is a pleasant activity for most consumers.

Developing a low-cost promotion strategy

Chapter 8

Developing a low-cost promotion strategy

What you'll find in this chapter:

⟹ Coordinating behavior and communication

⟹ Choosing the appropriate media

⟹ Understanding consumer's needs

⟹ Selecting a message

⟹ Considering the psychology of color

For most small businesses, promotion advertising causes frustration. Most entrepreneurs feel those activities are too expensive and find that the technical aspects of putting an ad together are beyond their abilities. Also, there is free help from the media itself in putting together effective promotional packages. The following discussion should help the reader to select and evaluate types of media and promotion techniques.

> *note* Actually, promotion can be used extremely effectively by the small business person, and at lower costs than might first be expected.

In the United States, monopolistic competition and oligopoly are the most common market structures. Product differentiation, either of a physical or psychological nature, is essential if the firm is to be an effective competitor. Successful differentiation of the physical aspects of the product is very difficult. Competitive protection—using patents or special production

processes—is typically short-lived in this rapidly changing technological environment.

Psychological differentiation, on the other hand, is much less easy for competitors to combat. Attempts to copy successful psychological differentiation may result in reinforcing the consumer's perception that the originator's product really validates the consumer's own image. Consider the luxury image of Cadillac. If a competitor like Mazda tried to develop a similar image, it would only reinforce the Cadillac owner's feeling that the Cadillac image is a favorable one. Such duplication probably would sell more Cadillacs.

Advertising is an extremely effective tool for developing differentiation among products. Its use encourages a variety of products to appear on the market and old products to be improved. It makes consumers aware of new innovations and new images. Old products are then forced to innovate if they are to retain their customers and gain new ones.

Advertising is the most effective means of communicating product appeal to consumers. Without advertising it would be impossible to sell the large volume of products produced by American industry today. The American Association of Advertising Agencies has determined that the average person can notice only 75 advertisements a day. Since he is exposed to 1,500 messages a day, this 5 percent success rate is quite discouraging. This, coupled with the fact that the quantity and cost of advertisements are going to increase rapidly in the next ten years, will probably result in a critical communications squeeze, making it more necessary than ever for the marketer to use his advertising dollars in the most successful ways possible. It is essential that the marketer understand the communications process and the best ways of reaching the consumer.

Definition:

Communication is the transmission of information, ideas, and emotions by the use of symbols—words, pictures, and figures. Advertising should be understood to be synonymous with communication.

In support of the traditional view of the communications process, nearly every communications textbook presents the same general model. According to this view, the stages of the process are as follows:

- the idea to be transmitted

- the idea translated into a language

- the physical transmission of the idea

- the movement of a signal over a particular medium (radio, television, or newspaper)

- the decoding process (comprehension of the idea)

- the successful transmission of the message

Traditional communications theory assumes that a common field of experience must exist for both the sender and the receiver. The message must employ signs or symbols that reflect that common experience, both at the source and at the destination, in order to transmit meaning. If the sender is speaking in Japanese and the recipient only understands English, no common field of experience exists and communication fails. Many college graduates have difficulty communicating with people who have not gone to college. This lack of a common field of experience is one reason that much advertising is written for, and tested on, sixth graders. Many people's educations do not develop significantly beyond this level. Also, the consumer's particular activity during exposure to the message may result in an uncommon field of experience. If an audience has just viewed a romantic episode on television, its frame of reference is not sensitized for viewing and comprehending a hemorrhoids commercial.

A behavioral view of the communications process

One may wonder, after considering the traditional communications process, why communication about a product is so difficult. The answer lies in the fact that both the communicator (advertiser) and the recipient of the message (consumer) behave and react in a certain psychological manner.

 Consider the psychological makeup of the consumer. He is deluged by promotional messages from every conceivable direction. If he were to comprehend and analyze each message he is exposed to, he would be

frustrated and would have no time for work or relaxation. Therefore, the individual develops psychological processes which aid him in screening out those communications stimuli that (according to his perceptions) will not enhance his well-being. In studying techniques of mass persuasion, some principles have evolved.* These principles are valuable to the marketer who wishes to understand some of the psychological characteristics that influence the consumer's acceptance of the advertising message.

- *The message must reach the sense organs of the desired audience.*

Simply going through the acts of advertising does not assure that the potential customer is listening or that the message is being perceived. The message must reach the customer when his attention is focused on the medium. This is one reason why the audio portions in commercials are usually louder than the regular programming. This is also why advertisements in color have greater impact on television and superior readerships in magazines and newspapers. Because of the realism of color, such advertisements gain the attention of more consumers.

- *The consumer must be interested in the general category of the information before it will be perceived.*

The consumer must be interested in purchasing an automobile before an automobile advertisement can be effective, or must be reinforced in his desire to purchase an automobile.

- *Consumers are interested in only the general categories that reinforce their attitudes.*

A consumer will generally expose himself only to those ideas that reinforce his beliefs. A Presbyterian does not care to hear about the religions of others and Democrats will only go to Democratic rallies. Ford owners usually notice only Ford advertisements.

- *A message, in order to be accepted, must be seen as appropriate to one's attitudes.*

---

* Dorwin Cartwright, "Some Principles of Mass Persuasion," in W. Edgar Vinacke, Warner R. Wilson, and Gerald M. Meredith, eds., *Dimensions in Social Psychology* (Chicago: Scott, Foresman, 1964), pp. 298-304.

A person without children will not be interested in an advertisement for children's books. A message which states that the individual is doing something foolish (the warning on cigarette packages) will not be accepted by smokers.

- *When a message is inconsistent with a person's prevailing attitudes, it will either be rejected or distorted so as to fit or produce changes in the cognitive structure.*

If a consumer is exposed to an advertisement with which he does not agree, he will dismiss it as invalid, or he will interpret it the way he wants to. Take the following example. John just purchased a Ford automobile. He is visiting Fred and they are watching a football game. An advertisement for a foreign-made import is shown. The foreign compact runs more quietly than a Ford, has more standard options, and costs less. Fred owns a foreign automobile and agrees with the advertisement, but the message is incongruent to John, the Ford owner. He may simply ignore the advertisement (selective forgetting) and the comments of his friend, or he may tell himself that foreign products are cheaply made, that he does not care about the foreign car options, or that his friend never did show good judgment.

> **HOT spot** So it goes with incongruent messages: They will be rationalized, distorted, and repressed so that congruity within the cognitive structure will be established.

- *Needs activate the creation of goals, which in turn aid in the development of attitudes.*

A given action will be accepted as a path to a goal only if the connection "fits" the person's entire cognitive structure.

Take, for example, an advertisement for a compact car that stresses the car's ability to save gasoline. If the consumer who hears this feels he is "on the way up" socially but has not yet arrived there, he may consider a compact automobile detrimental to this goal of achieving a high position. A large and gas-guzzling automobile may fit this individual's goals and cognitive structure better than a compact car.

• The more goals perceived to be attainable by a single path, the more attractive that alternative will be.

Consumers will take the path of least resistance in achieving goals. The more favorable physical and psychological attributes that can be attached to a product, the greater the probability that the product will be accepted. Thus, the more ways of projecting a specific image, the better. You would not attach a low price to a high-status product, nor would you sell a high-status product through a sleazy outlet.

 it is important to consider the price, package, advertisement, and channel of distribution—to assure that each factor reinforces the image.

• The easiest, cheapest, or most desirable action will be taken to achieve a goal.

When the consumer is confronted with relatively similar products, the most readily attainable, the least expensive, or the most desirable action perceived will be taken. If, for example, the consumer sees that two makes of automobiles are equally attractive, the ease of purchase, the price, or perhaps the value of available service may be the deciding factor. If quality is the important factor, the higher-priced product will be selected.

The communications mix

Experts have analyzed the communications process and their studies suggest that four variables influence this process significantly. These predispositional factors are bound by content, topic, appeal, argument, and style.

For effective communication to exist in the marketing effort, the ingredients * of the "communications mix" must be carefully developed. These communications ingredients are as follows:

- **Communicator-source effect.** This refers to the belief that the effectiveness of a communicator depends on the recipient's

* Jon Eisenson, Jeffery J. Auer, and John V. Irwin, *The Psychology of Communication* (New York: Appleton-Century-Crofts. 1963), p. 168.

evaluation of that communicator. This includes the affiliation of the communicator and the fact that he is perceived differently by different members of the audience who have preconceived opinions about the nature and characteristics of the communicator. Certain sources are more believable and trustworthy than others. Such campaigns as "Progress is our most important product," and "You can be sure if it's Westinghouse" are attempts at making the source more credible. Many nonprescription drug advertisements use individuals who appear to be doctors to sell their products. Robert Young was extremely effective for selling decaffeinated coffee because of his high credibility.

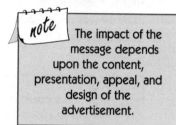

note The impact of the message depends upon the content, presentation, appeal, and design of the advertisement.

- **The media effect.** Some consumers will be more responsive to communications through magazines and newspapers, while others will be more readily influenced by radio and television programs and movies. In other words, some people are more receptive to visual media than they are to audible media. The channels of communication are themselves important to the successful transmitting of the message. The consumer can select the messages he receives by selecting the media to which he allows himself to be subjected.

- **The content-message effect.** In general, clear and simple messages communicate most effectively, but an understanding of the psychological realm increases the chances of successful communication. Let's consider these variables in greater detail.

The source effect

There are several sources of promotional communications. One source, as perceived by the consumer, is the manufacturer, who is usually represented by the brand name. Manufacturing organizations have specific goals that are reflected by the image they project. General Foods, Pillsbury, and General

Electric are examples of firms with strong brand images. The advertising department or agency is usually responsible for developing the actual image. The advertisement is the message to which the consumer is exposed. While each of the sources mentioned contributes to the message, the consumer is usually confronted only with the actual advertising message and the brand name presented. He may confuse the channel (medium) used with the source, since the channel certainly influences his acceptance of the source. Successful communication is highly dependent upon the consumer's perception of the source. Credibility of the source depends upon its trustworthiness and expertise—as perceived by the consumer. Two social scientists, Herbert C. Kelman and Carl I. Havland, have come to the following conclusions:*

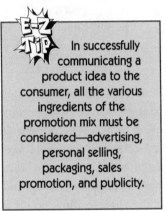

In successfully communicating a product idea to the consumer, all the various ingredients of the promotion mix must be considered—advertising, personal selling, packaging, sales promotion, and publicity.

- A highly credible source is more effective than a source with low credibility.

- Attitude change is greater for the highly credible source in the short run, but its advantage disappears over a period of time (three weeks in the research).

- Recall is significantly higher for the medium credible source than for either of the high or low credible sources.

- A highly competent, highly trustworthy counter-advertisement is more successful if presented after a period of time (two weeks) than if presented immediately.

The media effect

There are a number of ways of communicating a product idea to the consumer. Research by Thomas S. Robertson has indicated that the various media are not equally effective at all stages of the purchase-decision process.**

* Herbert C. Kelman and Carl I. Havland, "Reinstatement of the Communicator in Delayed Measurement of Opinion Change," *Journal of Abnormal and Social Psychology* Vol. 48, 1953, pp. 327-335.
**Thomas S. Robertson, *Innovative Behavior and Communication* (New York: Holt, Rinehart and Winston, 1971), pp. 154-161.

Media channels often perform varying functions for the individual and provide different kinds of information. Use of several media channels tends to reinforce the idea and increase the likelihood of purchase. Different media channels produce different behavioral changes.

Advertising is an impersonal medium and does not allow any feedback. With this relatively one-sided form of communication, the consumer has no way of asking for any clarification and may in turn distort or misunderstand the message. The advantage of advertising is the low cost of reaching the mass market through many channels. It is easily accessible to most consumers and it can usually influence general attitudes.

The advertising mix is composed of:

> **HOT spot** The printed medium has a longer-lasting effect than the broadcast medium. Printed matter can be reviewed, passed along, and even saved. Research shows that the printed medium is more believable because it symbolizes the desire of man to communicate, learn, and discuss.*

- printed media (direct mail, leaflets, handbills, and publication advertising, including newspapers and magazines)

- broadcast media (radio and television)

- position media (billboards, non-standardized signs, and transportation advertising)

- point-of-purchase displays

- other media (advertising on films and directory advertising)

Magazines appeal to rational thinking. Different magazines appeal to different consumers; each has its own personality and appeals to specific personality types. Magazines are personal and it is often difficult for the consumer to throw them away. They are usually read in the privacy of the home; at his leisure the reader can compare alternatives and select the products that suit his self-conception.

* Harper W. Boyd, Jr., and Sidney J. Levy, *Promotion; A Behavioral View* (Englewood Cliffs, NJ: Prentice-Hall, 1967), p. 88.

Newspapers deal more with daily activities in local environments. One study characterizes newspapers this way:

> The newspaper is an integral part of the everyday life of a community. A citizenry identifies with the community via its newspaper. Further, there is a faith in the newspaper; this faith is a confidence in the integrity and believability of the content, and that which appears in its pages can pretty well be accepted as true.*

Newspapers are points in the decision-making process and are used as a source of immediate product information. Because of the serious nature of the news content and the fact that the consumer uses advertisements to compare products, a more rational, descriptive advertising approach is generally used. Prices and special features are usually mentioned.

HINT: Because of the credibility factor, newspapers are effective for introducing new products. They are an excellent medium for small businesses.

The basic weakness of this medium is its short life. Because of the relatively poor reproduction capabilities, development of advertisements of high emotional impact and appeal are almost impossible.

Broadcast media (radio and television) have one common problem—how to present the advertisement so that it will be recalled. Most advertisements run for 15 to 30 seconds on radio and 30 to 60 seconds on television. This is a very short period of time to get a message across. The consumer has no way of saving the message for later reference, as he can with magazines and newspapers.

E-Z TIP: Radio programming varies broadly, and FM has been particularly effective at pinpointing certain target markets for small companies at low cost.

The transistor has made the radio medium more personal. Radio requires the listener to develop his own image.

---

* Social Research, Inc., *A Study of the Functions of Newspapers for Their Readers* (American Newspaper Publishers Association, 1954), pp. 15-16.

> **note**
>
> Television advertising is rather expensive and not commensurately effective for a small firm, although many entrepreneurs have used it with good results.

These images can be long lasting. It is the marketer's task to make sure the images are favorable, and that they lead to a sale. Also, it is easy to reach a particular target customer. Popular music stations are effective for reaching young people, while talk show stations reach the bored housewife and freeway commuter. FM stereo probably reaches upper-middle-class and affluent listeners.

Television reaches large audiences with great realism. A network program may capture the attention of millions of consumers. Television appeals to both visual and auditory senses. Because of its realism, television can present products as they truly are and can show them in actual use.

Three types of television viewers have been identified by social scientists Harper Boyd and Sidney Levy: * embracers, protesters, and accommodators. *Embracers* watch television often and accept it as an everyday part of life. Embracers are usually among the working class and find television an escape from their routine jobs and lives. Television is also an outlet for aggressive feeling. It enables the working class to vicariously enjoy upper-middle-class activities.

Children watch a lot of television for the same reasons. It is an escape from responsibility and makes children aware of the grownups' world. Senior citizens, too, watch a lot of television for escape purposes as well as for entertainment.

> **E-Z TIP**
>
> With self-service retailing so predominant today, it is important to have a package that attracts attention, expresses the characteristics of the product, and sells the product.

Protesters feel that television is a waste of time. They are typically of the upper-middle class. They feel that television interferes with productivity and social and cultural growth, and they consider most programming and all commercials demeaning to their

---

* Harper W. Boyd, Jr. , and Sydney J. Levy, *Promotion: A Behavioral View* (Englewood Cliffs, NJ: Prentice-Hall, 1967), pp. 92–93.

intelligence. Parents of this class resent the interference of television in their children's lives.

Accommodators do not spend a lot of time watching television. They are selective and consider television as one source of information among many. They watch the better shows and enjoy good commercials.

Personal selling is of a face-to-face nature (two-way communication). The customer can ask questions and there is less chance of distortion. The sales message can be geared to the individual, the product, and the situation, and the salesman is available when the product is displayed and at the very important moment of buying. Personal selling is an expensive way to reach the consumer, but it is often used by entrepreneurs. A major problem is the bad reputation personal selling has gained from unethical sales practices; skepticism on the consumer's part can reduce the effectiveness of personal selling. Packaging is an important communicative device. It acts as a silent salesman.

> **HOT spot** The marketer must understand what it is that truly motivates the buyer.

Sales promotion is usually considered a supplement to advertising and personal selling. Contests, giveaways, displays, even skywriting are used to reinforce other media. Like advertising, sales promotion is impersonal, but it is likely to result in an immediate purchase. An increasingly large number of convenience goods and shopping goods are purchased on impulse—usually as a result of displays. It is estimated that 85 percent of grocery products are purchased on impulse, although that practice has been sharply curtailed by rapidly rising prices in times of inflation.

DEFINITION

Publicity is any form of non-paid communication. News items and editorials are examples. Usually, publicity takes the form of product information expressed as news. News is more readily accepted as being true than is regular advertising, but publicity can become a problem because the businessperson does not always have a great deal of control over what is said. Small local papers are often starved for interesting publicity, and it comes to them free.

The message effect

The message is the persuasive communication designed to sell the product. Satisfaction is presented through symbolic characters and images are developed to match the consumer's own self-image. Bardin H. Nelson says that "the product image which attracts a consumer is the image which expresses what the consumer thinks he is, or wants to be." * The following variables should be considered in the formation of effective imagery:

- People are not exclusively rational creatures. Their behavior may be determined by inconsistent feelings and unconscious drives.

- People respond to situations in ways that protect their self-image.

- Various images and reference points (or anchorages) already exist in the minds of a particular group or society upon which other images may be built.

- If an image appears stable, and if reference groups surrounding the individual continue to support the image, it will remain highly resistant to change.

- If an image is marked by doubt, uncertainty, or insecurity, it is on unstable ground. Present a new image in a form that will dispel anxiety and doubt.

> **E-Z TIP** A symbol is appropriate—and the product enjoyed—only when it meshes with, adds to, and reinforces the consumer's image of himself. The consumer's choice between products becomes easier when one object is symbolically more harmonious with his goals, feelings, and self-definitions than another.

- Place the desired image in the most favorable setting. If at all possible, clothe the image in already accepted values.

- Finally, to stimulate development of a new image, attract the attention of large numbers of potential consumers.

* Bardin H. Nelson, "Seven Principles in Image Formation," *Journal of Marketing*, January 1962, p. 67

The thoughtful businessperson must also be aware of the growing use and influence of symbols. People are faced with advertising alternatives motivating them in conflicting directions. As behavior in the marketplace becomes increasingly elaborate, it also becomes increasingly symbolic.

Dr. Steuart Britt * suggests that to be effective, a symbol should promise a unique and distinctive quality, competitive prices in the range of the product it represents, and continuous market study to keep the product abreast of prevailing tastes and fashions.

Illustrations form emotional bonds that pull a person into the advertisement. An illustration should symbolize something of importance to the reader: status, beauty, success, variety.

People tend to think in symbols. They convert everything they come in contact with into symbols, and they communicate with symbols. The products they buy are symbols of the form of satisfaction they crave.

 Make an effort to notice the use of lines in advertising. Lines help symbolize various images. Heavy, dark lines and sharp angles are usually symbolic of strength and masculinity, while smooth, softly shaded, thin lines represent the feminine qualities. Straight lines convey formality while jagged ones express informality. A vertical line symbolizes growth, striving, spiritual uplifting, balance, honesty, and dignity. The horizontal line represents calm, rest, stability. The diagonal line symbolizes motion, excitement, progress, and change.

Angles are useful for directing attention. Convergent lines direct the eye inward or outward, providing depth and dimension. The square implies unity and harmony, while the triangle, because it appears to be in motion, symbolizes liveliness. A circle is continuous and flowing and is perceived to be soft and feminine. The oval, pleasant to the eye, is also gentle and feminine.

 Take particular notice of color in advertising, too. We live in a colorful world where bland colors get lost easily. Irritating colors or inharmonious combinations of colors may discourage a consumer from purchasing a product. When Color Research Institute wanted to determine if different colors had a significant impact over product purchases, they gave identical but differently packaged detergents to women to try in their homes. When the

* *The Spenders* pp. 139–146.

soap was rated, the detergent in the yellow box was too strong, the detergent in the blue box allegedly left clothes dirty, while the detergent in the blue and yellow box was overwhelmingly considered outstanding.*

Colors appeal to the emotions and can substantially add to the perceived value of a product. They can produce chilling or warming effects. They can express danger, love, or death. Colors may also influence the quality image of the product. For example, in the low-priced line for toothbrushes, red ones constitute 50 percent of all sales. In the high-priced line, amber toothbrushes are more popular. This preference may be due to the education level of the consumer. Educated persons prefer more subdued colors. Certain colors are nearly universal in their appeal: Ivory, blue, pale green, pink, and yellow sell well all over the country. Other colors are subject to local taste.

These differences may be due to general climactic conditions. Consumers in cloudier regions seem to prefer warm and luminous colors, while those in sunnier climes prefer blue and gray.

 Colors, properly used, have strong identities and are more easily remembered than words. Specific colors have acquired definite meaning and connotations. The following are some colors and the symbolisms and associations we attach to them:

- Green is symbolic of safety, fidelity, nature, ignorance, and youth.

- Violet denotes dignity, royalty, sorrow, despair, and wealth.

- Red is symbolic of danger. It possesses maximum attention value and is associated with warmth, passion, virility, life, excitement, power, and bravery. Men prefer this color.

- Blue is symbolic of achievement. It is associated with coolness, calmness, freshness, cleanliness, melancholy, truth, purity, depth, and restraint, and is preferred by most women.

- Yellow makes an object look large. It is exciting, cheerful, bright, youthful, and optimistic. It has high attention value.

- Orange has high attention value and indicates tastiness, abundance, harvest, and mid-life.

* Vance Packard, *The Hidden Persuaders* (New York: McKay, 1957), p. 11.

- Black denotes mourning, mystery, strength.

- White symbolizes cleanliness, fear, purity.

- Gray denotes depression, old age, dignity.

- Pink appeals to women; it is associated with sweetness, tenderness, and poetry.

Colors in advertising have the advantage of making things seem more realistic than is possible in black and white.

Guidelines for effective advertising

A superb guide to effective communication is the AIDA principle developed by Wilber Schrammed.* AIDA is an acronym for attention, interest, desire, and action:

- *Attention.* An advertisement must be designed and delivered to gain the attention of the receiver. Gaining attention is part of a complicated psychological process involving perception which in part refers to awareness and is a sensory phenomenon. Attention is most easily gained through illustrations. Because sex is such a good attention-getter, it is often used in advertisements.

- *Interest.* The ad must invite interest—the result of favorable attention—or the major ideas may be missed. Interest involves comprehension of the significance of the idea. Effective copy and typography can generate interest and draw the consumer's attention to the detailed message of the advertisement. Block type is more effective for appealing to men, and script to women. Roman lettering appeals to the more traditional, prestige-conscious consumer.

- *Desire.* The advertising message must arouse needs and desires in the receiver and suggest some way of providing satisfaction. Develop desire by providing copy that makes the consumer wish or long for the product.

* Wilber Schrammed, *The Process and Effect of Mass Communications* (Urbana: University of Illinois Press, 1954). p. 13.

- **Action.** The advertisement must suggest ways of fulfilling the needs it arouses. Action implies motivation toward a particular goal: An advertisement must motivate the reader to purchase the product and must suggest ways of attaining it. "Consult the *Yellow Pages* for the nearest dealer" and "Call this toll-free number" are appeals for action.

Entrepreneurs should always test their advertising against the AIDA formula. Psychologists have developed rules of learning that can be applied to advertising. Psychologist Steuart Britt* adapts these rules this way:

1) *Unpleasant things may sometimes be learned as readily as pleasant things: but the most ineffective stimuli are those which arouse little or no emotional response.*

An annoying radio or television commercial works better than a dull one, but not as well as a message which promises the audience a rewarding experience.

2) *The capacities of learners are important in determining what can be learned and how long it will take.*

Bright people can grasp a complex message that is incomprehensible to those who are less bright. They grasp short messages in a shorter time, too.

3) *Things that are learned and understood tend to be better retained than things learned by rote.*

Mere repetition of ads is of no great value unless the message is understood by the people. Extensive drilling is important in getting facts across. Understanding is even more important.

4) *Practice distributed over several periods is more economical in learning than the same amount of practice concentrated into a single period.*

In planning a campaign, the prospects should usually be exposed to the advertising over a relatively long period. High pressure campaigns are wasteful.

---

* Steuart Henderson Britt, "How Advertising Can Use Psychology's Rules of Learning," *Printer's Ink*, September 22, 1955, pp. 74-77 and 80.

5) *When teaching people to master mechanical skills, it is better to show the performance in the same way that the learner would see it if he were doing the job himself.*

Write the copy from the "you" standpoint; take a camera shot over the shoulder.

6) *The order of presentation of materials to be learned is very important.*

Points presented at the beginning and end of the message are remembered better than those in the middle. If four reasons are given, the two most important reasons should be first and last.

7) *If materials to be learned are different or unique, they will be better remembered.*

A television or radio commercial employing unusual sounds tends to stand out. The man in the Hathaway shirt will be long remembered as the first model who wore an eyepatch.

8) *Showing errors in how to do something can lead to increases in learning.*

The effectiveness of a demonstration on television might be increased by showing not only "what to do" but "what not to do."

9) *Learning situations which are rewarded only occasionally can be more efficient than those where constant reward is employed.*

It is more efficient to offer deals or premiums over fairly short periods than over extended periods. "Sales" that run all the time cease to attract attention.

10) *It is easier to recognize something than it is to recall it. Make the name of your product easy to recognize.*

The detergent All for automatic washing machines is a good example of an easily recognizable name.

11) *The rate of forgetting tends to be very rapid immediately after learning.*

Continuous repetition of the message is desirable. It takes a lot of advertising in the early weeks of a campaign to overcome rapid forgetting.

12) *Messages attributed to persons held in high esteem influence change in opinion more than messages from persons not so well-known, but after several weeks both messages seem equally effective.*

It is not essential to employ high-priced, well-known talent in testimonials if you are trying to build a long-range favorable climate for your product.

13) *Repetition of identical materials is often as effective in having things remembered us repeating the same story but with variations.*

The implication is that exactly the same advertisements can be run over and over again with real sales effectiveness each time.

14) *In a learning situation, a moderate fear appeal is more effective than a strong fear appeal.*

A fear appeal that is too strong is likely to put up a barrier of defense mechanism and lead to a rejection of the whole sales message.

15) *Knowledge of results leads to increases in learning.*

Advertisers should use this principle by telling the consumer what specific benefits he will get from the product or service advertised.

16) *Learning is aided by active practice.*

If you can get your audience members to participate in your sales message, they are much more likely to remember your brand. Get consumers to repeat key phrases, fill in coupons, or sing songs.

17) *A message is more easily learned and accepted if it does not interfere with earlier habits.*

A sales theme that draws upon the prior experiences of the audience will help the learning of the sales message.

18) *The mere repetition of a situation does not necessarily lead to learning. Two things are necessary—"belongingness" and "satisfiers."*

DEFINITION

Belongingness means that the elements to be learned must seem to belong together; there must be some form of relationship or sequence (organic unity) in the total advertising message. *Satisfiers* are real or symbolic rewards.

19) *When two ideas are of equal strength but of unequal age, repetition increases the strength of the earlier idea more than that of the newer one.*

If there are two ideas of the same strength but of unequal age, the older idea will not be forgotten as rapidly as the new. Older brands will not be forgotten as easily as newer ones.

20) *Learning something new can interfere with remembering something learned earlier. (Retroactive inhibition)*

It is better to sponsor one program than to run multiple advertisements, especially if competing, similar products are being advertised.

Advertising is most effective when it demands minimal attitude change—changes that do not pose a psychological threat. Defense mechanisms are not enacted, and ideas are accepted. This limited attitude change is not true for new products where general attitudes may be nearly nonexistent. Advertising information for new product ideas can have a significant impact.

If the perceived risk in purchasing a product is high, more information (from more sources) is required. Personal selling and other forms of interpersonal communication then become important. The businessperson must always remember that successful communication must be aligned with consumer attitudes.

Understanding the consumer's needs

Human beings are goal-oriented. Goals originate from needs. In order to obtain customer patronage, advertising must appeal to consumer needs. Needs are usually the result of internal mechanisms of which the average person is not aware.

> In order to develop effective advertisements, the entrepreneur must understand and consider the needs that influence those goals, which, in turn, result in people buying a product.

Among the universally important primary needs are those for food and drink, freedom from fear and danger, physical comfort, attraction of the opposite sex, welfare of loved ones, social approval, and a long life. A. H. Maslow's famous hierarchy of needs was built up from the primary needs to the highest:

- physiological needs (hunger, thirst)
- safety needs (security, health)
- social and love needs (affection, belongingness)
- esteem needs (self-respect, prestige)
- self-actualization needs (self-fulfillment)

Maslow maintains that as a lower level of needs is satisfied, the next level becomes the important motivating force.

Physiological needs

People seek food and drink because of an internal mechanism referred to as homeostasis. The body seeks to maintain a constant balance of water, salt, sugar, protein, calcium, fat, oxygen, and other necessary elements. When the body lacks one of these, the individual will develop a specific appetite or hunger for foods containing the missing ingredient. Many foods that are bought on impulse appeal to this process.

Eating is a pleasurable experience in itself. The ritual of eating several courses is well-defined in our culture; dessert is the reward for appropriate eating behavior. Eating is associated with friendship. "Let's get together for lunch" is the common call. Drinking alcoholic beverages is more of a social appeal, which puts it on a higher level in the hierarchy.

Safety needs

The usual threats to safety are war, the environment (the elements, wild animals), and assault on one's person. Society organizes to protect its citizens from such threats. Parents tend to be very protective of their family and home. Advertising gives consumers confidence in products, brands, and stores by making them familiar and building trust: "You can be sure if it's Westinghouse." Most health products appeal to the safety need. People load their homes with appliances, recliners, and air conditioners because of this need.

note In modern society, the threats of losing one's job, health, money, or life are real concerns: "What would your family do without you?" is a typical advertising theme.

Social needs

A feeling of belonging (to groups) can be very strong. Social acceptance may direct an individual's entire behavior. This is particularly true of strong reference groups. For example, professional business clubs expect members to wear neckties. Such group membership is projected by dress, language or jargon, type and location of a home, make and model of automobile, hairstyle, and general life style.

Social needs were an extremely important motivation in the 1960s and early 1970s. These needs continue to be strong among blue collar workers. Generally, the college experience of white collar workers and professionals brings out the next level of needs, the need for esteem.

The need for esteem

Every person also wants to have a favorable self-concept and to have others perceive him favorably. Women want to appear beautiful, men want to

believe they are attractive to women, and everybody wants to be perceived as capable and successful. Success and confidence can be projected through products.

Esteem needs have been a phenomenon of the later 1970s. "Do your own thing" and "Express yourself uniquely" have been the themes. Some feel that there was a return to social needs in the 1980s.

TV is a poor medium for projecting an esteem message because it appeals to predominantly blue collar workers.

Magazines, FM radio stations, and specialty publications such as *The Wall Street Journal* and *Christian Science Monitor* are more effective for appealing to people's needs for esteem. Specialty stores cater to this group most effectively.

> **E-Z TIP** The strongest advertising appeals are those which show a consumer how he or she can achieve a more favorable self-concept.

The need for self-actualization

As individuals come to be accepted by their reference groups, they then desire to formulate an individual identity. Success gives rise to a longing to fulfill one's potential, a striving to make one's self-concept real.

Saul W. Gellerman, in his book *Motivation and Productivity*,* puts it this way:

> Self-actualization is to live in a manner that is appropriate to one's preferred role, to be treated in a manner that corresponds to one's preferred rank, and to be rewarded in a manner that reflects one's estimate of his own abilities.

Advertising that shows the individual how to be free of dependence will appeal to this need. Most automobile advertisements show a person how to be independent.

The psychology of communications

The total communications process begins with the sender gathering and interpreting the thoughts to be transmitted into images which in turn are

* American Management Association, 1963, pp. 290-291.

transformed into symbols. This development phase is influenced by the sender's own self-image, his attitudes about the subject and the receiver, his past experience, and his perceived objective of the message.

> **E-Z TIP** It is the task of the advertiser to seek out his potential customer's reading, listening, and viewing habits and to cater to them rather than interfering with them.

As the information is transmitted, the receiver (consumer) decodes the signal from his own viewpoint, interpreting the information through his own psychological filtration process. A conscious and subconscious screening process takes place that is based upon the receiver's image of the sender and the message, his expectations based on previous experience, and his own self-image. Sometimes this process does not go smoothly. There are many reasons for breakdowns in communications. Problems can occur in each phase, whether it be newspapers, books, radio, television, board meetings, or simply person-to-person conversation. The wise businessperson will try to understand these deterrents to successful communication and learn how to avoid them.

The lack of face-to-face contact is a considerable drawback in every facet of advertising, with the exception of personal sales. The advertiser is unable to know whether or not his message is being accepted at the time it is printed or broadcast. The respondent is, of course, by the very nature of media, prevented from seeking further information from the advertisement. This factor may often cause misunderstanding of the message, or may distort it entirely. Generally speaking, people tend to be governed by habit. They usually are accustomed to reading the same newspapers and magazines and viewing the same television programs.

Sometimes money problems can plague a marketer. If he had an unlimited supply of funds, he would have little trouble reaching his audience, but funds are usually limited and must be utilized in an optimum way. This can be accomplished by making sure the advertisement reaches the target customer, successfully communicates with him, and causes him to buy the product.

Many advertisers feel that consumers attentively read and listen to their advertisements, but that is usually not the case. People concentrate and learn under specific conditions, and then are motivated only in reference to a particularly interesting stimulus. Since motivation—a learning device—is necessary for action, the advertiser must find a way to present facts so they will be viewed in a favorable light.

People's modes of thinking—their attitudes and beliefs—develop from experience. When the consumer's experiences are different from the advertiser's, two separate frames of reference exist. Normally, the consumer's mental world is composed of the circumstances of his everyday life—his neighborhood, occupation, and social circle—and he is, therefore, not necessarily equipped to understand a language which represents a different way of life. Thus, the advertiser must adapt his language to the particular consumer he is trying to reach.

It is often difficult to find words that adequately express the aspects and ideologies of one's perceived experience. Words have different connotations for different people. For this reason, it is difficult to create images through words. For example, how does one make a basically impersonal product seem personal? How does one convey an impression of trustworthiness and friendliness to a General Foods cake mix? These semantic problems are important to the sales message and must be carefully considered by the advertiser.

 Remember, also, that beliefs in stereotypes—ideas that a person consciously, or unconsciously, has about products, firms, advertising media— are also gained through experience. These stereotypes must be understood in order to communicate favorably with the consumer. This is particularly true in changing false impressions and creating new ones.

It should be stressed that good communications are essential to the advertiser. Marion Harper, Jr., reported in *Printer's Ink* recently that "marketing is almost entirely communications. In fact, without communications, marketing barely exists." There are obstacles to be overcome to achieve good communications, but understanding the problem is a big step toward its solution. The advertiser is becoming increasingly pressured to make his advertisements more effective.

Developing a promotional strategy

Although the communications system is the main system in promotion, it must be stated that this system consists of subsystems involving the consumer, the advertiser (the communicator), and the media. Since the consumer is integral to the communications process, emphasis will be placed on the understanding of his role.

Consumers are continually confronted with different appeals and are obliged to choose between competing products. The character of marketing itself helps to develop this process, for marketing is almost exclusively communications. It is important, at this point, to define the communications objectives that are necessary for advertising success. The following are general criteria for this goal:

- The aim of the marketer should be to serve the interests of the consumer.

- Communications goals should be made specific, and their effectiveness measurable.

> **HINT**)))
> If an advertising strategy is to be successful it must lead the consumer through the stages of awareness, interest, evaluation, trial, and, finally, adoption of the product.*

- Individual goals for sales, advertising, and public relations should support a central communications purpose.

- Advertising communications should be related to short-term, as well as long-term, profitability.

Consumer behavior is fraught with motivational dimensions. Before a successful advertising strategy can be developed, the marketer must select—and understand—his particular target customer. This can be accomplished by questioning the target customer in depth by using the sophisticated techniques that have been developed for analyzing data. Analysis of variance, for example, will indicate the dimensions that caused a particular desired result.

---

* Everett M. Roger, *Diffusion of Innovation* (New York: Free Press, 1962). pp. 281-286.

Consumers are unaware of new products and are often resistant to new ideas. Initial awareness may be of a negative nature: "Oh, that new product is probably too expensive" (or too dangerous, or it doesn't work properly). Interest in the product may develop as more information is provided and more people adopt the product.*

After several exposures to the product, the consumer will have to decide whether it is desirable, or whether he will not concern himself with it. If the decision is favorable, the consumer will decide to try the product when the proper circumstances present themselves. This opportunity may arise when he receives a free sample, redeems a coupon, or actively reaches for the product. During the trial stage, the consumer will evaluate the product. If it satisfies his expectations and contributes to his self-concept, adoption will probably take place.

Planning a promotional program

Once the target customer has been selected and his behavioral characteristics analyzed, that behavior must be carefully defined and a symbolic product image carefully developed. Elements of that product image, in the advertising context, include the physical characteristics of the product (price and quality), the context in which the product is shown, its color, and the symbolism used in the package, trademark, and brand. The image of the sender must be defined with great care. The most important elements of the product image are the media used and the nature of the symbols used to transmit the message. Finally, the appropriate promotional medium must be selected, and feedback developed to ensure that the desired objectives are being achieved.

One approach to developing an effective promotional program is to take the following steps: *

- Analyze your marketing objectives.
- Isolate the role of promotion.
- Develop promotional objectives.
- Define the target audience.
- Analyze alternative approaches.

* Adapted from Donald J. Massnick, "Massnick on Communications," *Industrial Marketing* January 1971, pp. 34-38.

- Select optimum use of elements of promotion.
- Determine general message content and desired image.
- Select appropriate media vehicles.
- Determine frequency and timing of the message.
- Implement the plan.
- Measure results and give feedback.

A strategy for advertising

The objective of advertising and promotion is to sell. An advertising strategy involves a complex process of informing and persuading the consumer to purchase a particular product. It involves understanding the psychological makeup of the customer and then developing a campaign that will pierce the many defense mechanisms and the sales resistance the consumer brings to bear. Strategies are not static, but occur over a period of time. The process of introducing a product can be described through the product life cycle concept of growth, maturity, saturation, and, finally, decline.

Otto Kleppner, a prominent advertising man and author, developed the concept of the advertising spiral.* He believed that different forms of advertising were required during the different stages of the product's life. These stages are: The pioneering, the competitive, and the retentive; the new pioneering, the new competitive, and the new retentive.

When a product concept is presented to the market, a great deal of sales resistance may be present simply because of the consumer's unfamiliarity with the product. This sales resistance may be due to fear of the product's safety, as was the case with the microwave oven and some of the new cosmetics. New products may require a person to change habits; it is often difficult for a man to adopt a new hairstyle. New products that have not yet built an image may lack image appeal. Usually such products will appear overpriced because image usually adds value to a product.

The purpose of the pioneering stage in advertising is to develop primary demand for the generic product. For example, we can speak of a primary demand for automobiles, hairstyles, motor homes, or freeze-dried coffees. Emphasis of a brand is hardly necessary at this stage; no significant

* Otto Kleppner, *Advertising Procedure* (Englewood Cliffs, NJ: Prentice-Hall, 1973), pp. 77-97.

competitors exist in the introductory stage. Pioneer advertising must alleviate fears and reduce sales resistance by educating the consumer to the advantages, safety, and use of the product.

In order to stimulate primary demand, publicity is very important. Editorials and newspaper articles may be circulated about the "new and exciting breakthrough." Journals for professionals such as *Fortune, Gourmet,* and *F.M. Stereo* may run articles about new products to look for.

As the product becomes better known, competitors enter the market. With the primary demand successfully developed, the second stage in the product life cycle involves developing selective (sometimes called secondary) demand. This demand relates to the specific brand name. Here, images are attached to the products. Consumers form segments around the particular image which closely matches their own self-concept.

Brand superiority may be gained by promotional methods such as introductory offers, point-of-purchase displays, and advertisements in periodicals such as *Business Week* and *The Wall Street Journal.*

As the market begins to mature, there is a scramble for customers. Much of the promotion and advertising is now designed to retain those customers who have already adopted the product. Coca-Cola spends millions of dollars to retain its customers. Retention of the customer is achieved by reminder advertising in magazines and on television. Promotional tools include billboards, dealer sales promotions, and contests.

At the saturation stage, there is widespread indifference to the product. The marketing manager must now decide whether to continue with retentive advertising (and gradually lose market share) or to innovate the product and begin a new mini-product life cycle. If the go-ahead is given, a new product or image feature must be developed. This may mean a dramatic change such as the rotary engine, or a simple one such as Tide's green crystals. The change may be purely psychological. Marlboro cigarettes found penetration of the female market discouraging, and concentrated on the male market with a different and highly successful image.

Pioneer advertising will be needed to promote an innovation or change. More or different customers may be attracted to the market, and the sales curve may go through all the stages again. Mass media advertising using

magazines, newspapers, radio, and television can be used effectively to attract attention to the new facelifting of an old product.

Some products go through the cycle many times. Tide has seen many changes over the years and is still going strong. Sophisticated models have been developed to aid the marketer. One of the most sophisticated is the AID (Automatic Interaction Detection) Model, which identifies the characteristics of those market segments with the highest probability of buying a brand.

Gerald Stahl, in an article in *Journal of Marketing** almost 20 years ago, wrote:

> Marketing executives today are authorizing . . . the expenditures of millions of dollars to contradict the specific corporate product and brand message they are spending other millions of dollars to promote.*

He goes on to explain that brand identifications are often visual contradictions of symbols projected in advertising: "Packaging is hindered by complicated and outmoded symbols and trademarks which weaken consumers' recognition and acceptance of products." Stahl feels that planned visual communication is "the visibly distinctive and consistent projection of related company, division, and product identity into its markets."

Only with each medium visibly supporting the others can consistency of communication be achieved. Mr. Stahl feels that the advantages to this consistency are many. He contends that it will aid in building strong brand loyalty, will strengthen merchandising confidence, and will enhance the marketing (profitability) of new products because of the already created familiarity and trust. Qualified designers should be hired to determine and create the desired image to be projected. This image must be appealing, unique, and easy to identify, understand, or remember. It must be clear and easy to communicate or transmit. The company must then coordinate the entire firm to the projection of the image. Each segment of the

> **E-Z TIP**
> Advertising must project the same corporate and brand image as the packaging, literature, visual commercial, and letterhead.

* Gerald Stahl, "The Marketing Strategy of Planned Visual Communication," *Journal of Marketing*, January 1964, p. 7.

firm must be oriented toward this focal point. Management has a responsibility to keep abreast of the contemporary approach to marketing communications.

Most important is the behavioral science approach—striving to understand the consumer more fully so that advertising may achieve its link in the chain of purpose: company profit. Management must be capable of visualizing the business as a whole with the hope that advertising communications may be related to the company's mission: success. Both the consumer and the producer may be described as engaging in creative activity. One is fashioning a "style of life" while the other is fashioning a specific product to fit this style. If they are to collaborate, they must communicate. Failure to do so harms both.

In order to promote effectively the marketer must understand the communications process—a process where product ideas are communicated to the consumer in the form of symbols. Communicating with symbols involves developing a product image through the use of colors, symbols, copy, and general layout. Many factors may impede the success of communications attempts.

> **CAUTION** The marketer must never forget that much of advertising falls on deaf ears. Probably less then one-tenth of all marketing communications reach the desired target-market consumer. Even reaching the potential customer does not necessarily result in a sale.

The consumer may be negatively influenced by the source of the message, the channel of communication, or the way the message is presented. Or he may not be influenced at all. A promotional strategy must be developed that successfully communicates the product image. This involves a proper balance of advertising, personal selling, packaging, sales promotion, and publicity. An appropriate mix of the various advertising media is also essential. Each medium has its own personality and its own kind of effectiveness.

Marketers must also learn all they can about their target customer's needs and desires. A study of the potential customer's self-concept is necessary, so that the product image can be developed to enhance the customer's own self-concept. Only after all these factors have been considered can a strategy be developed that will achieve the goal of the promotional campaign—that of persuading the consumer to purchase the product.

How to price for maximum profits

9

Chapter 9

How to price for maximum profits

Pricing is probably the most important ingredient in the marketing mix. It is, however, often neglected by the entrepreneur, who may see price only as revenue and, ultimately, as profit. Price is more than that; it is a vital element of the product image.

Small businesses often fail because the wrong prices are attached to the products or services. If a product is priced too high, the demand curve (Figure 9-I) shows us that it will not sell. When the price is too low, revenues and margins will be too low and there will be no profit. Somewhere in between lies the right price.

DEFINITION

The most common methods of pricing, and perhaps the worst, are known as "follow the leader" and "cost-plus." *Follow-the-leader* pricing occurs when the entrepreneur copies the prices of his competitors. This should only happen when your product is similar to that of the competition and there are only one or two competitors. This pricing policy assumes that the competitors know what they are doing (which is seldom the case) and neglects what the consumer is willing to pay.

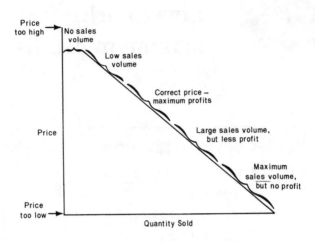

Figure 9-1. The demand curve for a product.

Cost-plus is the practice of determining the cost of production or doing business and then adding some percentage return. This method of pricing is useful only for determining the minimum price one is willing to charge for doing business; it, too, fails to consider the consumer.

The economics of pricing

The sensitivity of demand, as price changes, is known as elasticity of demand. Some products will sell nearly as well at one price as another (inelastic demand). The demand for milk does not change very much as the price is raised. For other products, demand reacts violently to price change. (See Figure 9-2.)

The secret of optimum price setting is to determine what the consumer is willing to pay for your product. The steps are fairly simple:

1) Determine the minimum price you can offer your product for (cost-plus) and still remain in business.

Figure 9-2. The elasticity of demand.

INELASTIC DEMAND

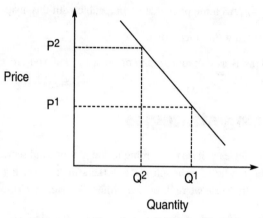

When price is raised from P^1 to P^2, there is a small
decrease in demand from Q^1 to Q^2

ELASTIC DEMAND

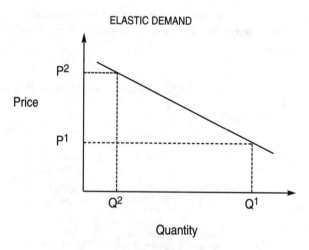

When price is raised from P^1 to P^2, there is a large
decrease in demand from Q^1 to Q^2

2) Select the market segment you desire to satisfy (target market).

3) Determine an image for the product/service that will satisfy that target market.

4) Attach the price that is compatible with this image.

5) Test the price.

This is a foolproof means of assuring that you are maximizing your profits.

Pricing strategies

Strategies will vary according to the product and service characteristics and the timing of your introduction. Let's look at pricing in terms of the product life cycle we've discussed earlier. (See Figure 9-3.)

In the introductory stage, skim pricing (starting with a relatively high price) is most common. By the growth stage of a product/ service life cycle, pricing should be similar to that of any major entrants and competitors.

For companies entering established markets with significant competition, it may be necessary to enter with a penetration pricing strategy (a lower price). Usually the price is raised after successful entry into the market.

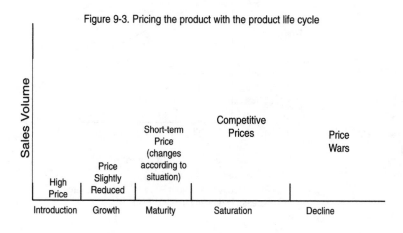

Figure 9-3. Pricing the product with the product life cycle

Penetration pricing may also be used at any stage of the product life cycle when it is believed that competition may enter the market. The low price may discourage competition from entering as quickly.

 Here is a guide to help determine when to charge a high price or when to meet the competition price:

Charge a higher price than competitors (skim pricing) when:

- Your product/service is new or unique.

- Your product/service is difficult to copy.

- You have a monopoly on some aspect of the product (source of materials, parts, a franchise for exclusive sales).

- It is a status product.

Charge what competitors are charging when:

- Your product has been around for a while and is similar to that of your competitors.

- Your product is easy to copy.

- You have an oligopoly situation, with no differentiated product/service and few competitors.

- You have a purely competitive situation with little product differentiation and many competitors.

The psychology of price

Price, in its strict form, is the amount of money a person pays for a product. Psychologically, however, it goes much deeper. To the consumer, price may be a "dis-utility"—a negative aspect which detracts from the product. The exception to this would be a status product, where a higher price projects a more favorable image. For most consumers price means giving up spending power (the ability to purchase other goods).

While price can be a negative aspect, it does communicate a great deal about the product. It tells the consumer the quality and status potential of the product and it communicates expectancy of satisfaction. A $5,000 cruise will probably yield more psychological satisfaction than a $1,000 voyage. Based on experience, a consumer develops a complex set of attitudes and expectancies about the relationship between price and product satisfaction.

> *note* It is the challenge of the marketer to surround price with enough positive attributes of the product image so the product will be purchased, used, and purchased again.

A child quickly learns that money is the means to acquire products that satisfy his wants, needs, and desires. Money is used to reward him for good effort and it is also perceived as a source of tension, especially if the child is raised in a home where limited incomes have caused anxiety.

HOT spot

A consumer's willingness to spend or not spend money is part of that person's self-concept. A person who is confident that he can earn money and that the economy is sound will be more inclined to spend money and will not be overly concerned about savings. A person who is insecure about his position and does not trust the environment will tend to be miserly. While money may enforce one's self-concept, many rich persons are insecure within their environment and miserly in their spending habits. Money does not necessarily make a person either secure or insecure. As the consumer develops his self-concept, he develops enduring attitudes toward money.

> **E-Z TIP** Research has indicated that in cases where no perceived differences are evident, consumers will select the higher-priced product, believing it has the best quality.

Most people have been raised to believe that there is a direct relationship between price and quality. Persons who generalize this way will select products according to the, price. They may assume that a relatively high-priced product has greater quality. This is not always the case, but many consumers feel this

way. Most private brands are lower in price, but are of the same quality; only the brand name is different. For example, much of the gasoline sold by independents comes from the refineries of the major brands. The price-quality impression is particularly strong when the consumer is concerned about the quality of the product medications and cosmetics, for instance.

There is a tendency to feel that consumers are always concerned with price. This is not true. A study by G. H. Haines * on why people purchase new products has discovered that 25 percent of consumers were not aware of the price of the toothpaste they purchased.

Many older persons in this country went through two serious depressions and have raised their children to be conscious of waste. It is common for such parents to be ultra-conscious of light bulbs left burning when not in use. Many believe that any form of extravagance or waste is sinful. A box or package that is thought to be too fancy may be considered wasteful or extravagant; the purchase of a Porsche automobile may seem outrageous.

The puritanical influence has had a strong impact on many of the children raised by such parents. Often, however, there is a backlash. One may leave the light burning all the time as an expression of independence and affluence.

> *note*
>
> To the modern consumer, extravagance is often a way of breaking away from parental influence. It becomes a release from the psychological suppression of the parent.

An enduring role for most consumers is that of the clever shopper. The housewife will justify her purchase of the red dress with chartreuse flowers as such a good deal that she could not turn it down. The male consumer likes to brag about how he "stole" that used car from the used-car salesman. It is not unusual for a prosperous individual to drive 20 miles to save 10 cents on a product. On the negative side, a consumer's realization that he was tricked or taken, or that he paid too much for a product, may be very harmful to his self-concept.

---

* G. H. Haines, "A Study of Why People Purchase New Products," in J. Engle, R. D. Kollat, and R. Blackwell, *Consumer Behavior* (New York: Holt, Rinehart and Winston, 1973), p. 253.

Most homemakers put emphasis on being shrewd shoppers. They diligently compare advertisements for the best prices and clip coupons for every bargain, sale, and deal.

In many countries, price haggling between the buyer and the seller is common. In this country, standard pricing has become accepted because of the strong impact of self-service, where there is usually no salesman to haggle with. A standard price also simplifies the buying process considerably.

> **HOT spot** Price haggling in the United States has been replaced by bargain shopping. The consumer probably receives the same form of satisfaction in finding a product on sale as he would in haggling the price down.

Consumers develop a feeling of "price zone" from past experience with other products. Within this zone, however, are a number of pricing possibilities; each may differ in its effectiveness in attaining consumer patronage. New products usually have broader ranges.

Prices below this level may give an impression of inferiority, and prices above may seem extravagant. A major national retail chain ran into this phenomenon with respect to a common hardware item originally priced at $1.19. Concluding that sales were not as good as they had hoped, they decided on a price experiment. They chose three groups of outlets for the experiment. In one group, the item was priced at 89¢, in the other at $1.09, and in the third at $1.29. The store selling the item at $1.09 sold far greater quantities than those listing it at either the lower or higher price. This mid-range price was apparently closer to the consumer's perceived fair-price standard.

Everyone is always looking for a bargain, but we all know that a low price does not always mean a good deal. Some consumers actually avoid low prices. They may feel that a lower price does not have a sense of status associated with it or that it projects a "bargain basement" image. The low price may imply to them that something is wrong with the product: it may be broken or old. A lower price may give the impression that no one else wants the item—it may not be stylish or in season—or that it is inferior to a higher-priced item.

Psychological pricing techniques

The prices which consumers are willing to accept are truly psychological in nature. Through cultural, social, and familial experience, consumers develop attitudes and beliefs about prices of which they themselves are not usually aware. The marketer who is aware of this price phenomenon should be able to develop a better pricing strategy than marketers who are unaware of the psychology of pricing.

Odd-even pricing

Marketers have long observed that products marked with even-numbered prices, like $2.00 or $4.00, reflect an aura of quality. Conversely, the odd-numbered prices of $1.99 or $3.99 give an impression of a "good deal" or a sale. These prices can also represent inferior quality, especially to a consumer who is more accustomed to buying products that are priced evenly. The implication to marketing is far reaching. A manufacturer or store seeking a quality product image can reinforce this image with an even price. Odd prices are effective for segmenting the market that appreciates a bargain or a good deal.

HOT spot It is not surprising that most discount houses and low-prestige stores use odd pricing, while high-status stores use even pricing.

This pricing phenomenon probably started with the belief that consumers with large discretionary incomes frequent high-status stores and are not concerned about spending a few more cents; therefore, a simpler form of even pricing is used. On the other hand, the consumer who has to count pennies may be more influenced by a $1.99 price which—psychologically— does not appear to be as much as the $2.00 price.

Number pricing

There is another interesting phenomenon in pricing. It has been discovered that certain numbers and certain ranges of prices are more effective in selling products than others. For example, in the discussion of odd-

even pricing it was noted that the bargain price of $1.99 might sell more products than a $2.00 price for those persons interested in bargains. But research by Benson P. Shapiro* has shown that the consumer sees little difference between $2.99 and $3.00. Products also seem to sell better at 19 cents than at 15 cents, or at 79 cents rather than 75 cents.

Oddball pricing

Many retailers have found that for special sales or promotions, oddball prices are effective: Three items for a dollar may sell many more products than the lower price of 33 cents apiece. Prices like $3.33 or $8.88 may sell a lot of products for special occasions, simply because they are so unusual. An executive of a large midwestern department store chain found that more merchandise was sold at $1.77 than at the lower price of $1.69. Special promotions selling a variety of tools for $1.88 have also been found effective.

Prestige and status pricing

Some consumers with almost unlimited incomes, and others who place a high value on status and prestige, actually look favorably on high prices. For them, the higher the price, the better the quality (within certain constraints). Such a response to price may be expressed in the famous "backward-bending demand curve" (see Figure 9-4). This curve indicates that the higher the price, the more items will be purchased by status-conscious consumers. Of course, there is some limit; the demand eventually begins to decrease at extremely high prices, causing the demand curve to bend back. Consider a gold-plated toothbrush. Very few of such a product would be purchased at $2.00; that is overpriced for a regular toothbrush, but not high enough for a prestige product. More may be sold at $5, $10,

Because higher prices give the impression of quality and status, they can be used to appeal to different classes of customers. The "bargain basement" of a large department store appeals to one particular group, but not to the customer who shops in the boutique on the fourth floor.

---

* Benson P. Shapiro, "The Psychology of Pricing," *Harvard Business Review*, July/August 1968.

and maybe even $15, but there would come a point (say, $100) where no one would be interested.

Habit and convenience pricing

A consumer may get used to a particular price, and such a price may be difficult to change. The 5 cent Coke and the 5 cent candy bar represent prices that were resistant to change. Candy producers found it wiser to decrease the quality and size rather than to increase the price. It got to the point that when one bought a candy bar, a few peanuts would roll out. Candy marketers were finally able to increase the price to 10 cents; even that price seems like ancient history today. Sometimes a situation dictates a convenient price. Most vending machines do not give penny change and therefore only accept coins in multiples of 5 cents. Concessionaires and vendors at sports events simplify their task by avoiding making a lot of change; they charge convenient prices which already include the tax. For example, one usually pays an even $1.00 for a program or 75 cents for a hot dog.

Quantum pricing

DEFINITION

If the quantity needs adjustment, it is important to determine the quantum price. The *quantum price* is the price above which the consumer will not go, no matter what the quantity. For example, a firm introduced a consumer specialty in three package sizes: 5 pounds, 10 pounds, and 25 pounds. Initially, the suggested retail prices were 69 cents, $1.29, and $2.65.

Figure 9-4. Backward-bending demand curve for status products

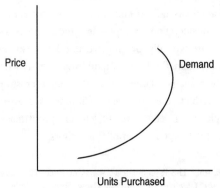

When it was decided to increase the price of the 25 pound box, increases to $2.75, $2.85, $2.95, and $3.09 made no difference to the amount purchased. However, $3.23 appeared to be the quantum price; after another increase sales dropped off substantially.*

Fair price

When a consumer feels that he can estimate the cost of a product, he will establish in his mind a fair or reasonable price image. Emphasizing such things as patent protection, uniqueness of the product, or some major differences may give the product more value to him. Showing many uses for the product may also add to its value. Anything plastic is thought to be cheap, while stainless steel or gold plating appears more expensive. Genuine materials appear more expensive, and real leather, fur, or pure ingredients add value.

Product price classifications

We have shown how consumers may come to perceive a product as a convenience good, shopping good, specialty good, unsought good, or new product. Let us now apply these consumer buying perceptions to some general pricing rules.

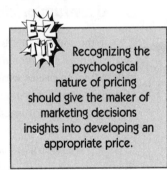

E-Z TIP: Recognizing the psychological nature of pricing should give the maker of marketing decisions insights into developing an appropriate price.

Convenience goods

Staples are the basic convenience items we normally purchase without a great deal of consideration. Examples are grocery items, kitchen utensils, and gasoline. They are typically low in price and the consumer will expend little effort in buying them. Hardly any brand loyalty exists when a staple product is not readily available. Rather than go to another store to purchase the unavailable product, the consumer will purchase a substitute brand or product. Staples are priced competitively and profit margins and prices are low because of the large number of competitors.

---

* Chester R. Wasson, "The Psychological Aspects of Price, *The Economics of Managerial Decision: Profit Opportunity Analysis* (New York: Appleton-Century-Crofts, 1965). pp. 130-133.

note

Staples are purchased often, and their importance to the basic diet or habits of the family causes marketers of such products to be very conscious of price.

Because of their importance, staples are effective loss-leaders for retailers. A two-cent decrease in the price of Morton Salt will increase consumer traffic appreciably. Other, more expensive, higher-margin products may then attract the consumer's eye and be purchased. Retailers are also turning to private labeling and selling such staple products a few cents lower than the nationally advertised brand.

Staples are competitive in price, and manufacturers with superior cost structures (economics of scale) and the ability to sell large volumes have a distinct advantage over the smaller, less efficient manufacturer. Psychological differentiation may be possible; it is desirable in terms of a higher markup. Morton and Chiquita have been very successful at differentiating their products (salt and bananas) in the eyes of the consumer. Volume may also be increased by selling through a private label (like Safeway or A & P) at a lower price.

DEFINITION

Impulse goods are convenience products which are purchased without any preconceived intent and usually because of sensory or psychological appeal and immediate accessibility. Ice cream, popcorn, and *Playboy* magazine are examples. These products can be priced relatively higher than their staple convenience counterparts because their appeal is more emotional. The price cannot be exorbitant, but the consumer does not go through any significant problem-solving process; his desire for the product is immediate and no appropriate alternatives are available, so no price comparison is made.

Such impulse products should be priced at the high end of the acceptable pricing zone. Since the appeal is sensory, visual appeal and pleasant fragrances should be emphasized. Everyone can recall the fragrance of freshly popped popcorn.

Emergency convenience goods are sought after because of the urgency of finding the product quickly. When a housewife finds herself out of coffee and guests are expected, or when a car breaks down in the desert, emergency

products and services are extremely important. Convenience and availability become more crucial than price. The 7-Eleven food stores that are always open and have a number of convenient locations cater to this form of consumer need.

 Since a specialized service is being offered, higher prices are usually charged. Emergency goods are purchased during an emotional situation when price is not the important consideration. Critics may say it is unfair to take advantage of the consumer in an emergency situation, but remember that a valuable service or product is being provided, usually with greater effort and at a higher cost. The industrious retailer or manufacturer who is able to satisfy emergency needs deserves higher margins. Take, for example, the gasoline station or restaurant that stays open all night to serve the night traveler. If these emergency services were not available, motorists would be unable to travel at night. In order to provide evening and early morning service, at least one additional shift, and often two, have to be added. Employees probably have to be paid time-and-a-half wages, and the volume of customers during these hours is usually much less than during normal business hours. Such emergency services and products deserve the higher prices charged.

Shopping goods

DEFINITION

Homogeneous shopping goods are products that the consumer perceives as being similar from one brand to another. One brand of color television might be considered identical to another. Most appliances and automobiles are also homogeneous in nature. Such products are significant purchases to most households, and consumers will usually shop to compare the available alternatives. Because the consumer perceives these goods as similar in quality and features, he will shop for the best price.

Manufacturers of these products may find themselves in a cost squeeze. The larger manufacturers with more favorable economies of scale will be able to win the price battle. Therefore, it is to the manufacturer's advantage to attempt to differentiate his product by quality, by patented features, or by appealing more specifically to a target customer. By such differentiation, price competition becomes only one of many factors, and higher prices and profits may be possible.

DEFINITION

Heterogeneous shopping goods are products which the consumer perceives as being different in quality and suitability. Clothes, mobile homes, and houses are examples. Like homogeneous shopping goods, these products represent a significant purchase for most families, and careful shopping takes place. Price is only one consideration, since quality, special features, and suitability are equally important. Many emotional factors enter into the purchase. A house might sell because of a carpeted bathroom or the color of the built-in appliances; a mobile home could sell because of its real wood-burning fireplace.

Because the purchase of heterogeneous shopping goods is psychological, and because brands are more difficult to compare, prices can be higher than the homogeneous counterpart and more varied from brand to brand. Price will depend upon the perceived quality, suitability, and uniqueness of the product, as well as the degree to which the brand image matches the target customer's self-concept.

Specialty goods

DEFINITION

Specialty goods are products for which consumers have a strong brand preference. Because of this brand loyalty, consumers are willing to wait long periods of time, exert special effort, or pay a higher price for the product than for comparable products that do not command the same brand loyalty. Cadillac automobiles, Michelin tires, and Polaroid cameras are examples of specialty goods. Achieving specialty status for a product is very desirable. Most marketers want to develop strong brand loyalty in their customers. Such customers resist competition and will go out of their way to purchase the favored brand. Many times this brand preference has psychological origins, though the consumer associates it with higher quality.

Unsought goods

DEFINITION

Unsought goods are products which the consumer does not perceive as something he wants or needs. Health insurance, encyclopedias, grave plots, and specialty items such as food choppers are seldom sought out. Consumers have to be sold personally and forcefully.

Unsought goods are usually sold on rather emotional appeals, using the door-to-door or direct-mail approach. Because of the inefficient, expensive personal sales method, such products are usually priced high. Commissions on direct sales range from about 50 to 100 percent of the retail price.

Price is the primary objection for the consumer, but experienced personal salesmen can surround the product with so many pleasant appeals that the price objection no longer becomes an important barrier to the sale of the product.

New products

A new product may be a copy of products already on the market, but with different features and some psychological differentiation, or it may be a unique and different product. In the case of the established market, a manufacturer may see potential profit by capturing a share of the market through product improvements or psychological segmentation.

Consumers are probably already using a particular brand, or are familiar with one. The only way for a manufacturer to penetrate the market is through a lower price. Because of competition, the relatively lower price may not be profitable over the long run and a higher price must eventually be charged. Customers usually resist price increases, and such increases may result in loss of customers. This is not true when competitors also raise their price or when inflation forces the entire industry to raise its prices.

There are several ways to enter the market with a low price and, after demand is established, raise the price without the consumer being resentful. Premiums or cents-off coupons are useful for enabling the customer to purchase at a lower price, but the higher price is still maintained. In extreme cases, a product may be given away through the mail, door to door, or at in-store promotions. The most common method is to give away or sell a small sample size of the product with a cents-off coupon enclosed so that the consumer will be encouraged to try to regular size after using the trial size.

When pricing a new and unique product, a high price is generally used. Innovators and early adopters can afford high prices and do not mind paying. They have come to expect high prices for new products and may even avoid

those that are perceived to be inexpensive. They have the income and the confidence to try unique products.

Planning your pricing strategy

Once the marketer has classified his product, considered his competition and his costs, and developed a general pricing policy, he is ready to develop a pricing strategy to achieve his long-run objectives—profit maximization and growth. This is accomplished by carefully planning the pricing strategy over the entire life of the product.

Pricing strategy changes over the period of time the product is sold. These changes can be followed through the product's life cycle. Let us follow the life cycle of a unique product, produced by a new firm, through its stages from introduction to decline.

Introduction

DEFINITION

In the introduction stage there is only one manufacturer. Product development, initial manufacturing, and marketing costs are great and losses are usually suffered. For these reasons, high prices are usually charged. Starting with a high initial price is called *skim pricing*.

In order to begin with this high price, the product must be new and unique with no direct competitors. If substitutes are available, the consumer might be discouraged from paying the higher price. There should be some major barrier to entry in the market by competitors. Special manufacturing processes or patents may slow the entrance of competitors. Finally, there must be some consumers who are interested in and financially able to purchase the product at the high price.

Innovators are in a high-income group, are cosmopolitan in outlook, and have a positive attitude about trying new products. Because they perceive themselves as successful, they are not afraid of making an unwise product selection.

Definition:

Individuals who are able and willing to pay high prices for new products are known as *innovators*.

It is very important for the marketer to reach this innovator group, since they influence the early adopters in the next stage. If the firm can succeed in this first stage, the channels are excellent for profits and an extended future. Between 50 and 85 percent of new products fail, however, and most failures occur in this introductory stage.

Growth

In the growth stage, sales begin to increase. The innovator has tried the product and broken the ice of newness, more persons have heard of the product, and a few competitors are probably entering the market. The first firm in the market has broken even and will experience healthy profits in this second stage. The price of the product may be lowered because of the newly introduced competition, lower manufacturing costs gained from experience, and economies of scale achieved from volume.

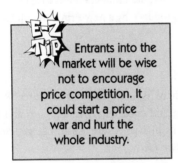

Entrants into the market will be wise not to encourage price competition. It could start a price war and hurt the whole industry.

Marketers who enter in this stage are at a disadvantage because the initiator has already recovered most of his expenses, while the newcomer's costs are just beginning.

It would be unwise to lower prices rapidly because the early adopter, who is the characteristic customer in this stage, is also psychologically willing and financially able to purchase the product at a relatively high price.

The early adopter is on his way up professionally; he is financially successful and aspires to the innovator group above him. Because of these conditions, he will purchase products that add to his status and prestige and give the impression that he is successful.

Maturity

Sales are increasing, but not as rapidly as they did in the growth stage. More competitors are entering the lucrative market. Most of these new firms will enter with a penetration price that will force prices and profits down for

the initial firm and the entire industry. They will also enter this established market against experienced competition. They can gain a substantial share of the market only by using a penetration pricing strategy. This strategy consists in starting with a very low price and, after gaining market share, raising the price to a competitive one, since the initial price is not profitable. Customers usually resist price increases by switching brands, except when competitors also raise their prices.

 There are several ways of applying a penetration strategy without giving the impression of raising prices. The most common method is giving customers coupons which, when redeemed, save the customer a few cents off the regular price. Sometimes trial sizes are introduced in special promotions. In extreme cases, products may be given away. Usually coupons accompany the free sample so that the consumer will be encouraged to seek out the product for himself after the free sample has been used.

The early majority consumer, who is susceptible to cents-off offers, is much more concerned about price than either of the groups above him. He is middle-class, and has learned about the new products from the leaders in his reference group (who happen to be early adopters). The early majority customer would not try a new and unique product; he cannot afford costly mistakes. He is more concerned about providing his family with a comfortable home and having a little money in the bank.

Saturation

In the saturation stage, most consumers have already purchased the product and the majority of the sales in this period are due to obsolescence of the product. Technical obsolescence results when dramatic innovations have taken place and consumers desire the new model. Psychological obsolescence occurs when style and appeal convince the consumer that the new model would be desirable and perhaps prestigious.

Most of the entrants have recovered their costs by this stage, and competition resulting from the large number of firms in the industry has forced the price down to a reasonable rate of return. Some of the less efficient firms may now go out of business. The latecomers who adopt the product for

the first time are called the late majority. These people waited before trying a new product because of their average incomes. They are very security-oriented and rarely try new products. Once the product has been adopted by many consumers, they regard it as a necessity.

Decline

In the decline stage, total sales for the industry begin to drop off. Other substitute products have been developed and only a few new consumers—who are called laggards—adopt the new product for the first time. They usually purchase on impulse because of the very low prices which have resulted from firms going out of business and dumping their product for whatever price they can get. Loyal customers who habitually purchase the product will continue to buy, but attrition will take its toll.

Profits can be healthy for the firm who has superior economies of scale and has developed strong brand loyalty, but care must be taken to avoid over-reaction to the low prices of those firms who are going out of business.

Engineering a product to a particular price

Sometimes a product must be manufactured for a particular price. The automobile industry and gasoline market operate in this manner: Because of competitive pressures, a particular price is required. In these cases, the manufacturer must work backward, starting with the price, manufacturing the best product possible, and then making the desired profit. This often forces a form of unplanned obsolescence: In order to manufacture the product at the competitive price, low-quality materials must be used. This pricing strategy is used when the marketer feels there are price ranges which competitors are not reaching, and when there appears to be consumer demand.

> **E-Z TIP**
>
> The pricing function is an important ingredient in developing a successful marketing mix. The traditional way of determining price is to consider the market structure and to establish the price according to supply and demand in the marketplace.

Because of the complexity of developing an optimum pricing policy, many firms tend to guess at the proper price to charge, use a cost-plus approach, or simply copy a competitor's pricing policy. These methods neglect the customer and the need to develop an appropriate product image.

 The marketer who is aware of the psychology of pricing is not as reluctant to use price as an important marketing ingredient. He is more likely to develop a firm pricing strategy, charge appropriate prices, and maximize his profits.

How to sell to the industrial market

10

Chapter 10

How to sell to the industrial market

The industrial market—the market for goods and services in commercial enterprises, nonprofit institutions, and other organizations—deals in turn with the consumer or with another industrial customer. The primary distinction between the industrial market and the consumer market is the intended customer: If the intended customer is a consumer, this is not the industrial market. Some would also include the government in their definition of the industrial market, but the government presents its own marketing problems, which will be discussed later.

Another distinction between the consumer and industrial markets is the kind of products sold. To the consumer we may sell perfume, clothes, or toothpaste, but to the industrial market it might be paper, pencils, capital equipment, laboratory equipment, component parts, raw materials, processed materials, and so forth. Since both the buyers and the products are different, the marketing methods must be adapted to this particular type of marketing. There are two major characteristics of the industrial market.

Industrial market sales are larger than those of the consumer market. Furthermore, of great interest and importance, there are fewer buying units in the industrial market: about 10 million versus more than 200 million in the consumer market. To sell to the industrial market, you do not have to

> **note** Currently the industrial market exceeds $700 billion a year versus $600 billion a year for the consumer market.

reach as many different people (10 million versus 200 million). On the other hand, once you have brought your sales volume to a certain level, it may be much more volatile because it is affected by a smaller number of buying customers than you would have in the consumer market.

Who the buyers are

The buyer for a single item or type of item in the industrial market may not be one single man or even one class of employees for a major industrial firm. While the physical act of purchasing may be done by one individual (a contract administrator), the decision to buy is usually made by a group consisting of the contract administrator, engineers or technical people in the customer's organization, and supervisors (managers and planners) who in some way come in contact with the item or service you are selling. What do these buyers look for, and what motivates them to buy? When an industrial buyer buys pencils, or nails, or a complete computer system for his company, he does not get the same personal satisfaction or need-fulfillment as the individual who purchases a book, soap, or a high-powered automobile for personal use. The industrial buyer's goals may actually be divided into three separate categories: the interest of the company that employs him, the personal interest of his organization, and, third, his own ego. Let's look closely at each one.

The company employs the buyer or other industrial customer and pays him or her for performing certain tasks. In return, the industrial customer must look out for the interests of the company. As fares his company, so fares he. If the company goes well, his job is secure, his salary increases, his retirement is secure, and he may be promoted. If the company does poorly, his salary increases may be withheld even though he is performing well, his

security may be jeopardized by layoffs, and various other negative things may happen to him. Therefore, his major concern is the welfare of the company as a whole.

The second category of goals of the industrial customer is the interests of the organization to which he reports. This organization is the unit which decides on his immediate status as an employee—his promotion, his next salary raise, and whether he is retained or discharged within the overall company organization. The *company* (as an organization) and the *immediate* organization (to which the buyer reports) may not always have identical interests. In a situation such as this the industrial customer must resolve a conflict as to which takes precedence the overall interests of the company or the interests of the organization to which he reports.

The third category of goals of the industrial customer is a more personal one. It is his own ego. Man is an emotional animal. Sellers, marketers, managers of all persuasions, and entrepreneurs have been taking advantage of this fact and exploiting the ego of the individual since time immemorial. There is no question that you can affect the ego of the industrial buyer to such an extent that he will do irrational things, which are in the best interests neither of the company nor of his immediate organization. The opposite is also true: You can affect the buyer's ego so that he will totally disregard his own self-interest in order to do what is in the best interests of his immediate organization or his company.

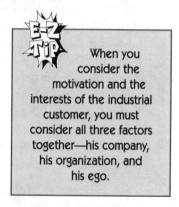

When you consider the motivation and the interests of the industrial customer, you must consider all three factors together—his company, his organization, and his ego.

Personal selling—the key to success

Your emphasis, as a marketer, must be on selling, if you want to be successful in the industrial marketplace. There are two types of selling you should know about: face-to-face selling and selling through proposals.

Face-to-face selling must be done with all the customers in the buying organization. It is essential that the actual buyer get to know you and your product, but it is also essential that other customers in this industrial organization—engineers or managerial people who may be using or coming in contact with your product—also become acquainted with you and with your product. Only in this way will industrial customers have confidence that you will deliver.

The actual buying, however, may not be done face to face. It is frequently done through a method of contracting based on written proposals and bids. The buyer will request competing suppliers to submit a bid and/or a proposal which will include such information as delivery schedule, what will be delivered, and a price. This required information will be specified in detail in the written request. Both methods of selling are dependent upon two very important theories. Consumer acceptance theory says that there are levels of consumer attitudes progressing from acceptance through preference to insistence. The *lowest level of acceptance* merely means that the consumer or the industrial buyer will accept whatever product or service you are offering. *Preference* means that the buyer will prefer your goods or services over those of your competitors. *Insistence* means that the buyers or the other customers in the industrial company will insist on your product or services, regardless of price or any other factor. Clearly, it is to your interest that the insistence level be achieved.

DEFINITION

According to consumer acceptance theory, the more positive the involvement with your product or service, the greater the chances of progressing from the lowest level of acceptance to the highest level of insistence. But which comes first, the chicken or the egg? What kind of positive involvement with your product or service is possible when you haven't gotten a contract with that industrial company? This is where face-to-face involvement in selling comes in. Clearly, this involvement must be created long before you actually submit a bid or a proposal.

> **E-Z TIP**
> Sometimes it makes sense to offer trial quantities of your product or service at a reduced charge— another type of face-to-face involvement with your product or service.

Think about this for a minute. In the consumer market, would you buy an automobile whose brand name you had never heard of? Not likely, and certainly not without a great deal of advertising or other selling. It is the same in the industrial market: You must spend time, energy, and resources in face-to-face contact so that the industrial customer will become comfortable with your product before you submit a serious proposal for a large quantity order.

The other theory that connects proposal/bid selling and face-to-face selling is merchandising theory. As it is used here, it concerns the fact that what you are offering to the customer and what he actually wants do not fit perfectly together, at least not at first. You may offer a product of a certain specification while the customer's specification differs somewhat from this. The critical factor is not how much it differs, but whether its difference is important for the purposes of the industrial customer. Merchandising theory says that, through a series of face-to-face meetings, you present your product or service in its best possible light; the customer provides you with feedback as to the acceptability of this product or service, its pluses and its minuses, its drawbacks; you then go back, modify your product or service, modify your presentation, and present it in a different light, according to the needs and wants of the customer. Eventually, you will close the gap between your product and his desires. You have merchandised your product or service to the point where what you offer and what the customer wants are almost identical. It is at this point that you respond to a request for proposal or an invitation to bid. You win this proposal because the customer realizes that what he wants and what you are offering are a good match. He accepts your product or—even better—prefers or insists on it.

If you are going to bid or propose, you should know that many industrial companies follow the government's lead and offer two classes of bidding: Invitations for Bids (or IFBs) and Requests for Proposals (or RFPs). An Invitation for Bid normally goes to the lowest bid submitted that meets the specifications, quantities, and delivery schedule required by the customer. In a Request for Proposal, price is but one factor. Technical performance and other factors may weigh even more heavily in deciding on a contract winner.

The actual format of either the Invitation for Bid or the Request for Proposal differs from customer to customer and the format of your proposal may differ slightly, depending upon the customer's lead, but regardless of what

you are bidding or proposing, it must be presold to the customer in advance: to the buyer, technical people, managers, and anyone else in the group making the buying decision. Further, everyone in that group must know the basic contents of your proposal long before you submit it, and the majority must be in favor of what you will propose.

Success in proposals depends on three factors: performance, delivery schedule, and the price. You have presold your performance, giving the customer confidence that you will meet his needs and requirements; you have established your credibility in that you will deliver on time and according to the customer's schedule; and you have made it known that your price is not only competitive but also realistic, and is a reflection of the image of your product or service. You have, of course, also presented this image during the prebid, preproposal stage of your selling, so that the customer is convinced that your price matches the image of your product, and that it is a fair price.

The industrial buying process

The process is divided into six stages. The first is need-recognition, and occurs when an industrial customer realizes the need for a particular product or service. Stage two, which develops over a period of time, involves identifying, both descriptively and by quantity, a solution or solutions to fulfill this need. The customer, perhaps an engineer, realizes that a certain widget is required to fulfill a requirement, figures out how many widgets he needs, and describes the widget.

> If you can help the industrial customer during the need-recognition, the solution identification, or the search-for-sources phase, so much the better.

The third step is a search for sources of this widget. How does the customer do this? He may consult the *Thomas Register of Manufacturers*, catalogues of industrial suppliers or supply houses, or suppliers of similar items with whom he is already dealing. In any case, he will search until he comes up with several sources that are likely to fulfill the need.

The fourth phase involves the acquisition of bids and/or proposals. This stage requires considerable work done ahead of time. In order for a Request for Proposal to go out, a data package must be prepared. This is usually done by the technical people with the close coordination of the company's buyer or contract administrator. Depending on the complexity and the sophistication of the product or services being bought, this data package may take anywhere from a few days to months to prepare.

> **HINT**
>
> If the buyer enjoys negotiating and would like to go back to his boss and say that he made you reduce your price between 5 and 15 percent, then you should overbid by 5 or 15 percent to allow for this reduction at the negotiation stage.

This is the time for you to do your face-to-face selling. This will also be the phase during which you can identify the fact that this solution is being sought and that a Request for Proposal or Invitation for Bid will eventually appear. You can use merchandising theory to promote your product or service. Then, by the time of the preparation of the data package and during the acquisition-of-proposals phase, you will be considerably ahead of your competition in understanding both the problem and the solution. You will be on the same wavelength as your industrial customer, and he on yours.

The fifth phase is the source selection and the negotiation of the actual contract. If you have done your marketing and selling job properly up to now, you will be the one selected. You and your industrial customer are both working toward the same end. What you have in mind to propose (and have described to your customer, at the price and delivery schedule you imagined, before a Request for Proposal or an Invitation for Bid is received), he has asked for in his request for proposal. You have met that need formally with your written proposal, which you have now submitted. By using these concepts and these marketing theories, you have placed yourself far ahead of your competitor who merely responds to an RFP or IFB and knows little, if anything, about the problem, the solution, the pricing, or what the customer really wants or needs.

When price is not the only factor in a request for proposal, you may be invited to negotiate along with other competitors who are within the general price range and who meet all aspects of the RFP. Again, if you have accomplished the processes of industrial marketing and selling correctly, the negotiation stage should be fairly straightforward. Your only decision, if you have competition, is whether or not to reduce your price. Here you really have to know your customer and his buyer fairly well.

You are now dealing with one of the motivations of the industrial buyer—the ego. If the buyer is this type of individual, and if his organization is the type that must achieve a 5 to 15 percent reduction in bid price, give it to him. If you do not grant the reduction, you will offend the buyer's ego, causing him to go against the personal interests of his organization or the interests of his company. Know your buyer, and know ahead of time whether or not to make the reduction if it is requested.

 You should consider the fact that the buyer is acting as an agent for the rest of the company.

If you have already convinced the company that your item is the one that will fulfill its need, it may be at the insistence level of consumer acceptance: It will insist on your product or your service. If this is so, you are in an extremely strong position in negotiating with the buyer. If you are asked for a reduction you may consider turning it down, firm in the knowledge that your item has insistence value with the customer. Even though the competition price range may be slightly lower, and you may offend the buyer's ego, you will win anyway. The relative strengths of these factors can be gained only by knowing your customer.

The sixth and final stage of the industrial buying process is feedback of your performance on the contract. Did you supply what you said you would supply, within the time frame and at the price you promised? If you enjoy a good relationship with the customer and have performed well on a contract, you can generally be assured of future contracts and future profits.

Let's look at this industrial buying process to see how we can integrate our marketing procedures to maximize our profits. Our first objective (as an

industrial marketing organization, an entrepreneur, or a marketer for a small company that wants to market to industry) is to find potential customers for our product or services. We may conduct our search in a fashion similar to the way the industrial buyer proceeds; we can look at the *Thomas Register of Manufacturers*, the *Commerce Business Daily*, or government publications. We can look at other catalogues and directories to find out who may be interested in our product.

Our next task is to make contact with these organizations. An initial contact might be by telephone, but the contact should not be limited to the industrial buyer. We should also strive to find out who is behind this buyer—the engineers, technicians, or other people who are specifying the ordering of these products or services—and make contact with them as well.

Our next job is to prepare a presentation for these buyers and the other people in the company who are part of the buying decision. This presentation should include a brochure or description of our

> **HOT spot** Remember that during these presentations we are not only dispensing information, we are also gathering information and utilizing consumer acceptance theory and merchandising theory.

product or our services. Additional presentations should be made as we continue to develop the sale during this preproposal phase of our marketing effort. We visit these individuals, study their problems and solutions, and attempt to find out what they are looking for and what they will be ordering in the future.

Next comes our proposal or bid in response to a request; then, finally, negotiation and a contract. The process does not end here. Now we must be concerned about our performance and begin our development of follow-on contracts.

Feast or famine

With the relatively smaller number of buying units (10 million versus 200 million consumer buying units), your sales may be much more volatile than

sales to the consumer market. For example, if you manufacture bottle-making machines and one machine makes 10,000 bottles, the individual selling these bottles (with a soft drink inside) to the consumer market will be affected by a

note There is one problem in dealing with the industrial marketplace that is not generally true of the consumer market. This is the problem of feast or famine.

10 percent reduction in demand and a 10 percent reduction in sales. But a 10 percent reduction in consumer demand may equate, as far as you are concerned, with your entire sale of bottle-making machinery to an industrial customer. While consumer items such as soft drinks or perfumes have predictably plottable peaks and valleys in ordering throughout the year, your peaks and valleys in the industrial marketplace, even when predictable, are generally much more extreme.

There can also be a much higher risk in the industrial marketplace than in selling to consumers. You could sell ten machines at $1 million each in January through March and have zero sales for the rest of the year. Or, perhaps you peak out every six months or every three months or in some other fashion. In any case, this can play havoc with your cash flow.

There are three possible solutions to this problem. The first is to produce several similar products or products that can be made on the same machinery and with the same raw materials you are currently using. For an example, I know a manufacturer of large plastic jacuzzis who also produces fiberglass cabs for trucks. I am also aware of a company that produces plastic police helmets and plastic clipboards. The idea is not to build yourself a mini-conglomerate within your firm, but to use your regular equipment and spread the risk over several different markets. If done correctly, your peaks and valleys will flatten out. When one type of product or industry has a peak, the other has a valley. The net result will be a smoother and higher level of sales throughout the year. Furthermore, if a drop in demand occurs in one market or for one product, the other product may be strong enough to carry over your cash flow until the weak product or market once again becomes healthy.

A second possible solution is to reach every customer you can with one single product. Again, if you do the planning of this industrial marketing correctly, your peaks and valleys from different customers can cancel one

another out. Of course, a drop in overall demand from one customer is not necessarily picked up by another, but you may be able to hold on with the other customer until things get straightened out. I read recently in *The Wall Street Journal* that a manufacturer of metallic products had gotten himself in a bind over a period of 10 to 15 years by selling solely to one of the large chain stores. Recently the demand for this product had decreased to the extent that it was no longer profitable for the chain store to carry it. Overnight this producer lost his entire market. If you can reach every customer or more customers for a single product, this will help solve this problem and lessen your risk. A third solution to high risk is to make your resources count.

No matter what kind of company you have, or how large or small it is, you will always have the problem of allocating a limited number of resources. Try to allocate your resources so that they pay double dues. For example, if you can use the same machinery or the same tooling to make similar products for different markets, you will lower your risk and save money. Use the resources you have, make them count, and double or triple their value.

> **E-Z TIP**
> Avoid taking on additional overhead or buying capital equipment for dissimilar products and markets.

Market research in the industrial marketplace

Market research is particularly difficult in the industrial market because you have more than one customer in one buying unit and because the customer may change during the buying process, especially if sophisticated or complicated equipment is involved. The process may then take months or even years. I have a friend who is a salesman for IBM. He sells complex computer and computer-peripheral equipment to large industrial companies. During one sale for several million dollars, not only did he have more than one customer, but many of these customers of this large industrial company changed during the several years it took him to make the sale. It was difficult to conduct market research during the process because the customers changed so often.

You cannot easily conduct a survey among customers to find out why they prefer a competitor's widget over your widgets or why they prefer to conduct business with a company other than yours, or why they prefer someone else's consulting services and not yours.

What you can do is to try to find out what the customer's problems are, what kind of solutions he is thinking about, what amounts of money and other resources he has for the project, and the time frame in which he is trying to operate. Also, remembering that there is more than one customer, especially for more complex programs, you must discover which customers are powerful in the buying organization and how the various organizations and groups in the company work to support one special interest within the total buying organization. It is no good talking to an engineer who proposes a solution of buying product X if the man has little power or authority to get his ideas accepted or implemented.

> ⚠ **CAUTION** Industrial market research cannot be done in the same way as consumer research.

Your research must be done not only in the problem and solution areas of the industrial customer, but also within the organization, so that you will know which customers are powerful and which are not. While it would appear that only in the face-to-face phase of selling can these market research procedures be accomplished, this is not actually true. Secondary research can often help you find out whether certain programs can be accomplished. You can analyze brochures of the company in which their annual budget and plans or requirements are given. You can read magazines in the particular area in which you are selling association magazines, technical magazines, and so forth. Valuable information can be gained by reading *The Wall Street Journal* or the business section of your local paper. Make contact with other companies with whom the firm you are interested in does business as a subcontractor, or perhaps other noncompeting or even competing companies.

Market research is absolutely essential in industrial marketing, for without it you cannot obtain the essential information about future programs of purchase. In addition, market research activities will provide the basic input for the direction in which to take your company and will guide your

marketing endeavors. It will develop additional sources of profit, perhaps through new products or services which you can offer, and it will certainly reduce waste in your marketing activities. It will provide a source for competitive intelligence about companies that are competing against you in the products and services you are selling, and it will serve as an insurance policy against unexpected changes in your market or marketplace so that you can allow for them ahead of time.

In order to be successful in obtaining your market research objectives, I would suggest making a list of them whenever you plan to have a face-to-face meeting with a customer. Ask the industrial customer for all the information he can give you, including brochures, annual reports, buying procedures, and organization charts. Always try to get the information by asking for it directly.

> **E-Z TIP** Sometimes you can get important intelligence and market research information from industrial customers with whom you develop a personal relationship.

Always make notes when you are visiting a customer. Write up these notes on a daily basis. After a week or so of making visits to industrial customers, and perhaps talking with three or four people at each company, all your information will seem to run together and you will have a difficult time documenting it when you return from your trip. What you don't document, what you don't write down, you don't actually have, so be certain to take copious notes during your talks and meetings with the customer and go over these notes and reorganize them so it is clear who said what. Use this information to decide which programs you will actually go after and whether you will deal only with bidding for low price or whether you will make a full proposal with other factors being of equal or greater importance. You can also use the information to forecast sales for each of your industrial customers. In sum, you will be able to decide which programs are likely to go, which ones you are likely to win, what the dollar amounts will be, and exactly when you can plan on submitting a bid or a proposal.

We are still left with one problem: how to hit a moving target. When our industrial customers in one particular company are continually changing due to transfers, promotions, hiring, and firing, we have to adjust. One company

> **E-Z TIP** The solution to hitting a moving or changing customer target is not an easy one, but you can help the situation by keeping abreast of changes in the customer's organization. When changes occur, consider yourself back at square one, grit your teeth, and start the whole merchandising process over again.

spent thousands of dollars in an effort to win a large industrial contract, then lost the whole thing when two key members of the potential customer's buying organization left and were replaced by new people. If it is profitable for you to go after the contract, it is worth the allocation of resources, time, energy, and money. Doing the job right means keeping on top of the contract until you win it. The industrial marketplace can be a very lucrative one for your company and one you can use either as the total market for your product or service or as a partial one that can complement the consumer sales that may be your mainstay.

How to sell to the government market

11

Chapter 11

How to sell to the government market

CAUTION

The United States government represents an incredible market for the small business—two hundred billion dollars or more every year. It also demands special marketing techniques and methodologies. If you know how to apply these techniques, you can make millions. If you do not, you can spend thousands of dollars in resources and end up without a single government contract. Let me tell you a couple of cautionary tales to give you an idea of what can happen if you are not careful.

The XYZ Company, located in New Jersey, made materials handling equipment and had sold it successfully in the industrial market for many years. It saw the big dollars available in the government marketplace and decided to go after them. Over a period of several years, it bid contracts for materials-handling machinery to the Navy, to NASA, and to the Air Force. But, despite having low bids in all these cases and going through a series of protests with each individual department and the General Accounting Office, the net result was not a single cent of government money.

Or you might consider the case of the Lockridge Map Strap Company.* Lockridge was a pilot flying for Hawaiian Airlines. He also flew F-4 fighter aircraft in the Hawaiian National Guard. Some years ago it was discovered that a serious problem existed with the kneeboard which a pilot strapped to his leg to hold maps and written materials. The straps frequently became entangled with the control stick during flight, and several fighter aircraft were lost. To remedy this problem, Lockridge invented a map strap, formed a company to build and market the device, and secured three different patents on his invention. Over a period of years he sold several hundred map straps to fellow pilots in his and other squadrons and offered his device to the Air Force for possible adoption for F-4 aircraft.

Lockridge spent thousands of dollars, not only in free map straps, but also in trips, demonstrations, and drawings which he gave freely to the Air Force for its testing of his invention. Finally, five years later, the

note Getting a new invention adopted by a government agency is no easy task.

Air Force decided to adopt Lockridge's map strap, which sold at $7.99 per unit as opposed to $19.95 for the kneeboard the Air Force had been using.

The government sent Lockridge a Sole Source Request for Proposal for procurement of 7,000 of his map straps. Lockridge proposed the $7.99 price that he had been charging to individuals, feeling that (1) he was totally protected by his patents, (2) he had expended a great deal of research and development and other costs in getting the map straps adopted, and (3) this price represented tremendous savings over the old kneeboard. The government rejected his price, canceled the request for proposal, and issued a competitive RFP, using Lockridge's own drawings with his name snipped off. The contract was awarded to another firm at a little more than $2.00 a unit.

Although Lockridge protested vehemently to the General Accounting Office, he was denied. It was said that the government contracting officer had no obligation to testify to the validity of patents. Although the Air Force bought several thousand of Lockridge's map straps over a period of several years, Lockridge was unable to receive either dollar or contract benefit. When he approached a well-known law firm dealing with government contracts, Lockridge was told that it was not worthwhile to sue; even if he won the

* James E. Lockridge, "U.S.A.'s Illegal Procurement Policy: International Infringement of U.S Patents," *SAFE Journal*, Vol. 8, no. 3, 1978.

suit—and this was not certain—he would only be awarded a 6 percent royalty, based not on his price of $7.99, but on the price for which the contracts were awarded. In effect, he would be paying more money to the attorneys than he could reclaim even if he won the case.

HOT spot Herman Holtz, a businessman who writes a newsletter in Washington, D.C., says that he has made over $86 million selling various types of goods and services to Uncle Sam. Other small businesses have also been extremely successful in learning how to work the government gold mine.

If a businessman takes the time to understand the government marketplace and how it works, he can avoid these disasters. The basic fact that you must understand about selling to the government marketplace and the government customer is that the process is far from automatic. You must market and sell just as you do in any other marketplace. Although the regulations state that you merely need to get on a bidder's list and wait for the bid to come in, or that you merely need to pick up a copy of the *Commerce Business Daily* and bid according to the specifications contained therein, this is not enough. You cannot do only this and expect to win, any more than you could in supplying a similar product (or perhaps the same one) to an industrial buyer who doesn't know you and hasn't done business with you previously. You cannot be a total unknown and expect to win.

The government buyer, no matter who he is, doesn't want to risk his career on someone he doesn't know or someone who has never dealt with the government before. You will have to plan to expend some resources in the right way in order to overcome this initial hurdle. Just as in other markets, once you have your first contract, other contracts will be much easier to get and at much less cost to you.

There is a process for winning government contracts which will make you successful. It will ensure that your win rate for RFPs is above 80 percent and it will enable you to make millions of dollars. Briefly, this process involves five phases: locating your customer, contacting the customer, planning your marketing presentation, submitting your proposal, and, finally, contract negotiation and post-contract follow-up.

Let's look at each phase individually.

Locating your customer

Regardless of what product or service you have, you will find that there are many government customers, both in the United States and abroad, who are interested in buying your product or service. These customers, who are found in every government agency and department, buy almost every product or service you can imagine.

Here are just a few:

Construction and Automotive

Plywood and veneer
Lumber and millwork
Pipe, conduit, plumbing fixtures
Electronics
Resistors
Capacitors
Filters and networks
Fuses and arresters

Diesel and gasoline engines
Cabs, frames, components
Transmissions, brakes, steering

Switches
Connectors
Crystals
Relays and solenoids

Fuel, Petroleum Products and Services

Gasoline and jet fuel
Fuel oils
Coal

Operation of government-owned terminals
Commercial storage

General

Chemicals
Pallets, wood
Sandbags

Scientific instruments
Service and trade equipment
Food preparation equipment

Industrial

Hardware
Metal bars, sheets, and shapes
Blocks, tackle, rigging

Chain and wire rope
Rope, cable fittings
Electrical wire and cable

Medical, Dental

Drugs X-ray equipment and supplies
Biologicals

Hospital furniture, equipment, utensils, supplies, and clothing

Subsistence

Meat, poultry, and fish
Fruits and vegetables
Coffee, tea, and cocoa

Dairy foods and eggs
Bakery and cereal products
Nonalcoholic beverages

Textiles and Clothing

Men's and women's clothing
Wool, cotton, and synthetic fabrics
Boots and shoes
Body armor

Sunglasses
Socks, undershirts, and other knitwear

If you want a complete list of products and government customers, order a copy of the *U.S. Government Purchasing and Sales Directory* from the Superintendent of Documents, Government Printing Office, Washington, D.C. 20402. Price is $28.00, and worth every penny.

Another way of locating specific customers for your product or service is through the *Commerce Business Daily*. It comes out five days a week and lists all contract awards above $25,000 for civilian contracts and $10,000 for military contracts. In addition, it has all requirements by various government agencies above certain dollar amounts listed. The *Commerce Business Daily* costs $80 a year mailed second-class, or $105 a year first-class. Remember that the value of the *Commerce Business Daily* is not that you will bid on the advertisements contained in it. In fact, you should not bid, no matter how closely you feel you can meet the bid requirements. The reason for this is that perhaps 98 percent of the awards made as bids advertised in the *Commerce Business Daily* are made to firms that have already made the preproposal contact and done the marketing that you will also do, later in this process, in order to win.

You could end up bidding approximately 100 times against advertised bids in the *Commerce Business Daily* and only win two, if any, contracts. The list of awards made and the advertisements of products and services needed is a tremendous source of potential government customers; these are the people who actually want to buy your kind of product and service. You can order the *Commerce Business Daily* from the same address as that for the *U.S. Government Purchasing and Sales Directory*.

All three military services also maintain offices to help managers of small businesses locate customers for research and development services. For example, the Navy has NARDIC, which stands for "Navy Acquisition Research and Development Information Center." The Army operates TILO, "Technical Industrial Liaison Office." The Air Force has "Information for Industry Offices." If you want to do research and development work with the armed forces, contact these offices. They will tell you who is interested in what, and exactly who to contact. Locations and phone numbers are listed in Resources.

A third way of finding government customers is to seek help from the Small Business Administration. The SBA is eager to help you find new customers in the government. Contact your local office and explain your

product or service and that you are interested in dealing with the government. They will make an appointment for you to talk with one of their management-assistance specialists.

Still another source is the government's purchasing agent, the General Services Administration, or GSA. The GSA buys thousands of products and services for government agencies and other organizations. The GSA has also established business service centers throughout the country that exist primarily to serve the entrepreneur in search of government contracts. You'll find a complete list of these service centers in the Appendix.

Contacting your customer

Once you have located a customer by government agency or other organization, the next step is to contact that agency or organization and get the name of the individual who is responsible for and interested in your goods or services. Sometimes you will have to go through several telephone numbers before you get the right one. Your general class of product or service is probably handled by several different people, and you must find the one who handles your specific item. Your first contact may be at the managerial level rather than the actual government customer, at the working level, that you are looking for.

When you have the right customer, explain your product or service and ask for a general idea of some of the items in which he or she is interested. This is especially true with research and development products or services, where general information about the customer's requirements is insufficient to enable you to understand what he is actually buying. Try to get as much information as you can from the customer over the phone. The main object of talking to this person is not to sell at this point, but merely to establish interest and to determine that this is truly the correct place for you to expend time and financial resources in making your first sale. Frequently you will find that, despite considerable screening by yourself and others 'in the government who have helped you, this is not really a customer for your product or service at all. This is the main point of the telephone call—to establish the fact that this is a bona fide customer who will be interested in buying from you.

During this initial telephone call you should arrange to meet the customer, if possible. This may be difficult if you are on one coast and your potential customer is on the other but, with few exceptions, face-to-face contact and a presentation of your capabilities are essential. This is absolutely true for research and development programs, and probably 90 percent true for all other programs. If you cannot set up an immediate visit, arrange to send a brochure describing your capabilities and request all information your potential customer can supply about his interests and the way his particular government agency is organized and does business. Indicate that you would like to get together with him to make a full presentation of your interests and capabilities in the near future and would like to call him the following week to set up an appointment.

> **HINT** Plan to make your selling trip as profitable as possible by arranging to meet not one government customer, but many.

Go through your list of all potential customers and make a final list of customers to visit. Locate the right individual in every case, describe your programs and your interests, and get as much information as you can about each customer's interests. Find a general period of time when each customer is going to be available, but don't set up a specific date yet. After you have worked your way through the list of customers and have some general periods of time when they can see you, go through the list and set up some tentative dates, along with alternatives, that allow you to see the maximum number of customers on one selling trip.

You will probably have to juggle back and forth between different customers in different places at different times, but it is worth it. Remember, though, that going from the East Coast to the West Coast to see a customer costs money and takes time and resources. If you can see two or three customers in one day, or several over a period of days, you can minimize your selling costs and maximize your profits.

Once you have your tentative list prepared, return to your list and call each customer to confirm the meeting that you have tentatively scheduled. Give yourself at least two weeks before the first customer visit so that you have time to prepare your presentations and any specific handouts that you wish to take with you.

Preparing a presentation

Preparing a special presentation for each customer, at each potential customer visit, can be tremendously effective in obtaining future government orders. Decide on the basic message you want to get across to your potential customer, make an outline, and prepare a few graphs, slides, or reproduction copies. Collect any samples you wish to show. Before you leave for the meeting, practice your presentation in front of someone who can criticize you. Let's go over these steps in detail.

Deciding on a basic message

The first point is to document the basic message that you want your customer to receive. This message may be "My widget is better than any other widget in the world" or "my widget is just as good as any other widget, but cheaper than any other in the world."

Outlining your presentation

> **E-Z TIP**
> Document your basic sales pitch to ensure that everything you say supports your basic message and that nothing you say is contradictory or irrelevant to the main point.

Start by noting the overall time you are allowed for your presentation. Your outline and your presentation will differ depending on whether you have one hour, three hours, or the entire day. Make sure that every point supports the basic contention that you have documented. Do not write the entire presentation as if it were a speech. A speech has to be memorized and does not allow for questions by the customer. Do not memorize your presentation. Work from an outline to ensure that all points will be covered.

Preparing viewgraphs, slides, or reproduction copies of your outline

Once you have the basic points documented and have completed the outline, the next step is to transcribe this outline either into viewgraphs, slides, or other formats that can be processed into printed copy. Which method

or methods you use depends on the size of your audience and which method you are most comfortable with. If you are making a presentation to only a few people, it is easiest to reproduce your presentation and give each person a copy to follow. If you have fifteen customers receiving your presentation at once, it is probably better to put your outline on viewgraphs or slides. (You may wish to give each a reproduced copy as well.) Availability of the projector for viewgraphs or slides is also a factor. If the government has no projector available (and you should check into this prior to your trip) you may not have any choice. In any case, if you leave a copy with your customers, they will be able to refer back to your presentation without having to depend on their memories or notes.

Collecting samples

Be sure that any samples you intend to take with you are available as you prepare your presentation. If you wait until after you complete the presentation and are ready to make your trip, you will sometimes find that the samples you wanted are not available and cannot be obtained, and you will have to change your presentation at the last minute. Gather all your samples (or "feelies," as they are called) right at the start.

Practicing your presentation

After you have assembled all your material, practice with it in front of someone else, either someone who works with you or someone at home. This will help your nerves when you do the actual presentation, and it allows your practice audience to criticize your presentation and suggest changes in what you say, what you have written on your slides, or the organization of your basic outline. Once you are able to go through your whole presentation smoothly, you are ready to go on the road and make your initial marketing contacts.

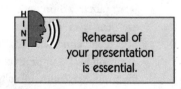

HINT
Rehearsal of your presentation is essential.

You may not immediately "sell something" on this first trip. Consider this initial contact an extension of your initial telephone call and a chance to become more familiar with your customer and his needs while he becomes more familiar with you, your capabilities, and the product or service you

supply. It is beneficial to understand the two marketing theories we discussed earlier and to keep them in mind as you make contact with your potential government customers.

Applying marketing theories

The two theories of marketing will influence your success in contracting with the federal government. As you recall, merchandising theory says that the

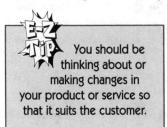

You should be thinking about or making changes in your product or service so that it suits the customer.

greatest potentials for profits are in the customer's needs and in the fulfillment of these needs. In order to best fill his needs, you must not only change or influence your customer, but you must also change your own product or service so that the two fit together. Every time you see the customer, you

present your product or service to him and he presents his need to you. To a certain extent, you influence him to alter or modify his needs slightly to better match your product or service.

Consumer acceptance theory, which was developed more than 30 years ago, describes how increased activity and interaction between your product and your potential customer increases the intensity of his acceptance of your product. At the very lowest intensity of consumer acceptance, he will simply tolerate purchasing your product if no other product is available and probably won't purchase it in preference to a competing product if one is available. At the next level of intensity—the preference level—your product is selected over competing services. The potential customer may still go to the competition if your product is higher-priced or if other terms tend to detract from his preference. Finally, your product reaches the highest level of consumer acceptance: insistence. At this point, the potential consumer feels that he must have your product or service and will insist upon it, regardless of price or other circumstances. Clearly, as far as you are concerned, this is the ideal situation.

It is important to remember, however, that this high level of intensity is reached only through successful interaction. The more contact of a positive nature that you can have with your potential customer, the more you are able

to explain your product or service to him. The more you merchandise the product or service to him, the better chance you have of reaching the highest levels of intensity. The more you reach the insistence level, the better chance you will have in government marketing.

Tracking a program to win

One of your main tasks, at the very first meeting with your potential customer, is to identify what future procurement programs are being planned. Once you have determined that these programs exist and the money is available for them, you should begin to track them. Tracking is done not only through contacts with this particular government customer, but also with other government customers who are knowledgeable about these programs. For example, your customer may be an engineer who is a candidate for the project's program manager, project engineer, or so-called program monitor. You can certainly track the program through him. You will also want to discuss this program with contracting personnel, the individual's supervisor, and, if possible, other commands or units associated with this program which are not at the same location.

For example, if you were interested in developing an ejection seat for the Air Force, your immediate customer might be the Life Support Systems Program Office in Aerospace Systems Division (ASD), located at the Wright-Patterson Air Force Base in Ohio. This would be the division where you would find the program manager responsible for ejection-seat programs and the one most concerned with obtaining the funding and directing such a program from the government side.

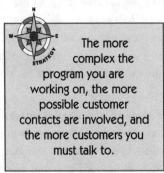

The more complex the program you are working on, the more possible customer contacts are involved, and the more customers you must talk to.

There will be many other engineers working on such a program and having an impact on its design; these people would be located at Wright-Patterson Air Force Base also, but in a different unit. You would also be concerned with other program offices at Wright-Patterson that might be interested in the new ejection seat—perhaps the F15 Systems

Program Office or the F16 Systems Program Office. It would also be a good idea to make contact at the Tactical Air Command Headquarters at Langley Air Force Base in Virginia where the ejection seat would ultimately be used. Additional information might come from the Air Staff in Washington.

In dealing with these people you will find some more ready to talk than others and you will find varying opinions and differing information. It is important that you really know the organization's involved—how they fit together, who has the money, and who has the power to act. When you identify these powerful individuals, you can then pay primary attention in tracking the program to them. Less complicated programs, of course, are much easier to follow. For example, if a production program has specifications which have already been established, only one government buyer or contracting officer will need to be kept totally aware of the program.

Over a period of months and using the principles inherent in consumer acceptance and merchandising theories, you will develop a rapport with the government customers in your product or service area and learn enough about their programs to submit a successful bid. If you track the programs this way, you will find that when the RFP or IFB or request for quotation actually comes to you, you will be fully prepared to answer with your proposal or bid in the specified period of time.

Writing a proposal

There are actually three types of government requests for bidding. With the IFB (invitation for bid), you need only bid the price: the winner is simply the low price bid. This type of request requires no proposal. An RFP (request for proposal) requires a formal proposal as well as a bid price, and the decision is made not only on the price bid, but also on your technical proposal. In addition, there is a type of proposal which government regulations allow you to submit known as the unsolicited proposal, a proposal that has not been formally solicited by the government.

The first thing you should know about an unsolicited proposal is that it really isn't unsolicited. If you have a great new idea that you think the government should buy, the most useless thing you can do is submit a truly unsolicited proposal. All you will do is waste your time and money, and

perhaps find that outstanding features of your proposal have been borrowed and used in future competitive solutions.

Consider the environment into which a true unsolicited proposal is introduced. First, there is no money to buy your proposal because the government organization's budget was prepared a year or more prior to your submission. Planning, which of course excluded your proposal, was done even earlier. Like a proposal in response to an RFP, you have only so many pages in which to make the sale. In fact, you can't make a sale in your proposal—you can only confirm it. Therefore, you cannot submit a true unsolicited proposal and expect to win, at least not often enough to make it worthwhile.

> **HINT** The key to winning with an unsolicited proposal—as in any proposal you submit to the government—is preproposal marketing. Use the principles of marketing so that your unsolicited proposal is actually invited and fully sold to your government customer before you ever sit down to write it.

Let's say that you have been sent an RFP and given 30 days to respond. You should already know, through your contacts with the government and your marketing activities, that the proposal was on its way and more or less what it would contain. Further, you should have already sold your main ideas to the government. The first principle of winning is to lay a groundwork for the proposal before you receive it. The government customer should have a pretty good idea of what you are going to submit and should not be surprised by anything in your proposal.

> **E-Z TIP** Your main proposal should contain the ideas that you have already discussed with the customer.

This raises a question: What if you have a brilliant idea after your last meeting with the government? Do you include this brilliant idea in the proposal or do you not? My strong recommendation is that you do not. There should be no surprises in your proposal. If something occurs to you which is so vital that you feel you

must include it in a proposal in a response to an RFP, make up two proposals, one of which contains the new idea as an alternative. The chances of winning with a proposal that includes significant surprises is very low. Even if you are overwhelmed with your new idea, present it only as an alternate proposal.

Why is this so important? For one thing, a proposal is a limited resource document. This means that it has a limited number of pages in which you can sell your ideas. You don't have enough space to sell any but the very simplest of your ideas. It is also more difficult to convince a government customer by the printed word when you are not there to answer questions he might have about a new idea. Even if this new idea is really great, and the government customer evaluating the proposal immediately recognizes it, he or she needs time to sell this idea to the boss. There is not enough time to do this during a proposal evaluation. During this period, a proposal evaluator has very little chance to talk to his superiors about new ideas.

What do you put in the proposal? The first section should be an executive summary—a summary of the whole idea of the proposal and how you intend to solve the government's problem. Next comes your technical proposal, in which you cover all areas in your customer's statement of work (a part of his RFP) and tell him exactly what you intend to do, in detail. Other important sections are the management proposal, which tells him how you are going to manage the contract; a biographical section containing short biographies of the major contributors to the project from your company; a facilities brochure or report which discusses the facilities you have for performing the contract; and a review of your past performance, showing contracts you have successfully performed for various agencies of the government in the past, if you have done any. Finally, your proposal contains a summary in which all the salient points of your proposal are reviewed and emphasized.

It is a wise move to use as many graphs and charts as necessary to illustrate each point. The cost proposal (or price proposal) is usually contained in a separate section. The government likes it this way so that their technical evaluation can be done separately from an evaluation of the relative prices of the different competitors. Let's look at each of these sections in turn.

The management summary

This brief statement is designed to be read by management personnel rather than the technical personnel who will go much deeper into the technical portions of your proposal. Therefore, while you should use appropriate technical language, you should write the management summary in such a way that it can be understood by individuals who are not working on the technical end of the project and who may not understand all the technical aspects of the requirements.

The technical portion

Make a checklist of the government requirements and follow it exactly, organizing your technical proposal in the same fashion as the government has organized its request for proposal. The reason for doing it this way is that the government evaluators will be going through your proposal, as well as your competitors' proposals, in a point-by-point attempt to ensure that every requirement of their RFP is met. The solution to a particular problem in the RFP may lose points with one of the government evaluators because he doesn't like it or isn't fully sold on it, but if you fail to include any solution at all, you will lose all the points. If the evaluator can't find your solution in that area, he may think you have not included it—and you will lose all the points.

Your technical proposal must be organized around the requirements in the government's Request For Proposal.

Make it as easy as possible for him to locate every requirement listed in the RFP. Many successful government contractors find that a special table of contents, in which the government requirements are set against your solutions and the page numbers given, is very useful in helping them to win government contracts. An example of such a table of contents is shown in Figure 11-1.

Your outline for a technical proposal has actually been provided by the government. But do you merely claim that you will fill all requirements? The

answer to that is no. Go down the line, requirement by requirement. Against every major requirement, list your solution and why it is the best one. For example, if one of the requirements for a fire extinguisher is that it should shoot a stream of water 20 feet, it is not enough merely to state that you propose a fire extinguisher that will shoot 20 feet; you must state how you propose to do this. Furthermore, you should mention other methods of achieving the same requirement that you have considered but rejected, and tell why you reject these alternatives.

Figure 11-1. Table of contents for a proposal, with RFP requirements.

Proposal Paragraph	RFP Requirement	Description	Page
1.0	1.0	Introduction	1
2.0	2.0	Design approach	2
2.1	2.1	Facepiece/Hardshell	2
2.2	2.2	Inhalation/Exhalation valve	3
2.3	2.3	Web-type suspension	4
3.0	2.4	Mask development	5
3.1	2.4.1	Faceseal development	5
3.2	2.4.2	Hardshell design	6
3.3	2.5	Mock-up	7
3.4	2.6	Prototype models	7
3.5	2.7	Final development models	8
3.6	3.0	Government-furnished property	9
4.0	4.0	Quality assurance	9
4.1	4.1	Quality assurance organization	10
4.2	4.2	Quality assurance program	10
4.3	4.3	Quality assurance test and evaluation plan	10
4.4	4.4	Acceptance test procedure	11
4.5	4.5	Systems safety	11
4.6	4.6	Maintainability demonstration plan	12
5.0	5.0	Corporate experience	12
6.0	6.0	Project personnel	24
7.0	7.0	Facilities and capabilities	25
8.0	8.0	Development schedule	35
9.0	--	Conclusion	37

There is a very important reason for doing this. Simply stating that you will meet a requirement does not convince government officials that you will do so; it doesn't give them any understanding of how you intend to do this, nor any basis for judgment between you and your competitors. You must state how you will actually meet the requirement of squirting the water 20 feet.

Why should you talk about alternative methods? Letting the evaluator know that you have considered alternatives shows that you have put considerable thought into your solution and have not merely proposed the easiest way or the first idea that came to mind. Since you have given reasons for rejecting these alternative solutions, any competitor who might offer one or more of your rejected solutions will suffer accordingly.

Wherever you can, illustrate your point by a chart or some other graphic means. Caption this so that it demonstrates and sells your point to the government. In the case of a fire extinguisher, you might want to show a comparison of your method and three other methods you have considered. Perhaps you have rejected the other methods because they are all costly. In that case, you might use this caption for your graph: "XYL Company's Proposed Valving for Achieving 20 Feet of Water Is Far Cheaper Than All Other Methods."

Evaluators, being human, sometimes tend to skip through the wording in the various paragraphs, but people look at graphs. A properly titled chart will get the point across to your customer even if he missed it when he read the paragraph with that information in it.

> **E-Z TIP**
>
> If you include a development schedule, the evaluator knows that you will complete the schedule as required because you have a firm plan for doing so.

Always include a schedule that shows the tasks needed to complete all requirements and when each will be done. An example of this is given in Figure 11-2. A development schedule is useful in demonstrating to your customer that you have really thought the entire project through, including all the steps necessary to do what he wants done within the required time frame. This gives you a tremendous advantage over competitors who do not include

Figure 11-2. Research schedule.

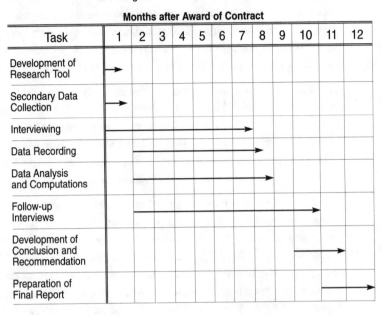

Months after Award of Contract

Task	1	2	3	4	5	6	7	8	9	10	11	12
Development of Research Tool	→											
Secondary Data Collection	→											
Interviewing							→					
Data Recording												
Data Analysis and Computations							→					
Follow-up Interviews										→		
Development of Conclusion and Recommendation										→		
Preparation of Final Report												→

development schedules and who expect the evaluator to take it on faith that they will complete the program within the desired time period.

The management proposal

A management proposal tells how you will handle the contract. It is necessary for all but the very simplest proposals. Any program that requires developmental work as well as production drawings, prototypes, or purchasing from outside the company requires good coordination and management. Even if you are technically qualified, the government wants to satisfy itself that you are capable of completing and managing a complex program. Again, some sort of picture or graph showing how you are going to manage the project can be

> **HINT** Make your management plan clear. Show that you have considered all the possibilities and contingencies and have developed alternative plans and alternative solutions.

very useful. An organization chart is also valuable here. Even if you are a small company of one or two men, you can draw an organization chart that shows the reporting relationship within your company as well as how outside organizations will be supporting you for various aspects of your program.

Show your management plan to other knowledgeable individuals who have not participated directly in writing the program to ensure the clarity of what you have written. Any questions about your chart or your method of management should be answered in your management proposal in anticipation of the evaluators' similar questions. For example, if certain raw materials are in short supply and you are proposing to deal with a source at the other end of the country, what will you do if there is a strike and you cannot immediately receive these raw materials?

Perhaps you are developing a project, but someone else must construct a set of tooling for you; he is located in Chicago and you are in San Francisco. You should indicate your solutions to potential problems, maybe in a weekly or even daily telephone conversation, or by sending an engineer to Chicago for several days or weeks while the tooling is constructed.

The biographical section

Include short biographies of all major personnel concerned with this program. If yours is a small company, this should include the president, whether he is directly involved in working on the program or not, other executives, and the program manager. One common mistake that many small companies make is to use a standard resume for every type of contract bid, regardless of to whom it is bid or what type of service or product is being bid. Instead of doing this, keep a basic resume of everyone on file, but tailor every biography included in your biographical section specifically for the contract you are bidding. You should keep a file of these biographies, should similar RFPs be received on which you desire to bid in the future.

The facilities section

List in detail all your facilities and capital equipment that have an impact on accomplishing the specific job under consideration. Do not take anything for granted here or assume that the customer knows what you have. Much of the equipment you consider commonplace or even obsolescent should be

explained and listed if it is useful for the job you are proposing. The more you can help convince the customer that you have the equipment and facilities to do a good job, the better your chances of winning.

Prior contracts

If you have had prior government contracts you should list them along with the name of a customer who is likely to give a favorable evaluation of the job you did (or are doing) for his government organization. Give his or her address and telephone number, too. Don't leave anything to chance. Even if you know that you have done a good job, someone who is unfamiliar with the program and the job may be contacted and may give a false or negative impression based on insufficient information or things he has heard from secondhand sources. If you have had no prior government contracts, list civilian contracts, again including name, address, and telephone number of someone who is aware of the program, knows it in some detail, and is likely to give a fair and favorable evaluation of your performance.

The price proposal

Not only should you learn how much money the government plans to spend on your project long before the RFP comes out, but you should also learn what amount the customer considers reasonable for the scope of work he anticipates. In any case, you must fully justify the price you bid to the government in your cost proposal, so that the customer not only knows why everything costs what it does, but also is convinced of the reasonableness of these costs.

There are certain rules and regulations for dealing with the government which limit the amount of profit you are allowed to take. However, costing figures are almost invariably open to judgment and interpretation. The first and primary rule should be: What is the customer willing to pay? Then work back and see if this price is profitable to you, either for this contract or in future

HOT spot Government pricing of contracts is just like the pricing of any other goods or services sold by a small business; it depends not only on the cost to you, but also and primarily upon what the government customer is willing to pay.

> **CAUTION** Any bid on a government contract costs money, time, and personnel resources. Don't use up these commodities unless you are going to win. If the government is unwilling to pay a price that is profitable to you, you will end up as a loser even if you are awarded the contract.

anticipated business. If the government is not willing to pay a price at which you can sell your product or service, either because of immediate business or other business on other contracts, then you should know this long before receipt of the RFP At that point you should have made this known to the customer and either changed the scope of the work he wanted done in order to reduce the cost or made him aware of the fact that what he wants will cost more. If you know that the price necessary for you to make a profit cannot be borne by the government, that there is no possibility of making this loss up on future contracts or on goodwill, and that you are unable to convince him to alter his price before receipt of the RFP, don't bid.

Negotiating the government contract

Once you have submitted your proposal, you wait for the government to evaluate it. If you are successful, your customer will contact you, usually for additional negotiations. To cover every aspect of negotiating with the government is beyond the scope of this book. There are books devoted entirely to this subject and I would like to recommend three of them to you: *The Negotiating Game*, by Chester L. Karrass (Thomas Y. Crowell Co., New York); *Negotiation of Contracts*, by Paul R. McDonald (Procurement Association, Inc., Covina, CA); and *Fundamentals of Negotiating*, by Gerard I. Nierenberg (Hawthorn Books, Inc., New York).

There are certain things about government negotiating that you should know before you start. For one thing, negotiations with the government are like negotiations with anyone else. The government customer will frequently assume that your price can be reduced by 10 to 15 percent or more. Sometimes he will intentionally enter into negotiation with several contractors at once in order to bid the price down, even though this is contrary to procurement

regulations. This is done by asking you for a "best and final offer." There have been contracts awarded by the government when no less than five separate "best and final" offers have been requested. One of the authors was once involved in a bid in which he tried mightily to bring the price down by 10 percent, only to discover at some later date that he had had no competition whatsoever.

You should think of imaginative ways to change the price or the costing of the program. For example, one of the authors once negotiated to retain the tooling (worth over $10,000) in return for lowering the price by $2,000. Another technique we have used is not to price out the required set of reprocurement drawings on a research development contract, but to offer the government a free set of drawings coincident with an order for a certain number of units in any one year. This lowers price by several thousand dollars, maybe as much as $10,000 or $20,000 as compared with that of competitors, and at the same time encourages the government to issue a contract at some future date in order to get the free drawings. The drawings are then charged against a future contract. If winning the present contract will lead to a future contract with big profits later on, you can afford to break even or lose a little money on this contract in order to make more money later.

You should also consider the fact that if you are going after a certain type of development contract for a new product, you are going to go through an improvement in the learning process; you will learn how to make the product faster and better than your competitors can, allowing you lower costs than your competition in the future.

The government market is huge. Once you learn how to locate potential customers in it and how to win government contracts, you are on your way to large sales volumes and big profits. The government market presents special problems, but also special opportunities. If you decide to market your product or service to the government, and if you follow the procedures outlined, you can make a fortune.

How to sell to the international market

12

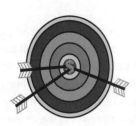

Chapter 12

How to sell to the international market

What you'll find in this chapter:

➡ Seeking government assistance

➡ Selecting a foreign representative

➡ Using an export management company

➡ Preparing international quotes

➡ Receiving payment

Only about 6 percent of American firms export, yet three out of five United States exporters are small companies with fewer than 100 employees. Incredibly, these small companies are doing a $60-billion-a-year business, and this business is growing at the rate of 11 percent a year. You can make a fortune selling in the international marketplace.

Exports can greatly increase the profits from your current business. Exports mean additional customers: If you export as well as sell in the U.S. market, you will have greater annual sales and a greater profit. By increasing sales through export, your overhead—which is amortized over all your sales—will be reduced on a per-unit basis. Your costs will decline, and this also will translate into increased

HOT spot
During the recession of 1974 and 1975, export sales were booming and American companies that were engaged in selling to the international market were able to overcome the setback in local markets.

profits. Exporting will continue to offer frequent opportunities, even when sales in this country fall off. Another advantage of exporting is that you can often extend the life of a product which is near the end of its life cycle. By extending the product's life you can reap additional profits. Also, many businesses are seasonal, or have peaks and valleys of sales throughout the calendar year. Through exports you may keep your plant operating or your people otherwise engaged in profitmaking activities during periods of local seasonal reductions in sales.

To encourage exports, government has programs which allow you to defer a percentage of the taxes on the profits of your export sales.

Measuring your chances for success

The key to success in selling to the international market is to make the right product available at the right time, in the right market, and at a price which the buyer can afford and which will bring you an acceptable profit. In most cases you will be able to do this, but not always; to understand the market better you should make an assessment of your chances of success.

First, do some market research and find out what the market is for your product or service abroad. Who is buying, who is selling, and at what prices are their exchanges taking place?

You should then assess your company's performance, considering the resources that you have available, to see whether you are in a position to undertake exporting. Evaluate how your present operations will be affected if you go into some form of exporting and analyze your product and service to determine which features will, and which will not, meet the needs of potential customers in other countries. You should also consider how this product or service can best be presented to foreign countries. The Small Business Administration has developed the following checklist for evaluating exporting opportunities in your business:

1) What domestic forces are likely to make exporting more attractive in the future?

2) At what level of commitment can the company most profitably enter exporting?

3) If exporting is undertaken, what strains would be created on the company and how can they be met?

4) What domestic sales and profit opportunities exist? What costs, risks, and returns can be expected?

5) What features of the product currently being sold in the United States provide a competitive edge in overseas markets?

6) Is the market being sought likely to be a nation or a group of buyers?

7) What kind of buyers is this product likely to appeal to? How can they be identified?

8) What are the consequences of product modification for the company?

You will note that item number two of the checklist speaks of levels of exporting. There are four levels: (1) export of surplus, where you are interested only in exporting a surplus of products, and not on an ongoing basis; (2) export marketing, where you actively solicit overseas sales for your product or service; (3) overseas market development, where you are willing to make major modifications in your products or services for export; and (4) technology development, where your firm develops products specifically for existing or new overseas markets. After making this analysis you should have a better idea of what exporting will mean to your company.

Finding the sources

Your biggest help for exporting information is the U.S. Department of Commerce (website: *www.ita.doc.gov/* or call the Trade Information Center toll-free 800-872-8723), which offers the *FT410* monthly statistics series, in which figures are provided on the quantity and the values of U.S. exports, listed by commodity and by countries of destination. Also of help for determining your market through statistics is the book *A Guide to the World's Foreign Trade Statistics*, published by the International Trade Center, Geneva, Switzerland.

The FET series, *Foreign Economic Trends and Their Implication for the United States*, is published semiannually by the Department of Commerce. It is a series of commercial reports prepared at foreign service posts abroad. These reports describe current business and economic developments in practically

To get started in exporting, decide whether there is a market for your product or service and, if there is, pinpoint where this market is located.

every country that offers a present or potential market for our products or services.

Global Market Surveys are in-depth reports covering 20 to 30 of the best foreign markets for a single industry or group of industries. These are also published by the Department of Commerce. Among the industries for which surveys can be obtained are electronics, computers, food processing, packaging equipment, metal working, finishing equipment, and process-control equipment. *Market Share Reports* give five-year statistical data on over 1,100 commodities classified by 90 different countries. They provide basic data to evaluate overall market-size trends, compare the competitive positions of American and foreign exporters, select foreign distribution centers, and identify other potential markets for our products and services.

Overseas Business Reports—known as the OBR series—provide background information on specific countries. Such information might include basic economic data, information on foreign trade regulations, market considerations, statistical reports on United States trade by commodities and by distribution channels, and customs peculiar to the country being analyzed.

Once you have completed your market analysis and decided which countries to concentrate on, you can proceed to identify and sell to customers abroad. The Department of Commerce has several programs that should be of tremendous interest and will be worth thousands of dollars in services to you. To make use of any of these services, contact one of the district offices listed in the Resources section. A trade specialist is usually on duty to help if you call. Let's take a closer look at some of these outstanding Department of Commerce programs.

World Trader Data Reports include general sales and some financial data about firms in other countries. They also provide credit information on foreign companies. If you anticipate selling to an importer or dealing through an agent in a foreign country, use the *World Trader Data Reports*.

Worldwide Trade List contains data on foreign credit reporting services that respond to requests received from American companies. The information given in the *Worldwide Trade List* includes the name and address of the firm, the name and title of an officer of the company, the year the company was established, the relative size, the number of employees, the telephone number and date of information, the telex number, the cable address, an item indicating whether the organization is a member of the American Chamber of Commerce, and Standard Industrial Classification (SIC) codes, indicating the complete range of products or services of the firm. If you are interested in this program, contact one of the district offices or the Department of Commerce Office of Export Development.

The Agent Distributor Service (ADS) can help you find interested and qualified agents or distributors overseas for your products or services. At your request, in markets of your choice, U.S. foreign service personnel will direct inquiries to appropriate overseas representatives to determine the interest of these representatives in your export proposal. The names and addresses of prospective agents and distributors then will be sent to you so that you may negotiate directly with them. This service should, of course, be used only after market indicators from your analysis point to an existing or potential market, and when your research shows that such factors as tariff barriers or other import restrictions would not preclude the direct export sale of your products through an overseas representative. When the foreign service personnel have completed an ADS search, the results are reported by telegram to the Bureau of International Commerce. The telegram is then sent to their district office which forwards it to you for information and action.

You can obtain additional information about this program and an application from your local district office or from the Bureau of Export Development, Industry and Trade Administration, U.S. Department of Commerce, Washington, D.C. 20230.

Under the *Foreign Buyer Program*, foreign business people who are visiting the United States may seek assistance in finding products or services

they are interested in. American suppliers are identified to match the business of the potential foreign buyer. To be listed as a supplier of a particular product or service costs you nothing. Contact any local office of the Department of Commerce.

The Foreign Traders Index, or *FTI,* is an automatic file of foreign importers and some exporters. It contains data on over 140,000 firms in 130 different countries. New information on firms and information on newly identified firms is constantly added to this tremendous file. Included in this index are manufacturer service organizations, agent representatives, retailers, wholesalers/distributors, and cooperatives. This information from the data bank can be retrieved singly or in any combination relative to any given product, group, or industry.

The FTI is specifically designed to produce lists of potential foreign business contracts. These lists include firms that import from the United States and/or have a high potential to become purchasers of American goods or services. They also include firms that are interested in representing American exporters. Information from the FTI is made available through the Export Mailing List Service or EMLS printouts. Lists of foreign firms by commodity classification are provided on a custom basis to you in the form that you request—on labels, computer printout, or magnetic tape. These lists include the name and address of the firm, the name and address of the chief executive officer, the type of organization, year established, relative size, number of employees, and product or service codes by SIC number. As of this writing, the cost of this service is nominal. A set-up charge of less than $25 is applicable to each list requested. An additional charge of approximately 10 cents per name listed is billed to you. The standard charge applies without regard to the number of countries, areas, or industries selected. To get more information about the mailing list service, contact your local Department of Commerce district office or write U.S. Department of Commerce, Bureau of International Commerce.

Trade lists are available in two forms—business lists that provide commercial data on selected developing countries, and lists of state-controlled trading companies which identify trading groups in countries where foreign trade is conducted through state-controlled organizations, such as the Communist countries. A free index of trade lists, including those released

since publication of this book, can be obtained from Department of Commerce district offices or by contacting the U.S. Department of Commerce, Bureau of International Commerce, Export Information Division.

The *Trade Opportunities Program* (TOP) is a computerized information service of the Commerce Department which provides American exporters with data on foreign firms that could act as agents or distributors for their products. For the latest costs on the TOP Program, contact your local Commerce Department district office.

Selecting a foreign representative

One major method of selling abroad is through a foreign representative. Selecting the right one is very important to your business. There are bad ones, dishonest ones, brilliant ones; foreign representatives come in all types, and can do good or bad service for your firm. Prepare a list of qualified firms. You can obtain this list from any of the Department of Commerce programs. Write to each of the firms you have selected that may be interested in being your representative. When writing, you should request information on a form, as illustrated in

E-Z TIP: Before selecting a foreign representative, establish criteria for identifying the type of firm or representative that fits your company's export needs.

Figure 12-1. Your next steps are to screen the representatives, narrow your choice, and make a proposal to the foreign representative you have selected.

There are many types of foreign representatives, including the agent, the importer, the wholesaler, the jobber, the merchant, the distributor, and the broker. These people all operate in different ways, and not necessarily in the same ways as similarly identified American companies operate. Therefore, when in contact with a potential foreign representative, be certain that you understand what job he is going to do for you.

A commissioned representative can be a good choice for an exporter of most types of equipment in a small company. This type of representative is usually not appropriate for exporters of inexpensive items where inventory

Figure 12-1. Representative's application form.

GLOBAL ASSOCIATES
Protective Armor Systems
San Carlo, California
USA

This application is for sales representation of Global Associates' armor product lines on a commission basis for the territory indicated.

Name of Firm _____

Address _____

_____

_____

Year Established _____ Number of Salesman _____ Annual Sales _____

Name of Managers or Partners _____

_____

Territory Covered _____

Territory Desired _____

References _____

_____

_____

Firms Now Represented/Products

_____

_____

_____

_____

turns over rapidly. It is important to know whether the representative plans to take title to your goods or not; his failure to do so is likely to mean that you will be responsible for the product reaching the final destination or the final customer. In such a situation you would be involved in customs problems, arranging for delivery, and so forth.

 Some representatives are importers who will purchase your goods or services at a certain time, but may not agree to handle your product on a continuing basis. This should affect your decision about whether to do your own product promotion in a foreign country. It does not make much sense to promote a product if its market will exist only as long as a certain importer decides to buy it. If the representative you contact buys for his own account, it is important to determine whether or not he will maintain an inventory or simply place orders when he receives firm commitments from his customers. Time required for export shipments may mean you will lose sales to other firms that maintain an inventory in that country.

You should also make sure that the representative interested in handling your product is not handling competing products on the same basis. In many foreign markets you will find that the best representatives are already handling competing products; in this case they cannot handle your product as well. Ask the firm for a list of major clients, or check through the *World Traders Data Reports* of the Department of Commerce and such sources as Dun and Bradstreet.

When considering representatives, try to get information that includes the year established, the number of salesmen, the annual sales, the territory covered, the territory desired, references, and major firms now represented along with their products. You might also want to get information about how the representative plans to introduce new products into his area, his capability to provide service for your products if required, what kind of product display area he may have available, and what other warehousing facilities he has available for your use. Firms that really want to do business with you won't hesitate to give you this information. To ensure that it is accurate, compare it with data from other sources such as business directories, Dun and Bradstreet reports, and so forth.

Many representatives will request territories considerably larger than their country of residence. For example, if you are dealing with a

representative in Italy, he may request all of western or southern Europe as well. It is my recommendation that you not give this representation to any individual until you have established a business relationship with him over a period of time. Representatives collect commissions for sales made in their area, whether or not you believe they had anything to do with making the sale. If you give a manufacturer's representative in Italy the entire territory of Europe and then make a sales trip in which you do considerable selling in West Germany, he would have the right to demand a commission for those sales, even though you were the actual salesman. Therefore, you do not want to grant this unless the representative truly has influence in the particular area involved.

Using an export management company

An *export management company* or EMC is an independent firm which acts as exclusive sales department for noncompeting manufacturers. An EMC works like a sales representative, except that it is usually located here in the United States, whereas a foreign representative is located abroad. The bottom line is that you make a deal with an EMC to manage your export business. An EMC may represent your entire product line, or it may represent only a part of it. The EMC usually, but not always, receives exclusive rights to sell in all foreign markets. Some EMCs act as agents and do not actually take title to your goods. In any case, the EMC helps the manufacturer of the product with details of the export transaction. Depending upon whether the EMC is acting as your agent or as your exclusive sales department, you may or may not have control of its prices; the company may not even know who its customers are. There are both large and small EMCs and they handle every product that you might imagine; there are 1,000 EMCs in the United States.

An EMC will charge depending on what type of EMC it is and the service you want it to perform. Some operate on a commission basis. Generally this commission is between 10 and 15 percent. Other EMCs act as distributors, actually taking title to your goods. Usually they will ask for your U.S. discount for distributors plus an extra discount, probably 15 percent in addition to the discount you offer within the United States. At certain times EMCs will ask for additional charges for special circumstances. For example, an EMC may ask

you to share the cost of overseas trade shows or the cost of advertising or other promotional activities. Sometimes EMCs will ask for a monthly retainer, although this is not frequent.

Using an EMC will cost you additional money. Is the service worthwhile? Export sales should come quicker because EMCs already have overseas agents, distributors, and customers in your area and your product line; if you are lucky, you

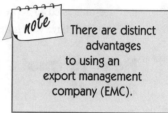

note

There are distinct advantages to using an export management company (EMC).

could get immediate sales. If you were to try to set up your own export effort, it would take you much longer to generate such business. Your out-of-pocket expenses should be lower because you will not have to pay for handling export transactions, identifying your best foreign markets, and setting up distribution in one or more countries.

Bear in mind that an EMC is a specialist and has the time to do the job. Any effort you make is an allocation of resources away from your normal operations. An EMC specializing in international trade and export can handle export problems much more efficiently than you can, and will allow you to allocate your time toward building your business. Finally, if you have not been involved in international trade before, you can learn from an expert.

How can you locate an EMC? There are several methods. One is the Department of Commerce district offices. They will know the EMCs in your area and will be happy to give you the names. Another is writing an associate of an export management company, as listed in the Resources. A third source is the *Yellow Pages* of your phone book under export. Still another way of locating EMCs is the *Directory of U.S. Export Management Companies* published by the U.S. Department of Commerce, from the Superintendent of Documents, Government Printing Office, Washington, D.C. 20402.

Once you have located some potential EMCs, write them letters and make your interest known. Give a full description of your product, including catalogue supply sheets if available. Tell the EMC who your most important American customers are and the most important market segments they are in. Enclose a sales brochure. Describe your company, including any exporting

experience you have had in the past or any inquiries you have received from abroad. Ask the EMC for a description of the firm how it is organized, the lines it handles, and the principals of the company. You can be sure there are EMCs that are interested in representing you. If you operate on the commission basis, you will have very little to lose and much to gain by contacting an EMC.

How to quote for the international market

When you send a quotation to a prospective foreign buyer, to an EMC who is acting as your distributor, or to a foreign agent, you are making an offer to sell your goods. The selling situation is complete when the buyer accepts.

Be precise in all the elements of your quotation—quantity, price, description, method of payment, and shipping terms. These definitions are, in general, the same as those carried out within the United States, with the exception of shipping terms (terms of delivery). These terms can be complex, but the most common are FOB and CIF. FOB stands for *Free on Board* and refers to your quotation price at the place named. For example, if you quoted "FOB Los Angeles," you would be quoting a price at Los Angeles. "FOB vessel Los Angeles" would include all expenses to get the goods aboard an international carrier in the port of Los Angeles. The buyer would pay the expenses from then on.

DEFINITION

The other common term of delivery you should know is CIF, which stands for *Cost, Insurance, and Freight.* This quotation includes the price of the goods plus all in-transit expenses to whatever port is mentioned CIF. The term "CIF Rome, Italy" would include the cost, insurance, and freight of the goods from the point of shipment all the way to Rome. The buyer would pay all expenses to any point beyond Rome where he wanted them shipped. Other terms, which are used less frequently but which you will encounter in international trade, are FAS, C&F, and Ex-dock or Ex-point of origin. Let's look at each of these in turn.

FAS stands for *Free Along Side.* Under this quotation you, as the seller, must get the goods alongside the vessel or a dock designated and provided for by the buyer. The buyer picks up the tab from then on.

C&F stands for *Cost and Freight*. It is just like CIF except that it does not include the cost of insurance. Under this quotation the buyer pays for his own insurance.

Under the term *Ex-dock* the seller quotes a price including the cost of the goods and all additional costs necessary to place the goods on the dock at the designated port of importation. In other words, you are responsible for shipping all the way to the foreign port. Ex-point of origin refers to the point of origin of the goods, such as ex-factory of ex-warehouse. Under this term the price you quote applies only at the designated point. The buyer must pick up the tab from there and get his goods shipped to wherever he desires.

Getting paid

It is often tricky to deal with someone you have never dealt with before and yet be sure he is not going to run off with your goods and neglect to pay you. The best way to avoid this problem is to use a Letter of Credit, and specifically a confirmed, irrevocable Letter of Credit. This type of Letter of Credit is opened on your bank at the time of order. When you present the documents proving that the goods have been loaded aboard ship, you will receive your money. In other words, the money is held in escrow for you by the bank. Other methods that can be used are partial payment or full payment up front. There are also various types of insurance which the Department of Commerce and all of the major banks dealing in international trade can help you with.

There are, of course, other methods of payment. Consult your banker or the Commerce Department about payment procedures prior to your quotation. The Foreign Credit Insurance Association, known as the FCIA, administers export credit insurance on behalf of member

You should be clear about how you will receive payment before you ship the goods.

insurance companies and the Export-Import Bank of the United States. This covers commercial credit risk, such as insolvency or prolonged payment default by an overseas buyer, as well as political risks, including such hazards as war, confiscation, and expropriation.

Your three friends in international trade

From the services that we have mentioned, you get some idea of the many things that the Department of Commerce does. Its trade specialists, trained in export techniques, can assist you in the business of exporting and help you locate an EMC, a foreign agent, and customers.

> *note*
> You have three friends in foreign trade: the Department of Commerce, your international bank, and your foreign freight forwarder.

An international bank can provide another full line of worldwide services, covering all aspects of exporting and foreign trade. Banks that deal in international trade retain their own experts who are knowledgeable about the various types of industries, transactions, and legal aspects of trade that you will be concerned with. International banks can arrange for export sales insurance, furnish you assistance with your documentation and letters of credit, offer financing for exporting, provide financial advice on your transactions, investigate credit backgrounds of foreign companies, and provide you with data on the business environment in particular countries.

In choosing an international bank, be sure that the branch you select will be able to help you. For example, the Bank of America is an international bank, but it is unlikely that you will be able to tap into these services at your local branch. You will have to find a large branch in a major city—Los Angeles or New York. The central branch of a bank dealing internationally, such as Bank of America, will certainly be able to help you. If you live in a small city, go to your local banker and ask him to point you in the right direction, either to locate the central branch of your bank or to help you find an international bank.

Your third friend in international trade is the foreign freight forwarder. These firms will handle a number of export services for you at quite modest costs. These services include compliance with all international trade regulations, arranging for warehouse storage, assuring suitable packing of

your products, handling shipping insurance, advising on consular and licensing requirements, quoting rates and related charges in advance, booking ocean cargo or air freight space, providing routing and scheduling information, and providing information on marketing and labeling requirements. You can also call on the foreign freight forwarder for assistance in making up your quotation. The cost of all these services is less than $100.

Exporting is an outstanding way for your company to increase profits while minimizing serious losses. The bad debt risk in overseas markets is no worse than that in the United States and can be insured against through various methods of financing. The only other possible losses you can sustain

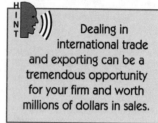

Dealing in international trade and exporting can be a tremendous opportunity for your firm and worth millions of dollars in sales.

are investments in analyzing and visiting foreign markets and promotional material and sample products sent overseas. Even these costs can be minimized through the commission method of payment.

A marketing plan to ensure your success

13

Chapter 13

A marketing plan to ensure your success

Without a plan, it takes a long time to get anywhere. Every business originates with an idea, usually initiated by the individual entrepreneur. Once this idea is conceived, it must be developed into a full-scale business. A marketing plan is the method of developing a particular idea, project, or program into a profitable, viable business endeavor.

The marketing plan will help the entrepreneur obtain financing, entice personnel, and gain customers. Even more important, it will enable all the firm's resources to be concentrated at the right place and at the right time in order to make the firm's marketing strategy successful.

> **HOT spot**
> It is vital that you develop a truly professional marketing plan.

There are both informal and formal marketing plans. An informal plan may exist only in the mind of the entrepreneur and may develop as needs and demands arise. Such an informal way of planning usually results in frustration, costly mistakes, and perhaps even failure.

A formal plan is written down in an orderly manner and details the specific requirements for success. In order to achieve one's objectives, a formal plan is usually necessary. Asa Candler bought Coca-Cola for $2,300; years after he bought the company, Coca-Cola became a multi-million dollar operation: Coke was sold in every state of the union. Candler used marketing plans to make his enterprise successful. Napoleon Hill in his multi-million copy bestseller, *Think and Grow Rich*, says, "Intelligent planning is essential for success in any undertaking designed to accumulate riches."

Your marketing plan is a written presentation of the marketing aspects of your business idea. It contains the essence of the strategy that will direct the business and shows the timing and ordering of conducting that business. It is a controlling device which enables the business aspirant to compare his results with his expectations.

Why have a marketing plan?

Your marketing plan is an essential element not only in planning but also in explaining and selling your idea to others. The plan must convince those individuals who are essential to the business: yourself, your prospective employees, financial lenders, suppliers, and customers.

Selling yourself

An informal marketing plan is usually a wish or a desire for a business. By formalizing a marketing plan on paper, you finalize your conviction that the plan is feasible—

note The marketing plan shows the conviction of its originator and indicates dedication of effort.

or find that it is not. By placing the plan on paper in the order of the development of the business, you can consider the logic of your plan and make the required changes. Others can then easily evaluate the idea and make suggestions for improvement.

Your family may be an important factor. Parents may want to help financially after seeing that a formalized plan has been developed.

Selling prospective employees

When the entrepreneur begins to think about bringing others into the business, he will have to convince them to give up whatever they are presently

doing and risk their time, energy, and income working in a small business. The entrepreneur may seek help from qualified friends, such as lawyers, engineers, and other professionals, but without a marketing plan it is difficult to gain help or procure new employees. With a plan, each individual can assess the potential success of the new business and determine if he has a place in it.

Selling financial lenders

Lenders are notoriously conservative. They want things in black and white whenever possible. Very few loans are made on a verbal pronouncement of the nature of an idea. A formalized marketing plan is essential.

When a firm fails, it is often because of a lack of adequate financing. With a detailed marketing plan it is much easier to determine the amount of funds required. A person experienced in finance can immediately assess the nature of the plan and the amount of money needed.

Selling suppliers

Relationships for manufacturing and obtaining natural resources or component parts must be developed early in the planning process. This means convincing individuals that they should align themselves with this new business venture. Suppliers are cautious about new or small businesses; if they involve themselves with too many failures, they may not survive. Since the entrepreneur frequently has no history of past business performance, he must sell the supplier on his idea. A properly developed, formalized marketing plan certainly has validity. The supplier can indicate how he may fit into the business and what services he is willing to supply.

Selling customers

In the initial stages of a firm, the first customers for the new product are the agent middleman or wholesaler and the retailer. These intermediaries are exposed to hundreds, and sometimes thousands, of businessmen seeking channels of distribution. Only the manufacturers with the greatest chance of succeeding will be accepted by the more vigorous, successful intermediary. The formal marketing plan is an excellent vehicle for convincing the intermediary to handle a particular product.

Developing your marketing plan

The marketing plan is your sales tool. With it you will obtain financing, personnel, products, and customers. To make it appear professional, you must follow several guidelines.

Grammar, sentence structure, spelling, and typing must be perfect. The folder in which the plan is bound must look expensive and professional. Most school libraries have the facilities for binding, printing, and duplicating at reasonable rates.

Layout is important. Large margins at the top, bottom, and left should be used. Everything should be double-spaced. Topical headings should be used to enable the reader to locate specific subjects easily—an average of one per page is common. Graphs and charts should be carefully designed and labeled. Pictures, pamphlets, letters, and other display items should be placed between plastic protectors, not glued or stapled to a page.

Finally, the report must be believable. This means writing in a conservatively optimistic manner. Too much puffery will make the entire plan suspect to the reader. Everything must be logical and realistic. This is particularly important when approaching money lenders.

Over the years, many formats for marketing plans have evolved. This arrangement has proved to be successful:

- Title Page
- Table of Contents
- Part 1—Background/Objectives/Summary
- Part 2—Service/Product Description
- Part 3—Management Audit
- Part 4—Market Potential
- Part 5—Marketing Strategy
- Part 6—Financial Requirements
- Part 7—Conclusion
- Appendixes

The cover page gives the title of the plan, who the report is prepared by, and the date. The word "confidential" placed on the page adds a bit of intrigue and professionalism. The table of contents should be detailed, listing in outline form the entire marketing plan. If many tables and exhibits are used, a separate list of these should be included.

Part I—Background/Objectives/Summary

This first section of your report will establish the reader's attitude toward your idea for the remainder of the report. It must be realistically optimistic, it must be interesting (so that the reader will want to go on reading), and it must summarize the major aspects of the plan. This first part should not be over three pages in length.

As background, give a short description of the proposed product/service or concept. Include the name of the owner, the nature and location of the business, and the proposed date of opening.

List your objectives. Begin with a lead-in paragraph: "The objective of this project is to establish locations in most of the major metropolitan areas in the United States. To accomplish this objective, we plan to:

- Obtain $100,000 to develop an experimental prototype located in San Diego.

- Open additional locations at the rate of approximately one per year for the first three years.

- Open other facilities at an expanding rate, utilizing the experience gained from the first three facilities."

HINT: Explain why the project is going to be a success. Be logical and very specific.

Your objectives should be very specific and clearly stated. Don't say "The objective is to make money." Order the objectives in a logical manner. If no particular order seems necessary, put the most important objectives at the beginning and at the end (since these will be the ones most likely to be noticed and remembered) and the less important in the middle.

Part 2—Service/Product Description

In this section, explain the nature of the product or service. If you are promoting a product, explain its physical nature. Include diagrams, patent descriptions, and other pertinent data. The nature of the promotion, channels of distribution, and pricing should be carefully detailed. Remember that you are not selling products, but rather product images, channels of distribution, price, and promotion.

If you are promoting a service, describe its nature and state where the service will be located. Relate each aspect to the general image you are trying to project. Justify each aspect.

Part 3—Management Audit

Because the success of a business depends upon its management, this section is extremely important. The major figure is the entrepreneur himself. State in detail those characteristics that will enable him to direct the business successfully. General characteristics, like those included on most resumes, should be mentioned. The best age range is 28-40. Married people are considered more reliable than single ones. A healthy business background, similar to the nature of the new business, is preferable. Any indications of managerial ability and leadership should be mentioned, along with experience in skillful financial handling. Ages below 28 or above 40 , should not be emphasized, nor should lack of experience or high job turnover.

 If the entrepreneur does not have an impressive background, it is necessary to show a strong reservoir of employees and connections who can fill the gap. This could include friends, family, or consultants such as lawyers and management consultants. Since most businesses require personnel, it is important to mention where your employees come from. Briefly describe their backgrounds. Any doubt that the entrepreneur can attract qualified personnel will weaken the plan. Include personnel data sheets whenever possible. These are usually appended to the report.

Part 4—Market Potential

To inspire confidence in the future of your business and to show that potential for your idea does exist, you must evaluate secondary sources,

conduct primary research, and develop a careful analysis of your market potential.

The demand for a product or service can be associated with the demand for some other service about which research is already available. For example, a demand for a unique darkroom product may depend on how many darkroom enlargers are sold. By determining the growth potential of the existing darkroom enlarger, you can estimate the nature of the demand for the new product. A demand for new products or services may also be

> **HINT** Present a strong case that the new product or service can successfully penetrate the market and maintain a market share.

associated with some particular characteristic of the consumer. For example, if the new service is a restaurant designed to appeal to teenagers, the potential of the restaurant can be associated with the number of teenagers located within driving distance of the restaurant. This section of your marketing plan should present concrete proof, or observed indications, of the need for your product. It is necessary to project this outlook to indicate potential in the future. Analyze your competition.

In some cases, no secondary information is available. Perhaps the product is so unique that no relevant information exists. In such cases, primary research should be conducted to give assurance that the product or service will gain customer acceptance and patronage. Research should seek to determine the nature of the customer (age, sex, income, location, buying habits) and the nature of the demand.

Part 5—Marketing Strategy

This part of your plan consists of the actual strategic steps involved in starting your business, operating it, and enabling it to grow and prosper. You should present:

- Pre-development activities—the product development, the location of the business, personnel training, advertisement of promotion, and pricing.

- The means for developing the physical facility or manufacturing the product.

- Details of the grand opening or trial stage. Mention the number of sales and potential profits to be expected.

- Growth strategy. If you hope to expand the business later, mention how this expansion will be achieved. Will stock be sold? Even if you are not really interested in expansion at this early stage, it should be included in the report. Most people like to be associated with a growing, dynamic business, and most businesses that succeed do grow larger than the entrepreneur originally envisioned.

Part 6—Financial Requirements

This section is extremely important for determining the amount of cash sought and the actual cash obtained for developing the business.

By developing a carefully planned financial analysis, the entrepreneur is forced to determine the amount of cash he needs to achieve success. These precise figures show the readers that the financial requirements have been carefully thought out and show the financial lender how much money is required and what it will be used for.

Begin your analysis with a statement of the financial requirements. List and justify the costs involved in developing the project. Follow this with a balance sheet and income statement. Figure 13-1 is a sample. The willingness of a lender to release funds for a business venture depends upon risk and return on investment: the greater the risk, the higher the expected rewards; but the higher the risk, the fewer the institutions that will provide money. Banks, for example, will invest money only in relatively safe ventures.

> **E-Z TIP**
> You should project incomes for the first five years in some detail and outline incomes for the life of the project.

Sometimes, the entrepreneur has had prior experience with the business and will have an income statement. If the historical records show a favorable financial future, it will be easy to get additional funds. If your records show a weak financial situation, carefully explain why this is so and state what changes will be made to improve the situation.

Include a breakeven analysis indicating how many units have to be produced or how many customers have to be served before your firm will break even. A time line can be attached to your analysis, showing how long it will take to achieve this goal. The chart can also show the extent of profits to be made after breakeven is achieved. To determine the length of time loan funds will be needed, determine how long it will take to pay back the investment. Investors are concerned with the return on investment (ROI). Investors in highly risky ventures expect an ROI of three to six times the original investment, usually within a five-year period.

Figure 13-1. Proforma Income Statement.

	First Month	For Second Year/Month	Second Year/Year
Assumptions:			
Number of Regular Members	100	200	
Retail Sales	$5,000	$10,000	$120,000
Less Cost of Sales	3,334	6,668	80,000
Gross Profits on Merchandise Sold	1,666	3,332	39,984
Locker Rental	400	800	9,600
Darkroom Rental	2,500	5,000	60,000
Studio Rental	450	900	10,800
Seminar Fees	100	200	2,400
Registration Fees	4,500	19,000	108,000
Gross Profits	9,616	19,232	230,784
Expenses			
Salary and Wages	1,250	1,250	15,000
Repairs and Maintenance	25	25	300
Rent (or Mortgage Payments)	750	750	9,000
Taxes and Licenses	200	200	2,400
Depreciation (or Equipment Loan Payments)	350	350	4,200
Advertising	250	250	3,000
Insurance	50	50	600
Legal and Accounting	50	50	600
Miscellaneous	50	50	600
Office	50	50	600
Outside Instructors	3,200	6,400	76,800
Telephone	25	25	300
Utilities	150	150	1,800
Total Expenses	6,400	9,600	115,200
Net Profit	3,216	9,632	115,584

Conclusion and appendices

The concluding section simply restates that the business venture does have merit and that it will succeed. The appendices contain bulky materials, or materials that would interfere with the clarity and flow of the business report. The appendices would normally include resumes of individuals associated with the firm, detailed and audited income statements, examples of advertising, detailed results of primary or secondary research, and brochures.

Many persons have valuable and profitable business ideas floating around in their heads, but until these are formulated on paper, they will remain only ideas or dreams. A business plan is just what it implies: a business idea on paper.

note You can develop a professional marketing plan for your small business—a plan that will convince yourself and others of the project's potential.

A marketing plan is an invaluable part of your planning and developing process. If it withstands the scrutiny of others, chances are that the project will succeed. For your business idea to come to fruition, your plan must be sold to investors, employees, suppliers, and customers.

Million-dollar marketing for a small business

It is said that small business represents the greatest risk of failure; failure rates as high as 90 percent have been quoted by various authorities and experts on the subject. Even if these figures are true, it is because of the risks and challenges of marketing for a small business that the payoff is so great. It was because of this risk, the potential payoff, and small business marketing techniques that mail-order entrepreneur Joe Cossman built a $25 million business starting with less than $100, that importer-exporter Brainerd Mellinger took in millions and made a fortune, that Asa Candler built Coca-Cola from a $2,300 acquisition, that Margaret Rudkin turned her Great Depression kitchen baking business into Pepperidge Farm, and that C. C. Criss, a medical student working his way through college by selling insurance, took

over a debt-ridden insurance company and made it into Mutual of Omaha. What others have done, you can do, too. You can make millions.

Marketing for a small business will bring you more than personal success. Small businesses produce 40 percent of the gross national product, employ 58 percent of the labor force, and make sales amounting to $8 out of $10 in construction, $7 out of $10 in retail, and $6 out of $10 in wholesale. Marketing for a small business is the essential ingredient in the free enterprise system. Without it, business in the United States would not exist as we know it. Success in marketing for your small business means more than financial gain to yourself. Without your success, even big business will not succeed.

If you act on the procedures, plans, and techniques contained in this book, you can succeed. Then, someday, your name will be included among those intrepid and successful businessmen who master successful small business marketing and contribute to the well-being of their fellow citizens while acquiring their own personal fortunes.

Resources

... Department of Commerce ...
District Offices

Assistant Secretary and Director General

U.S. and Foreign Commercial Service
HCHB 3802
14th & Constitution Avenue, N.W.
Washington, D.C. 20230
(202) 482-5777
FAX: (202) 482-5013

Principal Deputy Assistant Secretary

U.S. and Foreign Commercial Service
HCHB 3802
14th & Constitution Avenue, N.W.
Washington, D.C. 20230
(202) 482-0725
FAX: (202) 482-5013

Deputy Assistant Secretary, Domestic Operations

U.S. and Foreign Commercial Service
HCHB 3810
14th & Constitution Avenue, N.W.
Washington, D.C. 20230
(202) 482-4767
FAX: (202) 482-0687

ALABAMA
Birmingham
Medical Forum Building, 7th Floor
950 22nd Street North, 35203
(205) 731-1331
Fax: (205) 731-0076

ALASKA
Anchorage
World Trade Center, 421 W. First St. 99501
(907) 271-6237
Fax: (907) 271-6242

ARIZONA
Phoenix
Tower One, Suite 970
2901 N. Central Avenue, 85012
(602) 640-2513
Fax: (602) 640-2518

ARKANSAS
Little Rock
TCBY Tower Building, Suite 700
425 West Capitol Avenue, 72201
(501) 324-5794
Fax: (501) 324-7380

CALIFORNIA
Los Angeles
11000 Wilshire Blvd., Room 9200, 90024
(310) 235-7104
Fax: (310) 235-7220

* Newport Beach
3300 Irvine Avenue, Suite 305, 92660
(714) 660-1688
Fax: (714) 660-8039

** Long Beach
One World Trade Center, Ste. 1670, 90831
(310) 980-4551
Fax: (310) 980-4561

*** Ontario
3281 E. Gausti Road, Ste. 100, 91761
(909) 390-5650
Fax: (909) 390-5759

San Diego
6363 Greenwich Drive, Suite 230, 92122
(619) 557-5395
Fax: (619) 557-6176

San Francisco
250 Montgomery St., 14th Floor, 94104
(415) 705-2300
Fax: (415) 705-2297

* Santa Clara
5201 Great American Pkwy., #456, 95054
(408) 970-4610
Fax: (408) 970-4618

COLORADO
** Denver
1625 Broadway, Suite 680, 80202
(303) 844-6622
Fax: (303) 844-5651

CONNECTICUT
Hartford
Room 610B, 450 Main Street, 06103
(203) 240-3530
Fax: (203) 240-3473

DELAWARE

Served by the Philadelphia District Office

FLORIDA

** Miami

P.O. Box 590570, Miami, FL 33159
5600 Northwest 36th St., Ste. 617, 33166
(305) 526-7425
Fax: (305) 526-7434

* Clearwater

128 North Osceola Avenue, 34615
(813) 461-0011
Fax: (813) 449-2889

* Orlando

Eola Park Centre, Suite 1270
200 E. Robinson Street, 32801
(407) 648-6235
Fax: (407) 648-6756

* Tallahassee

107 West Gaines Street, Room 366G, 32399
(904) 488-6469
Fax: (904) 487-1407

GEORGIA

** Atlanta

285 Peachtree Center Avenue, NE
Marquis Two Tower, Suite 200
Atlanta, GA 30303-1229
(404) 657-1900
Fax: (404) 657-1970

Savannah

120 Barnard Street, Room A-107, 31401
(912) 652-4204
Fax: (912) 652-4241

Hawaii

Honolulu
P.O. Box 50026
300 Ala Moana Blvd., Room 4106, 96850
(808) 541-1782
Fax: (808) 541-3435

IDAHO

* Boise

Portland District Office
700 West State Street, 2nd Floor, 83720
(208) 334-3857
Fax: (208) 334-2783

ILLINOIS

** Chicago

Xerox Center
55 West Monroe Street, Suite 2440, 60603
(312) 353-8040
Fax: (312) 353-8098

* Wheaton

c/o Illinois Institute of Technology
201 East Loop Road, 60187
(312) 353-4332
Fax: (312) 353-4336

* Rockford
P.O. Box 1747
515 North Court Street, 61110
(815) 987-8123
Fax: (815) 963-7943

INDIANA
Indianapolis
Penwood One, Suite 106
11405 N. Pennsylvania Street
Carmel, IN. 46032
(317) 582-2300
Fax: (317) 582-2301

IOWA
Des Moines
Room 817, Federal Building
210 Walnut Street, 50309
(515) 284-4222
Fax: (515) 284-4021

KANSAS
* Wichita
151 N. Volutsia, 67214
(316) 269-6160
Fax: (316) 683-7326

KENTUCKY
Louisville
601 W. Broadway, Room 634B,
40202
(502) 582-5066
Fax: (502) 582-6573

*** Somerset
246 Poplar Avenue, P.O. Box 50,
42501
(606) 678-2029
Fax: (606) 678-2267

LOUISIANA
New Orleans
One Canal Place
365 Canal Street, Suite 2150
70130
(504) 589-6546
Fax: (504) 589-2337

MAINE
* Portland
145 Middle St., P.O. Box 8119,
04104
(207) 772-2811
Fax: (207) 772-1179

MARYLAND
** Baltimore
World Trade Center, Suite 2432
401 East Pratt Street, 21202
(410) 962-4539
Fax: (410) 962-4529

MASSACHUSETTS
Boston
164 Northern Avenue
World Trade Center, Suite 307,
02210
(617) 424-5990
Fax: (617) 424-5992

MICHIGAN
Detroit
1140 McNamara Building
477 Michigan Avenue, 48226
(313) 226-3650
Fax: (313) 226-3657

*** **Pontiac**
Oakland Pointe Office Building
250 Elizabeth Lake Road, 48341
(810) 975-9600
Fax: (810) 975-9606

*** **Ann Arbor**
425 S. Main Street, Suite 103,
48104
(313) 741-2430,
Fax: (313) 741-2432

* **Grand Rapids**
300 Monroe N.W., Room 406,
49503
(616) 456-2411
Fax: (616) 456-2695

MINNESOTA
Minneapolis
108 Federal Building
110 South 4th Street, 55401
(612) 348-1638
Fax: (612) 348-1650

MISSISSIPPI
Jackson
201 W. Capitol Street, Suite 310,
39201
(601) 965-4388
Fax: (601) 965-5386

MISSOURI
** **St. Louis**
8182 Maryland Avenue, Suite
303, 63105
(314) 425-3302
Fax: (314) 425-3381

Kansas City
601 East 12th Street, Room 635,
64106
(816) 426-3141
Fax: (816) 426-3140

MONTANA
Served by the Boise Branch
Office

NEBRASKA
* **Omaha**
11135 "O" Street, 68137
(402) 221-3664
Fax: (402) 221-3668

NEVADA
Reno
1755 East Plumb Lane, Suite 152,
89502
(702) 784-5203
Fax: (702) 784-5343

NEW HAMPSHIRE
* **Portsmouth**
601 Spaulding Turnpike, Suite
29, 03801
(603) 334-6074
Fax: (603) 334-6110

NEW JERSEY
Trenton
3131 Princeton Pike, Bldg. #6,
Suite 100, 08648
(609) 989-2100
Fax: (609) 989-2395

NEW MEXICO
* Santa Fe
c/o New Mexico Dept. of
Economic
Development
1100 St. Francis Drive, 87503
(505) 827-0350
Fax: (505) 827-0263

NEW YORK
Buffalo
1304 Federal Building
111 West Huron Street, 14202
(716) 551-4191
Fax: (716) 846-5290

*** Long Island
1550 Franklin Avenue, Ste. 207
Mineola, 11501
(516) 571-3921
Fax: (516) 571-4161

Rochester
111 East Avenue, Suite 220,
14604
(716) 263-6480
Fax: (716) 325-6505

** New York
6 World Trade Center, Rm. 635,
10048
(212) 264-0634
Fax: (212) 264-1356

*** Westchester
707 West Chester Avenue
White Plains, - 10604
(914)682-6218
Fax:(914)682-6698

NORTH CAROLINA
Greensboro
400 West Market Street, Suite
400, 27401
(910) 333-5345
Fax: (910) 333-5158

NORTH DAKOTA
Served by the Minneapolis
District Office

OHIO
Cincinnatti
550 Main Street, Room 9504,
45202
(513) 684-2944
Fax: (513) 684-3200

*** Columbus
37 North High Street, 4th Floor,
43215
(614) 365-9510
Fax: (614) 365-9598

** Cleveland
Bank One Center
600 Superior Avenue, East, Ste
700, 44114
(216) 522-4750
Fax: (216) 522-2235

*** Toledo
300 Madison Avenue, 43604
(419) 241-0683
Fax: (419) 241-0684

OKLAHOMA
Oklahoma City
> 6601 Broadway Extension, Rm.
> 200, 73116
> (405) 231-5302
> Fax: (405) 231-4211

* Tulsa
> 440 South Houston Street, Rm
> 505, 74127
> (918) 581-7650
> Fax: (918) 581-2844

OREGON
Portland
> One World Trade Center, Suite
> 242
> 121 SW Salmon Street, 97204
> (503) 326-3001
> Fax: (503) 326-6351

PENNSYLVANIA
** Philadelphia
> 615 Chestnut Street, Ste. 1500,
> 19106
> (215) 597-6101
> Fax: (215) 597-6123

Pittsburgh
> 2002 Federal Bld 1000 Liberty
> Ave., 15222
> (412) 644-2850
> Fax: (412) 644-4875

PUERTO RICO
San Juan (Hato Rey)
> Room G-55, Federal Building
> Chardon Avenue, 00918
> (809) 766-5555
> Fax: (809) 766-5692

RHODE ISLAND
* Providence
> 7 Jackson Walkway, 02903
> (401) 528-5104
> Fax: (401) 528-5067

SOUTH CAROLINA
Columbia
> Strom Thurmond Federal Bldg.,
> Suite 172
> 1835 Assembly Street, 29201
> (803) 765-5345
> Fax: (803) 253-3614

* Charleston
> P.O. Box 975, 29402
> 81 Mary Street, 29403
> (803) 727-4051
> Fax: (803) 727-4052

*** Upstate Export Assistance
Center
> Park Central Office Park, Bldg. 1,
> Ste. 109
> 555 N. Pleasantburg Drive,
> Greenville. SC 29607
> (803) 271-1976
> Fax: (803) 271-4171

SOUTH DAKOTA
* Sioux Falls
> 200 N. Phillips Avenue,
> Commerce Center
> Suite 302, 57102
> (605) 330-4264
> Fax: (605) 330-4266

TENNESSEE
Nashville

Parkway Towers, Suite 114
404 James Robertson Parkway,
37219
(615) 736-5161
Fax: (615) 736-2454

* Memphis

22 North Front Street, Suite 200,
38103
(901) 544-4137
Fax: (901) 575-3510

* Knoxville

301 East Church Avenue, 37915
(423) 545-4637
Fax: (615) 545-4435

TEXAS
** Dallas

P.O. Box 58130
2050 N. Stemmons Fwy., Suite
170, 75258
(214) 767-0542
Fax: (214) 767-8240

* Austin

P.O. Box 12728, Suite 300R
1700 Congress, 2nd floor, 78701
(512) 482-5939
Fax: (512) 482-5940

Houston

#1 Allen Center, Suite 1160
500 Dallas, 77002
(713) 229-2578
Fax: (713) 229-2203

UTAH
Salt Lake City

324 S. State Street, Suite 105,
84111
(801) 524-5116
Fax: (801) 524-5886

VERMONT
* Montpelier

109 State Street, 4th Floor,
05609
(802) 828-4508
Fax: (802) 828-3258

VIRGINIA
Richmond

700 Centre, 704 East Franklin
Street, Suite 550, 23219
(804) 771-2246
Fax: (804) 771-2390

WASHINGTON
** Seattle

Westin Building
2001 6th Ave, Suite 650, 98121
(206) 553-5615
Fax: (206) 553-7253

* Tri-Cities

320 North Johnson Street, Suite
350
Kennewick, WA. 99336
(509) 735-2751
Fax: (509)783-9385

WEST VIRGINIA
Charleston

405 Capitol Street, Suite 807,
25301
(304) 347-5123
Fax: (304) 347-5408

***Wheeling
1310 Market Street, 2nd Floor, ZIP 26003
PHONE (304) 233-7472,Fax (304) 233-7492

WISCONSIN
Milwaukee
517 E. Wisconsin Avenue, Room 596, 53202
(414) 297-3473
Fax: (414) 297-3470

WYOMING
Served by the Denver District Office

(^) EASTERN REGION
World Trade Center, Suite 2432
401 East Pratt Street
Baltimore, MD 21202
(410) 962-4539
Fax: (410) 962-4529

(^) MID-EASTERN REGION
9504 Federal Building
550 Main Street
Cincinnati, OH 45202
(513) 684-2947
Fax: (513) 684-3200

(^) MID-WESTERN REGION
8182 Maryland Avenue, Suite 1011
St. Louis, MO 63105
(314) 425-3300
Fax: (314) 425-3375

(^) WESTERN REGION
250 Montgomery St., 14th Floor
San Francisco, CA 94104
(415) 705-2310
Fax: (415) 705-2299

* - DENOTES TRADE SPECIALIST AT A BRANCH OFFICE

** - DENOTES A U.S. EXPORT ASSISTANCE CENTER

*** - DENOTES A DISTRICT EXPORT ASSISTANCE CENTER

(^) - OFFICE WITH MANAGERIAL AND ADMINISTRATIVE OVERSIGHT RESPONSIBILITIES (OFFERS NO DIRECT BUSINESS COUNSELING)

••• Bureau Directors •••

Can't find it here?
Call: Telephone Information/Locator: 202-482-2000
TDD: 202-482-4670

◆ **Bureau Of Economic Analysis**
Director 202-606-9600

◆ **Office Of The Associate Director For Regional Economics**

Associate Director 202-606-9605

◆ **Office Of The Associate Director For International Economics**

Associate Director 202-606-9604

◆ **Office Of The Associate Director For Industry Economics**

Associate Director 202-606-9612

◆ **Bureau Of Export Administration Office Of The Under Secretary For Export Administration**

Under Secretary 202-482-1455

◆ **Office Of The Assistant Secretary For Export Administration**

Assistant Secretary 202-482-5491

◆ **Office of Export Services**

Director 202-482-0436

◆ **Economic Development Administration Office Of The Assistant Secretary**

Assistant Secretary 202-482-5081

◆ **Economics And Statistics Administration Office Of The Under Secretary For Economic Affairs**

Under Secretary 202-482-3727

◆ **STAT-USA**

Director 202-482-1405

◆ **General Counsel**

General Counsel 202-482-4772
Administrative Officer 202-482-0490

◆ **Office of Inspector General**

Inspector General 202-482-4661
Deputy Inspector General 202-482-3516

◆ **International Trade Administration Office Of The Under Secretary For International Trade**

Under Secretary 202-482-2867

◆ **Assistant Secretary And Director General Of The U.S. And Foreign Commercial Service**

Director General 202-482-5777

◆ **Office Of The Assistant Secretary For International Economic Policy**

Assistant Secretary 202-482-3022

◆ **Office Of The Assistant Secretary For Import Administration**

Assistant Secretary 202-482-1780

◆ **Office Of The Assistant Secretary For Trade Development**

Assistant Secretary 202-482-1461

◆ **Minority Business Development Agency Office Of The Director**

Director 202-482-5061

... Export Management ...
Leading Associations

◆ **The Federation of International Trade Associations**

11800 Sunrise Valley Drive, Suite 210
Reston, VA 20191
800-969-FITA (3482)
Fax: (703) 620-4922

◆ **EMAC**

222 N. Sepulveda Blvd., Suite 1690
El Segundo, CA 90245
(310) 606-0161
Fax: (310) 606-0150

Save On Legal Fees

with software and books from Made E-Z Products available at your nearest bookstore, or call 1-800-822-4566

Stock No.: BK311
$29.95 8.5" x 11"
500 pages Soft cover
ISBN 1-56382-311-X

Everyday Law Made E-Z

The book that saves legal fees every time it's opened.

Here, in *Everyday Law Made E-Z*, are fast answers to 90% of the legal questions anyone is ever likely to ask, such as:

- How can I control my neighbor's pet?
- Can I change my name?
- What is a common law marriage?
- When should I incorporate my business?
- Is a child responsible for his bills?
- Who owns a husband's gifts to his wife?
- How do I become a naturalized citizen?
- Should I get my divorce in Nevada?
- Can I write my own will?
- Who is responsible when my son drives my car?
- How can my uncle get a Green Card?
- What are the rights of a non-smoker?
- Do I have to let the police search my car?
- What is sexual harassment?
- When is euthanasia legal?
- What repairs must my landlord make?
- What's the difference between fair criticism and slander?
- When can I get my deposit back?
- Can I sue the federal government?
- Am I responsible for a drunken guest's auto accident?
- Is a hotel liable if it does not honor a reservation?
- Does my car fit the lemon law?

Whether for personal or business use, this 500-page information-packed book helps the layman safeguard his property, avoid disputes, comply with legal obligations, and enforce his rights. Hundreds of cases illustrate thousands of points of law, each clearly and completely explained.

Whatever you need to know, we've made it E-Z!

Informative text and forms you can fill out on-screen.* From personal to business, legal to leisure—we've made it E-Z!

PERSONAL & FAMILY

For all your family's needs, we have titles that will help keep you organized and guide you through most every aspect of your personal life.

BUSINESS

Whether you're starting from scratch with a home business or you just want to keep your corporate records in shape, we've got the programs for you.

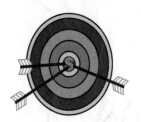

Index

Mar-Psy

Pul-W